THE COST (

LINDA SCOTT is an internationally renowned expert on women's economic development, and Emeritus DP World Professor for Entrepreneurship and Innovation at the University of Oxford. She is founder of the Power Shift Forum for Women in the World Economy, which brings together leaders from across sectors; and founder and senior advisor of the Global Business Coalition for Women's Economic Empowerment, a consortium of major multi-nationals working to empower women in developing countries. She was formerly Senior Consulting Fellow at Chatham House, and is a frequent consultant to the World Bank Group on gender economics. Linda Scott's work has been covered by *The Economist*, the BBC, the *New York Times*, the *Guardian* and the *Financial Times*, and *Prospect* magazine has twice listed her among their Top 25 global thinkers.

@ProfLindaScott

Further praise for *The Cost of Sexism*:

'One of the most objective, data-led, rigorously scientific and morally persuasive books of the year.'

Katy Guest, *Guardian* (Science Books of the Year)

'Like Virginia Woolf before her, Scott identifies female economic empowerment as the key to liberation . . . the coronavirus outbreak has made Scott's message more urgent than ever . . . Scott is practical and pragmatic. She has little time for hand-wringers of any variety, preferring to focus on briskly Getting Things Done. Fittingly, this is how she closes: with a step-by-step plan of tangible and precise goals we should – and most importantly, could – achieve.'

Caroline Criado-Perez, *Observer*

'Linda Scott's new book on the costs of gender inequality pulls no punches . . . shocking.'

David Chance, *Irish Independent*

'Shocking . . . a call to arms.'

Adam Rutherford, *BBC Inside Science*

'A strong counter to "lean in" feminism . . . fascinating . . . those who have had more than enough "fun" feminist books – frothy you-go-girl stuff by celebrity authors, or compendiums of inspiring women down the ages – may well find it a tonic . . . there's something curiously exhilarating all the same about the brisk, no-nonsense anger bubbling beneath the surface of the text.'

Gaby Hinsliff, *Guardian* **(Book of the Day)**

'An impassioned account of the personal and societal costs of denying economic opportunity to women.'

Barry Eichengreen, *Foreign Affairs*

'A thought-provoking, data-rich argument for what society and world economies sacrifice by excluding women. This is a crucial book on a crucial subject.'

Dr Phumzile Mlambo-Ngcuka, Executive Director
of UN Women

'This book is the practical rallying cry we need to address the most significant challenge of this century and a great resource for anyone fighting for women's equality.'

Laurie Adams, CEO of Women for Women International

'Linda Scott has done a great service to women (and men) as she outlines how, by empowering women economically, countries can

accelerate their growth and enhance the well-being of all citizens
. . . Her book skewers myth upon myth about patriarchy, male
dominance, and women's historical roles in society . . . a logical and
fascinating read.'

Laura Liswood, Secretary General, Council of
Women World Leaders

'A must-read for anyone interested in understanding why gender
inequality exists today and why it may take us centuries to fix . . .
Scott uses sobering real-life anecdotes alongside hard data and facts
to engage, educate and inspire readers. Full of insight and embed-
ded with a call to action, this book is a timely input for discussions
from boardrooms to book clubs to business schools.'

Arancha González, Executive Director,
International Trade Centre

'A powerful presentation on the costs of gender inequality for all of
society . . . As Linda Scott shows, this is the great imperative of our
time.'

Melanne Verveer, Executive Director of the Georgetown
Institute for Women, Peace and Security, and the former U.S.
Ambassador for Global Women's Issues

THE
THE
COST OF SEXISM

THE
COST OF SEXISM

How the Economy is Built for Men and
Why We Must Reshape It

LINDA SCOTT

faber

First published in the UK in 2020
as *The Double X Economy: The Epic Potential of Empowering Women*
by Faber & Faber Limited
The Bindery, 51 Hatton Garden
London EC1N 8HN

This paperback edition first published in 2022

First published in the USA in 2020
by Farrar, Straus and Giroux
120 Broadway, New York 10271

Printed and bound by CPI Group (UK) Ltd, Croydon, CR0 4YY

A CIP record for this book
is available from the British Library

ISBN 978–0–571–37459–5

MIX
Paper | Supporting
responsible forestry
FSC® C013604
www.fsc.org

Printed and bound in the UK on FSC® certified paper in line with our continuing
commitment to ethical business practices, sustainability and the environment.
For further information see faber.co.uk/environmental-policy

Our authorised representative in the EU for product safety is
Easy Access System Europe, Mustamäe tee 50, 10621 Tallinn, Estonia
gpsr.requests@easproject.com

10   9   8   7

For Jim, Catherine, and Paul

The truth will set you free, but first it will piss you off.

—GLORIA STEINEM

CONTENTS

THE
COST OF SEXISM

1 | THE DOUBLE X ECONOMY

As the car whirled through the unlit streets of Accra, my heart pounded. The driver explained the scenes moving past us, his voice full of rage and sorrow.

Hundreds of homeless adolescent girls moved like shadows in the night. Some were half-naked, bathing in buckets because they had nowhere private to go. Others slept in piles. "They run from the villages," the driver said. "Their parents want to sell them to a man they don't know, to be a wife who must work like an animal by day and submit sexually by night. They run to the city, believing they can escape."

Many had pregnant bellies or were holding infants. Rape was a fact of daily life in the villages, he said, but these streets were no safer. "We have a generation growing up, from birth, on the street," the driver said in anguish. "They will never know a family or a community. How will they learn right from wrong? What will happen to Ghana when these children become adults?"

Many girls worked in the markets carrying shoppers' purchases in baskets they balanced atop their heads, but some fell into prostitution. Still others became trapped in a nightmare of ancient stature: the slave trade that still emanates from West Africa and feeds the vast crime rings of the world.

In my hotel lobby, I felt as if I had stepped back from another dimension. I have been doing fieldwork among the world's poor for a long time, but I have never observed anything that disturbed me more than what I saw on my first night in Ghana.

I had arrived that afternoon to start a promising project: my team from Oxford would test an intervention to help rural girls stay in school rather than drop out. It was a simple thing—providing free sanitary pads—but definitely worth a try. Retaining girls through secondary school was already known to be a powerful economic boost for poor nations. Educated females add to the quality of the labor supply, as well as its size, which stimulates growth. But girls who complete their education also have their first child later and so have fewer children, which slows the overwhelming rate of population expansion. Educated women also raise their own children differently, insisting they finish school, eat well, and are given adequate health care. These mothers act as a brake on the pernicious cycle of poverty that grips Africa.

But that evening I met someone who showed me what happened when the forces pulling girls out of school also made them run away. These girls in desperate flight produced a downward spiral that radiated danger and suffering for generations in the entire region. That destructive force, I knew, rolled across the world, carrying violence and instability to other countries—because human trafficking is one of international crime's most profitable activities. My experience that night forever changed the way I thought about my work. And it gave me a sense of urgency that I have never lost.

The unlikely truth that equal economic treatment for women would put a stop to some of the world's costliest evils, while building prosperity for everyone, is at the core of this book's argument. In these pages, I will tell more stories like this one from the shadows of Accra. I will draw on personal experiences from the villages of Africa to the slums of Asia, as well as the boardrooms of London and the universities of the United States. Throughout, I will show how the same plot of economic exclusion repeats itself in each of these places, always with negative impact.

An unparalleled influx of data since 2005 reveals this reality: a distinctive pattern of economic inequality marks the female population of every nation, each with the same mechanisms holding the disadvantages in place. Everywhere, the barriers to women's economic inclusion reach beyond work and salary to encompass property ownership, capital, credit, and markets. These economic impediments, combined with the cultural constraints usually imposed on women—limited mobility, reproductive vulnerability, and the ever-present threat of violence—form a shadow economy unique to females: I call it "the Double X Economy."

If the global community chose to dissolve the economic obstacles facing women, an unprecedented era of peace and prosperity would follow. Over the past decade, a small movement has begun, propelled by the intention to do just that—eliminate the barriers. Though its numbers are still few, this women's economic empowerment movement now has global reach and counts a rising tide of the world's most powerful institutions among its partners: national governments, international agencies, large foundations, global charities, religious organizations, and multinational corporations.

I have been part of the women's economic empowerment movement from its beginning. My role began with research that tested ideas for helping women gain financial autonomy. Initially, I worked in rural areas, especially in Africa. I tested my own ideas, as well as those of others, and worked face-to-face with women in different countries and under varying circumstances. I also hosted an annual gathering of women's economic empowerment specialists called the Power Shift Forum for Women in the World Economy, where people working on this cause could share what they were learning. In 2015, my focus shifted. Though I continue to conduct research in remote areas, I now also participate in high-level policy conversations about implementing global reforms that take me to the capitals of the world.

I am frequently dismayed by what I observe. The national finance ministers who manage the world economy undermine women's advocates by treating them like a ladies' auxiliary. The Asia-Pacific Economic Cooperation (APEC) and the G20 may hold a "women's week" or start an "engagement group" and even put a phrase about women in their communiqués, but they won't accommodate the distinctive needs of half their citizenry in their plans. They refuse to learn how the exclusion of women hurts their economies or how including women in their national budgeting could bring the growth they so desperately seek. They sideline the Double X Economy on the basis of nothing more than prejudice.

That's why we need you. By writing this book, I hope to recruit many voices, hands, and minds to the cause of women's economic inclusion. I propose concrete, reasonable, and effective action. I ask you to join this movement regardless of your sexual and gender identity, race, or origin. I'm reaching out whether you work in a factory, in an office, on a farm, at home, or online. In this book, every time I say, "*We* should do this . . ." or "*We* can infer that . . . ," I mean *all* of us.

Why are we only now learning about this shadow economy? There have been two obstacles: an absence of data and a blinkered way of thinking about our exchange systems. Economic measurement focuses on the exchange of money, but much of women's economic contribution, like household production or farm labor, goes uncompensated. Furthermore, the smallest unit of data we usually record is the household, in which women's earnings are typically attributed to a male head. For these two reasons alone, our systems do not pick up women's economic activity most of the time.

To make matters worse, institutions from universities to governments have not generally collected or analyzed data by gender. At the time of the women's movement of the 1970s, very few females were in academia; as a consequence, no discipline had given women much thought. Over the past fifty years, as women scholars rose in both numbers and prominence, one discipline after another— history, anthropology, psychology, sociobiology, archaeology, medicine, and biological science, to name just a few—was transformed when the simple question was asked, What about the women? But there are a few fields as yet untouched by this wave of intellectual change: economics is one of them. Meanwhile, the absence of consistent gender data has meant that comparing the welfare of women *here* with those *there*, or even *now* with *then*, has been impossible to do systematically.

The biggest obstacle, however, has been the deep contempt that economists hold for women, which has kept them from taking up the question. Those who manage the cogs and wheels of national economies train in the Ph.D. programs of university economics departments, where they learn to think of the economy as a disinterested machine operating far above the ground where issues like gender exclusion occur. It is also in the universities that economists learn to demean and dismiss women as a class.

Male economists' animus toward women has recently been the subject of essays in *The New York Times*, *The Washington Post*, the *Financial Times*, and *The Economist*. Press attention was sparked by a study that revealed, in shocking detail, what economists say about women in private. A million posts from an online discussion group where economics students and faculty gossip about their colleagues were analyzed to see whether, in unguarded moments, economists spoke about men and women differently. The words most frequently used about a female colleague were *hotter, lesbian, sexism, tits, anal, marrying, feminazi, slut, hot, vagina, boobs, pregnant, pregnancy, cute, marry, levy, gorgeous, horny, crush, beautiful, secretary, dump, shopping, date, nonprofit, intentions, sexy, dated,* and *prostitute*. The terms used in connection with males were *mathematician, pricing, advisor, textbook, motivated, Wharton, goals, Nobel,* and *philosopher*. Female economists told journalists these word lists reflect the way senior economists teach junior members to disparage women.[1]

Economics is the most male-dominated field in the universities worldwide—more so than even the science, technology, engineering, and math (STEM) fields. Because of rising numbers of women in science, more than half of Ph.D.s in scientific fields now go to women in some countries—like the United States—but less than a third of economics doctorates do.[2] Women's representation hasn't improved in decades because economists don't see a problem with their gender mix. As explained by the economist Shelly Lundberg, "Conventional wisdom in most disciplines is that diversity per se is good. Mainstream economics tends to reject that—a reflection of the willingness to believe that lack of diversity is an efficient market outcome. Economists are much more likely to believe that if there aren't many women in the field, it must be because they're not very interested or not very productive."[3]

The culture of economics departments, however, strongly suggests a different explanation. Forty-eight percent of female economics professors say they have experienced sex discrimination on the job. There is a pervasive atmosphere of bullying: many point to the economics research presentations required of new recruits, junior professors, and doctoral students, which are always subject to hostile scrutiny by the male faculty "trying to nail the speaker to the blackboard." At academic conferences, 46 percent of women say they will not answer a question or present an idea for fear of being treated unfairly. In 2018, the American Economic Association acknowledged that misogyny in the field resulted in "unacceptable behavior [that] has been allowed to continue through tacit toleration." Leah Boustan, a Princeton economist, explains that economics professors see women as an inferior class whose entry into the discipline threatens their status. These academics therefore intimidate women, hoping they will leave—so as to keep their own prestige intact.[4]

Economics as a discipline has an outsize impact on society because of its role in advising governments. "If systemic gender bias skews the way the field looks at things," said *The Economist*, "that has implications for the policymakers and others looking to academic economists for analysis, advice or indeed wisdom."[5] Economics professors' bias against real women translates into a negative attitude toward the topic of women's economics, making it hard for the Double X Economy to win a place on the global agenda.

The philosophy that underpins this intransigent stance also presents an imposing barrier. The first principle is that the economy is built on the collective actions of rational, informed individuals who act independently to make free choices in their own interest. Such an economy, if left to its own devices, is said to aggregate into the optimal outcomes for everyone—no matter how unequal things may look—as if guided by Adam Smith's famous "invisible hand." If someone has not benefited from this economic dexterity, then she either has some inborn deficit or has self-selected into her disadvantages.

The Double X Economy struggles with conditions so opposed to these basic premises that they falsify the entire philosophy. As we shall see over the course of this book, women, as a class, have severely constrained choices, have important information actively withheld from them, and are punished for showing anything like self-interest. Indeed, when it comes to economic choices, women can seldom act independently; rather, they are often coerced into acting irrationally—that is, against their own best interests. Women contend with economic *exclusion*, not merely unequal economic outcomes—a circumstance that the dismal science doesn't even have the tools to conceptualize. And the only explanation the prevailing philosophy can offer is that (a) women are biologically inferior when it comes to any kind of economic engagement or (b) they have *chosen* to put themselves in an underprivileged position in *every* country and *every* domain in the world economy, a proposition that is as bigoted as it is implausible. So, right at its roots, the global market's economic philosophy can't even address half the world's people. As a female economist writing in the *Financial Times* warned, "It is just as bad to have mainly male economic research and policy advice as it is to test medicines mainly on men. The results will fail at least half the population."[6]

Because of this stubbornness in academia, the data analysis that revealed the Double X Economy's profile has been done by gender groups within large international agencies, not universities. Early in this century, major institutions like the United Nations Development Programme and the World Economic Forum began comparing measures of women's status (education, employment, leadership, health, legal rights) with the performance data of national economies.[7] Given the basic assumptions of economics-as-we-know-it, they were surprised to discover a striking correlation between gender equality and national economic viability (Figure 1). Where gender equality was high, national incomes and living standards were also high, but where gender equality was low, countries were trapped in poverty and conflict.

At first, people said, "Oh, well, in the poor countries, they have to worry about survival, so it is necessary for the men to be dominant. The rich nations are more comfortable, so they can afford to let the women have more freedom."[8] Yet there was never any evidence that male dominance is necessary for survival. In fact, we can now say, with considerable evidentiary support, that excessive male dominance is actually a destabilizing factor that reduces the chances for survival, especially

WOMEN'S ECONOMIC OPPORTUNITY AND NATIONAL COMPETITIVENESS

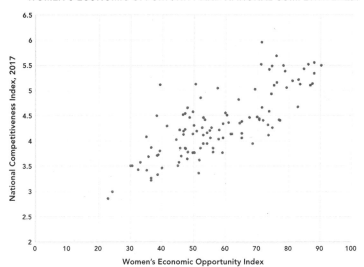

WOMEN'S ECONOMIC OPPORTUNITY AND GDP

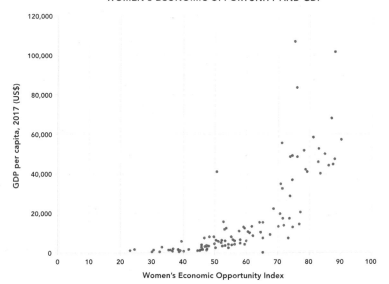

because it so often leads to conflict. But the default explanation that gender equality was a luxury—and that male power somehow made populations better off—fit people's beliefs, so, at the time, folks just accepted it.

In 2006, however, the World Economic Forum's annual *Global Gender Gap Report* began framing the economics of gender differently, taking the stance that including women equally in national economies spurred growth and that, without fair inclusion of women, countries would stagnate. The solution for poor countries, therefore, was to emulate the rich nations by embracing gender equality. The lesson implied: it's not that the rich nations could afford to set their women free, but that setting the women free made them rich.

Still more data has now been generated and further analysis done by the International Monetary Fund, the World Bank, UNICEF, and several global think tanks.[9] By 2018, all this material had converged to show gender equality positively influencing country wealth and overall well-being, while also showing the negative influences of male economic monopoly. During the same period, smaller practical studies—such as ours in Ghana—examined the mechanisms that produce gender inequality and tested interventions to find "what works" to lift the limits on female participation. Ultimately, our understanding of women's role in economics changed drastically.

FIGURE 1. (opposite) Each dot on the two graphs shown here represents a country's Women's Economic Opportunity Index score as related to either readiness for growth (top) or GDP (bottom). There are approximately one hundred nations shown in each graph; all those for which the data was available were included. In the top graph, the upward-right direction of the dots indicates that more economic freedom for women corresponds positively to national competitiveness, a measure of a country's readiness for growth. On the bottom, there is a similar pattern between GDP per capita and women's economic empowerment. These two graphs taken together, showing the "before" and "after" of rising GDP, imply that women's freedoms have a positive effect on national wealth. Other data has converged to reach the same conclusion.

Sources: World Bank Database for GDP at purchasing power parity; Economist Intelligence Unit for the Women's Economic Opportunity Index; World Economic Forum for the National Competitiveness Index

The Double X Economy can be grasped in a way similar to the underground economy, the gig economy, the information economy, and the informal economy. Each of these is an identifiable part of the world system, though none is completely self-contained; all have an effect on the global economy and will play a part in its future, for better or worse. The Double X Economy is an economy composed of women. It has certain ways of doing business, as well as typical products and services. And, while it is as invisible as the underground economy to many, the Double X Economy will affect the future, just as it has the past. The goal for the women's economic empowerment movement is to make that future better, not worse.

In the beginning of the women's economic empowerment movement, we usually made the case for supporting the Double X Economy on the basis of the expected boost to economic growth. That strategy appealed to the audience—mostly economists and finance ministers who were interested in growth but unmoved by appeals to social justice for women. Over time, we began to use GDP as shorthand for the magnitude and direction of any large-scale effect when women were included (or not). That is how I will use GDP. I am not suggesting that we should empower women for growth alone. The indiscriminate drive for more growth is a defining feature of patriarchal economics; it should not be our main goal.

The numbers show that the Double X Economy is huge; only resolute blindness causes economists to miss it. To illustrate, if the Double X Economy in the United States were its own nation, that country's economy would be big enough to join the G7. Women already produce roughly 40 percent of global GDP, and their contribution will soon match that of men. Women produce almost 50 percent of worldwide agricultural output. Despite accounting for half the species, half the national income, and half the food supply, women are nevertheless treated as bit players by economists and policy makers.[10]

The Double X Economy is also the most reliable source of economic growth. When great numbers of women in North America and Western Europe entered the labor market during the 1970s, they caused an economic upswing that made their countries the powerhouses you see today. The capability that working women have to create prosperity has now been proved using data from 163 countries.[11] Men, in all countries, form the bedrock of the economy because pretty much all of them work, more or less all the time. That means, short of a revolution in productivity, growth is not going to come from male labor because men are maxed out. Women, however, are often an untapped or underutilized resource, so getting more females engaged causes the economy to grow. The data shows that women's entry into the labor force is additive, so the new trend does not result in employment losses for men, as is often feared. The belief that economic inclusion for women is a zero-sum game—that is, that gains by one sex happen at the expense of the other—has proved false.

By helping countries to prosper, women's economic empowerment produces a better environment for all citizens. But the reverse is also true: where women have no freedoms, everyone suffers. In the poorest and most fragile countries, indicators of gender equality are lowest and the effects of women's economic exclusion are devastating, perpetuating poverty and contributing to violence, as well as increasing hunger, denying children's needs, wasting resources, feeding slavery, and encouraging conflict. The destructive impact of extreme male dominance in these societies is felt by everyone on earth.

Enabling women is now a proven strategy in the fight against suffering. "As study after study has taught us, there is no tool for development more effective than the empowerment of women," wrote Kofi Annan, Secretary-General of the United Nations, in the opening of UNICEF's *The State of the World's Children* report in 2007. "No other policy is as likely to raise economic productivity or to reduce child and maternal mortality. No other policy is as sure to improve nutrition and promote health, including the prevention of HIV/AIDS. No other policy is as powerful in increasing the chances of education for the next generation."[12] Yet, despite the known capability of economically enabled women to alleviate distress in poor countries, only the thinnest slice of international aid is aimed at females.

All over the globe, the opportunity cost of excluding the Double X Economy is steep. For instance, the rich nations' failure to invest in childcare forces millions of women who prefer full-time jobs to work part-time or quit completely, leaving billions in GDP on the table. "The motherhood penalty" is also the single biggest contributor to the gender pay gap. The World Bank estimates that, because of unequal pay, the global economy loses US$160 trillion every year,[13] while penalizing the Double X Economy for some of its most important economic work—the cultivation of human capital.

An educated, healthy population is the most valuable resource a modern economy can have. The West, however, has come to see children as private luxuries rather than public assets. Parents must pour money and effort into their children until they can sustain themselves. Once children are grown, they are seldom expected to provide economic support to their parents. So, raising children feels like consumption, not investment. Perhaps that's why people in rich nations have lost sight of how important each rising generation is to every cohort ahead of them—we all must rely on *other people's children* to be our firefighters, police, and construction crews, not to mention the teachers, doctors, musicians, and librarians who make our lives safer and happier.

The Double X Economy lays the groundwork for a positive future by its judicious spending on families and communities. Though the prevailing wisdom *everywhere* is that women are frivolous consumers who blow their money on clothes and cosmetics, while men are rational and responsible economic beings, evidence reveals this belief to be straight-out gender ideology. Men, as a group, often choose to spend money on their own indulgences, rather than sharing it with their families, even prioritizing expenditures on vices such as alcohol, tobacco, gambling, prostitution, and guns above their children's education. By contrast, women, as a group, spend first on their families, especially children, and communities. A report by Goldman Sachs's Global Markets Institute argued that the BRIC (Brazil, Russia, India, and China) and "Next 11" countries (Bangladesh, Egypt, Indonesia, Iran, Mexico, Nigeria, Pakistan, the Philippines, Turkey, South Korea, and Vietnam) must achieve gender equality in order to create a middle class, which every market economy needs for stability. Goldman Sachs argued that women's spending money on improving household welfare—nutrition,

education, medical care, clothing, childcare, and household durables—
is what builds the middle class.[14] Research has demonstrated repeatedly that, even in the poorest communities, economically empowering
women increases spending on education, nutrition, and health care,
strengthening countries in the process.

Despite women's centrality to our material well-being, the Double
X Economy is consistently undervalued. This is because a worldwide
conviction persists that females simply deserve less. You can see it, for
instance, in the Wage Equality for Similar Work data collected each
year by the World Economic Forum.[15] In the WEF's Executive Opinion Survey, managers in 132 nations are asked, "In your country, for
similar work, to what extent are wages for women equal to those of
men?" The sum of their answers is not a direct report of actual pay,
but an estimate of what normative practice is in that country—what
women are customarily and, implicitly, *fairly* paid. As you can see in
Figure 2, there is no country on earth where the custom is to pay the
sexes equally for the same work. A global rule of thumb says that a
woman is worth only about 65 percent of what a man is, whatever job
they are doing. This prejudice drives women's subordination in every
economic domain.

In every type of work in every sector, every occupation, and every
country, women are paid less than men; every source of pay information, collected by every method, ends in this conclusion. Only through
dishonest manipulation of the data can you show any other finding.
Unfortunately, plenty of apologists for male dominance are willing to
do that, just so they can push out a meme claiming that "the gender pay
gap is a fiction." These trolls massage pay data to control for influences
that are clearly gendered, especially the impact of housework and childcare on women's careers, then announce triumphantly there is no such
thing as gender discrimination.

In truth, the crux of the Double X Economy's plight is its burden of
servitude; so-called "obligations" at home penalize women in the workplace and increase their personal economic risk. Women in every country work as many total hours as (or even more than) men, but because
females carry the burden of unpaid household labor, they have fewer

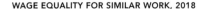

WAGE EQUALITY FOR SIMILAR WORK, 2018

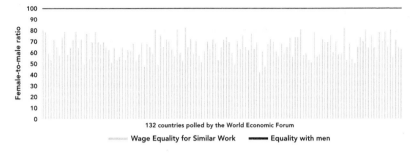

FIGURE 2. The Wage Equality for Similar Work measure is expressed as the percentage of men's pay that women are paid for the same or similar work. The black bar marks the level at which women would be paid equally to men. You can easily see that women are not customarily paid equally for the same work in any country in the world. Countries are shown alphabetically, starting with Albania and ending with Venezuela.

Source: World Economic Forum, *The Global Gender Gap Report*, 2018

hours to devote to paid work, as well as to leisure time. Men can work longer paid hours—and garner the economic benefits—because women are serving them at home.

Cross-national comparisons demonstrate this trade-off for women and governments. As illustrated in Figure 3, women's participation in the labor force has led to higher GDP per capita in wealthy countries like Sweden, the United States, and the U.K., all nations where women work in numbers nearly equal to men but put in fewer paid hours. Women in these countries still do more housework than men—from 30 percent more in Sweden to nearly double that figure in the U.K. So, women and men work an equal number of hours in total, but the men are getting paid for most of their time, while the women are doing more unpaid. Mexico, Turkey, and India have lower female labor participation and, consequently, lower GDPs. Women at home are a significant opportunity cost to these nations. Their women do three to seven times more housework than men. The domestic burden is so skewed in Turkey and India that women work at home for an hour to two hours more

PAID AND UNPAID LABOR BY GENDER

	Labor force participation (female-to-male ratio)	GDP per capita (thousands of US$)	Time per week spent in unpaid work (female-to-male ratio)	Total hours worked per week (female-to-male ratio)	WEF Economic Participation and Opportunity rank (out of 144) in 2017
SWEDEN	95	51.5	1.3	1.00	12
U.S.	86	59.5	1.6	1.01	19
U.K.	87	44.1	1.8	1.04	53
MEXICO	59	19.9	2.8	1.02	124
TURKEY	44	26.9	3.6	1.15	128
INDIA	35	7.2	6.8	1.21	139

FIGURE 3. The percentage of women working varies from the top to the bottom of this table, more or less matching the GDP per capita of each country. This is the connection between working women and national wealth. The third column shows the proportion of time women in that country, as compared with men, spend in unpaid work. In the fourth column is the relationship between all hours spent working, whether paid or unpaid, as compared with men. The fifth column shows each country's rank in the World Economic Forum's Economic Participation and Opportunity Index. The more housework women do, the fewer opportunities are made available to them.

Sources: World Economic Forum, *The Global Gender Gap Report*, 2017, for labor and Economic Participation and Opportunity rank; CIA, *World Factbook*, 2017, for GDP per capita; Organisation for Economic Co-operation and Development database for time use, accessed November 2, 2018

than men every day—they're still mopping floors while their husbands are watching TV.

Women's economic viability is therefore inversely related to their position at home: the more housework women do, the less economic opportunity they have. Subservience in the household also imposes disproportionate losses and risks on women. They are typically expected to subordinate their own ambition to that of their husbands. It is virtually *always* the woman who quits or shifts to part-time work when children come; he continues building his career while hers flounders or goes up in smoke. Women turn down opportunities to advance because their husbands refuse to relocate, even though women are usually expected to relocate for their spouses. Women's "responsibilities" in the home gradually result in lower pay and less advancement at work, but the impact does not stop there: if a couple divorces or the husband dies, the woman and her children will experience economic hardship, and often fall into poverty. Because of a lifetime's accumulation of economic disadvantages, a woman's pension or retirement account will be significantly smaller than a man's, so women are more likely to be poor in old age, becoming a burden to their families and their governments.[16]

The work that women do at home is essential for the functioning of the economic system. However, the practice of measuring only money as a proxy for economic activity has meant that work done in the home does not have a value attached to it. Unfortunately, that omission has developed, over time, into a propensity on the part of economists to treat that labor as if it were without value entirely. That's why feminist economists and women's economic empowerment activists are pushing hard to get governments and their advisors to calculate the value of this unpaid work and include it in their models.

The Double X Economy has never enjoyed an equal share of the wealth it helps produce, largely because women have not been equal owners in family assets. Globally, less than 20 percent of the world's landowners are women. Because land has for so long been society's main store of wealth—and women have nearly always been prohibited from owning it—females now hold much less capital worldwide than men do. Even as wealth expands and some women become rich, they still don't get a fair share.[17]

Another reason women hold less wealth today is that they haven't had the means to keep money safely and privately, nor the ability to invest it. The Double X Economy has been barred from the financial system for centuries; only in the 1970s did women in the West win the right to have bank accounts and credit cards in their own names. Today, women in the developing world push for those same rights. Unfortunately, disrespect for women is still the order of the day in finance, even when it is in the sector's best interest to be welcoming. Bankers protest that females are risky investments, that they care about babies not business, that they are unprofitable financial customers—any excuse they can think of. But nothing the financial sector says to disparage women should be taken seriously, because these institutions do not separate their records by gender and so their views are based on stereotypes rather than evidence.[18] They literally don't know what they're talking about.

In a world given to congratulating itself on open exchange and free trade, the Double X Economy routinely struggles against gender-based barriers to market entry. Guilds, unions, cooperatives, and marketing boards historically have barred women in the West, something that is still true in other parts of the world. But at the level of global exchange, where the markets and profits are very large, the exclusion of women is nearly total. Very few women participate in international trade or win large institutional sales contracts, both areas of the economy in which men control a staggering 99 percent of business. Yet, according to the International Monetary Fund, introducing better gender balance to global trade would be beneficial, because such diversity makes economies more resistant to downturns and more prone to innovation.[19]

The Double X Economy is also constrained in the marketplace because women have limited access to productive resources. Everywhere, females have difficulty commanding the equipment, labor, and materials needed to found and grow their own enterprises. Customers and suppliers believe it's permissible to cheat women, who then may be unable to turn the same profits as their male competitors. Though the constraints are systemic, female entrepreneurs are often criticized for slower business growth; detractors insist that "women just don't know anything about business" or that "women really aren't serious about growth."

The efficient operation of a market assumes the free flow of information. Even in the digital age, however, women have less access to data. While women in developed nations use resources like the internet and mobile phones in numbers equal to men, there has been a large gender gap in the rest of the world in access to information communications technologies. The gap stems from long-standing habits of keeping women at home and controlling their communication with the outside world.

Due to historical gender barriers to learning, the Double X Economy has always had limited access to information. Since the invention of writing and mathematics, societies have limited women's education. Ancient cultures forbade them literacy; today, adult women are more often illiterate than any other segment of the world's population. Over the millennia, education for girls—where it existed at all—focused on household arts, leaving issues of law, medicine, finance, government, and management to boys. Women were not admitted to universities until the nineteenth century, and some disciplines, usually science and mathematics, were off-limits to them until after World War II. When women closed the achievement gap in these subjects during the 1990s, it was because governments had at last given them equal access to higher math classes.[20] Any alleged cognitive deficits had been caused not by inferior female brains but by men who denied women schooling.

Today, the world's women are approaching equality to men in education for the first time in history; indeed, in the developed nations, they are already educated to an equal or greater degree than men. Yet women are still held back from realizing their potential. Consider that among the G7 countries—the United States, the U.K., France, Germany, Italy, Japan, and Canada—women between the ages of twenty-five and fifty-four are 10 percent more likely to have completed higher education than men of the same age (Figure 4). Though female labor force participation is very high and women occupy an equal number of the professional and technical jobs that require the most specialized training and skill, they have not advanced at a rate commensurate with their qualification: men are twice as likely to hold leadership posts in the public or private sectors. This lack of advancement is one reason why, across the G7 countries, women earn only 62 percent of what men do. Meanwhile, young women in the G7 are currently enrolled in higher education nearly 20 percent more often than men are. Unless the barriers that blocked the previous generation are removed, the next cohort of young women will move through their careers slowly and be underemployed at every stage.

Think about what goes into educating these women. Family savings. Government loans and scholarships. Gifts to universities. Taxpayer

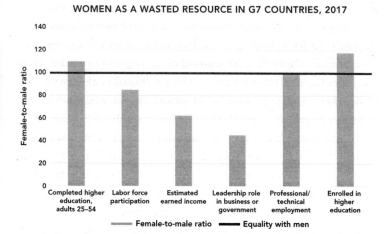

FIGURE 4. The columns show key economic measures as female-to-male ratios. The black bar marks where women would be equal with men. Where the column rises above that bar, women have exceeded men; in the columns that fall below the bar, equality has not been reached. So, from the left, women in the G7 have exceeded men in completion of higher education by 10 percent; are 85 percent of men's representation in the labor force; are paid 62 cents on the dollar; are in less than half the leadership posts men are; are equally likely to be in employment that requires specialized skill; and are now enrolled in higher education nearly 20 percent more often than men are.

Source: World Economic Forum, *The Global Gender Gap Report,* 2017

contributions. These nations are deploying significant resources to educate women, yet they are underutilizing female talent.

Ironically, the G7 countries face the imminent prospect of slow or even zero growth, a problem that better inclusion of women would solve. There is also a skills gap looming in which new jobs will require highly skilled labor, but there won't be enough who meet the qualifications—in part because the G7 countries are throwing some of their best people under the bus. The Double X Economy may well be the world's most wantonly wasted resource.

Just as important to national economies, however, is the power of gender equality to reduce costs that drag on growth. For instance, domestic violence, a phenomenon closely linked to economic gender inequality within communities, is extremely expensive for nations. Over and above the inestimable price of human suffering, there are the police calls, emergency room visits, women's shelters, lost work days, and psychological counseling, which all have price tags that can be used to calculate the aggregate costs. In 2014, the Copenhagen Consensus Center estimated that intimate partner violence against women costs the global economy US$4.4 trillion annually, or 5.2 percent of GDP. To put that into perspective, it's about the same percentage that nations spend on primary education, and thirty times what the world spends on international aid. Because domestic attacks are so often witnessed by children—and boys tend to repeat the behavior as men—their economic impact continues far into the future.

Globally, this phenomenon is dramatically skewed, however, with higher levels of intimate partner violence in the poor, conflicted countries where gender equality is lowest: in Sweden, for instance, 24 percent of women have experienced violence at home; in Afghanistan, it's 87 percent.[21] Certainly, 24 percent of Swedish women enduring violence is much too many. But let's focus on the 76 percent of Swedish men who have not hurt their partners and, indeed, have probably never been violent at all, compared with only 13 percent of Afghans we might say that about. To be sure, men, as a group, are dramatically more violent than women, as a group—and violence is always costly. But violence of *all* kinds is lower in the nations with high gender equality. Even interstate violence has been declining, worldwide, in the decades since World War II.[22]

The reduction in global violence over the past seventy-five years is now referred to as "the Long Peace" in scholarship and international policy. The formal institutions that underpin that trend include the United Nations and the European Union, which were founded in the 1940s with the intention to avoid another conflagration like World War II—the bloodiest war in human history, at 58 million casualties. These organizations, designed primarily to achieve peace, have charters that include gender equality as a top priority. Indeed, experts attribute the decline in interstate violence since the war to three main factors: the expansion of international economic activity, the spread of democracy, and the dramatic rise in gender equality.[23]

The postwar order aspired to repurpose economic activity away from military spending and toward international trade, as a way of maintaining peace. Unfortunately, by the early 1950s, the West was forced to rearm in response to the aggressive stance taken by the Soviet Union. Speaking of this rearmament, General Dwight D. Eisenhower, president of the United States, lamented:

> Every gun that is made, every warship launched, every rocket fired signifies, in the final sense, a theft from those who hunger and are not fed, those who are cold and are not clothed. This world in arms is not spending money alone. It is spending the sweat of its laborers, the genius of its scientists, the hopes of its children . . . This is not a way of life at all, in any true sense. Under the cloud of threatening war, it is humanity hanging from a cross of iron.[24]

Though international trade grew and the Long Peace held, the Cold War brought a massive arms race. The world still spends heavily on arms: today, the United States allocates more than half its discretionary budget to its military, an amount increasing steeply under President Trump. Think what good could be done with even a partial reallocation of that money. In this book, I will often discuss the links between warrior economies, male dominance, all forms of violence, and the distribution of essential resources.

The constraints on the Double X Economy are enforced by threats of violence. We know now, however, that male violence is *not* part of our biological package. If male violence were a hardwired condition we could not change, the number of attacks on women would not vary by geography or over time. Certainly, you would not see whole societies, such as Sweden, where the overwhelming majority of men are not violent.

The evidence at hand, in fact, compels us to begin making a distinction between two groups of men: those who support gender equality and those who don't. In the Western nations especially, surveys show that most men have bought into basic principles such as equality of access, pay, and advancement. There are still, however, those men who retain hostility toward women's presence in the economy and women's subsequent rise in status. These guys are often quick to anger when the topic comes up, which then influences the behavior of the men around them. Furthermore, economic institutions often perpetuate gender inequality in ways that are invisible to these short-tempered males, who too often have authority over more reasonable men, largely because the organizations they're in still treat aggression as the preferred material for leadership. I believe that these group behaviors and institutional norms perpetuate the economic gender gap in a big way, but their effect goes unnoticed in the rush to find fault with women. So, going forward, I will be emphasizing the role of groups, as well as making the distinction between *some* men and *most* men.

A tragic outcome of women's economic exclusion is that women are themselves traded as commodities. The slave trade I mentioned in the opening of this chapter is a global phenomenon, bigger than ever in history. The vast majority of slaves, about 70 percent, are female. Though economic vulnerability is what usually causes females to become human trafficking victims, the trade is not limited to poor nations, as the recent revelations about Jeffrey Epstein's sex trafficking ring illustrate. And, as became clear in that tragic case, the institutions meant to protect vulnerable females often fail them. That's one reason why Kevin Bales, the leading expert on human trafficking, advises that the only way to rid the world of slavery is to economically empower the victims.[25]

The Double X Economy also suffers from hostility in workplaces and markets all over the world. Most women have either experienced sexual assault at work or know someone who has, but this reality was swept under the rug for so long that the #MeToo movement caught people by surprise. Sexual predators exist in factories and high-tech companies, just as they do in Hollywood. Supervisors stalk female agricultural workers, attacking them in open fields where they can't be seen or heard. Venture capitalists try fondling women seeking investment and then refuse to support them if they do not comply. Commuter violence puts women in danger every day. There is no industry and no country where women are safe.

The Double X Economy is also consistently undercut by everyday bigotry. Businesses and other institutions avoid confronting this reality, instead hiding behind flashy but insincere "diversity programs" and euphemizing bigotry as "unconscious bias." Unconscious bias is a specific cognitive phenomenon in which well-established habits of perception produce shortcuts in the brain's processing. Those shortcuts do sometimes result in unconscious acts of unfairness, but the reason that happens is that the cerebral connections were already imprinted by years of learning that women are less worthy. The term is now widely used, however, as a blame-free smoke screen for anyone committing discrimination, whether unconscious or overt, to hide behind. Labeling all discrimination "unconscious bias" only provides cover for those who are consciously biased to continue in unrepentant acts of prejudice.

In companies where males are more dominant—as a rule of thumb, where 70 percent or more of the employees are men—there is more sexual harassment and discrimination against women. However, there is also a marked propensity to mistreat male employees in these organizations. Bullying and autocracy become the order of the day. In male-dominant sectors, the employers are more likely to be "greedy institutions"—that is, they demand an unlimited lien on all the individuals' mental and emotional energy, compelling employees to put their work first, laying claim to all private time, and devaluing other forms of activity, including family life and sleep. Men in such organizations have a significantly higher incidence of health problems, especially heart disease. Here is where we see what the Japanese call *karōshi*—literally, "overwork death."[26] The toxic environments in such firms can be attributed, in part, to the group dynamic *among* the men, which, as the tension accelerates, tends to produce more aggression as well as negative attitudes toward women.

Gender balance makes workplaces friendlier and fairer, while also spurring superior business outcomes. Study after study shows that the best results come from work teams composed of both women and men:

they produce better products, more innovation, and stronger financial returns. Corporate boards with at least 30 percent women show vastly improved performance, with higher financial returns, reduced risk, better governance, improved accountability, fairer personnel management, more transparency, more environmentally sustainable operations, and less inclination to award outrageous salaries or bonuses.

Governments and the public benefit from diverse corporate leadership because the improved transparency and risk reduction protect the stability of the overall economy. A number of social and environmental benefits are also attributable to the values women bring to corporate leadership. A 2012 study from the University of California at Berkeley showed that companies with higher numbers of women on their boards are more likely to invest in renewable power, to actively measure and reduce the environmental effects of their production and packaging, to implement carbon-reduction programs among their suppliers, to integrate the impact of climate change into their planning and financial decisions, to help customers manage climate change risks, to work actively to improve their operations' energy efficiency, and to minimize and mitigate biodiversity disturbances.[27]

The Double X Economy therefore brings an ethic of leadership that could quell the worst impulses of the patriarchal system. Having been excluded from the world of high finance and quick riches throughout history, women appear to assess risk more realistically than do men. Having been charged with the cultivation of children, they seem to have a longer horizon than their male compatriots for return on investment, as well as a greater aversion to long-term damage, such as is happening to the environment. Perhaps because of their historical emphasis on home and connection, women are more likely to invest in their communities, to give to charity, and to demand social responsibility from both the products and stocks they buy.

In the rich nations, including the Double X Economy increases efficiency and performance while reducing risk and waste. In the poorest nations, enabling the Double X Economy can act as a counterweight to the unrelenting pull toward disaster that extreme male dominance causes. But the greatest potential may be in the middle: the "emerging economies"—places like Brazil and Turkey—all rank somewhere between the comparatively better gender conditions of the rich countries and the despair in the conflict zones. These middle-income economies are working successfully toward achieving stability and prosperity, but they remain vulnerable, not least because half their population is so deeply disadvantaged by discriminatory economic practices. Women's economic empowerment within the households of emerging economies can equalize family decision-making, lift livelihoods, reduce interpersonal stress, and open opportunities for all members.

Women are economically disadvantaged in every country in the world. Indeed, it appears that women are economically unequal *within* every group on the planet. There are no religious, ethnic, class, or racial groups in which women, as a class, are as economically autonomous as men. It's because females are unequal in every group that a program to better include women economically would benefit all segments of the world population, including the most marginalized people.

Never in history have we had such a vivid blueprint for eliminating suffering, achieving justice, and ensuring peace. Never before has it been possible to troubleshoot one problem and solve so many others. What we can achieve is worth every effort we can make, every new tool we can invent, and any funds we have to invest. Now is the time for all women and men to join the movement to empower the Double X Economy.

2 | BEHIND THE BIG DATA

Graphs describing the Double X Economy can tell us what happened but not why. If we are going to work for meaningful change, however, knowing what lies behind the data is essential; otherwise, we'll take practical steps that fail or even cause harm. So, once we have seen the big data, we want to get as close as we can to the subject and look for something more like a narrative than a spreadsheet. Let me illustrate by telling you the rest of the story of our sanitary pads project in Africa and then a very different tale from the American business schools.

At the beginning of the sanitary pads work in 2008, we hoped to answer a question that was already getting a lot of attention in policy circles: early data showed a strong connection between secondary-level education for girls and rising GDP, but in the poorest countries, girls seldom made it past primary school. No one really knew why girls dropped out, but many explanations were floated: girls were needed for chores at home, parents preferred to spend money educating boys, and older girls cared for younger siblings.

Local wisdom in Ghana held that teenage girls dropped out of school because they were too materialistic; girls would trade sex, they said, for new clothes and mobile phones. And girls were "rightly punished" when they became pregnant and were forced to leave school, or so I was indignantly told. As self-satisfied as this story sounded, I had to admit that it explained another phenomenon, where adolescent fertility dropped as school enrollment rose. This inverse relationship between enrollment and pregnancy seemed logical enough, but it was as yet unclear why either factor would produce rising GDP (Figure 5).

Our hypothesis was that girls in poor areas lacked adequate sanitary care, and so once they began menstruating, they stayed home several days a month. We speculated that absence from school made the girls fall behind, become discouraged, and finally drop out. Once they had given up school, they had no options other than to get married and start a family. If we could break that pattern, more education among girls would lead to more female participation in the labor force, which would stimulate growth—and the girls would have more choices. Livelihoods would improve and the tax base would grow; if governments provided pads, they might reap benefits that would offset the expense.

Ours was not an unreasonable hypothesis, because if you look at the moment *in life* that girls drop out (Figure 6), instead of the moment *in school*, a link between menarche—the first occurrence of menstruation—and leaving school seemed likely. Despite this logic, we met with resistance from professionals in international aid—people working for charities, as well as governments and international agencies—because no one from a poor village had ever raised a problem about menstruation to them.[1] The U.S. Agency for International Development (USAID) dismissed our idea as frivolous. Others tossed aside our scenario as a figment of Western imagination. Yet the consensus approach to the dropout rate then revolved around poster campaigns intended to convince parents that girls' education was a great idea—and it was not working.

When my British colleagues joined me on the ground in Accra, we began meeting with the government to get permission for the fieldwork, seeking ethics approval, and visiting local nongovernmental organizations to ask for their help in implementing our field test. When we began visiting the NGOs, however, we hit a roadblock. We struck out every time. NGO personnel told us the women already had sanitary

FEMALE SECONDARY SCHOOL ENROLLMENT AND GDP, 2015

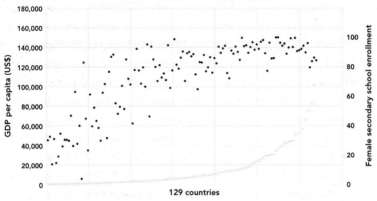

GDP per capita • Female secondary school enrollment, percent of all females in age group

ADOLESCENT FERTILITY AND GDP, 2015

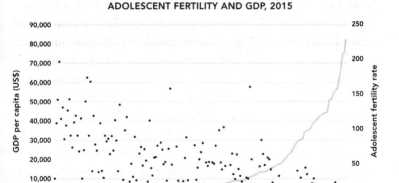

GDP per capita • Adolescent fertility, number of births per thousand among females 15–19

FIGURE 5. The graph at the top shows that GDP increases as more teenage girls remain in school. Notice that the benefit is attached to enrollment, not graduation. Every year a girl is in school helps her and her country. The graph at the bottom shows that GDP also goes up when fewer teens get pregnant. So, as enrollment goes up, teen pregnancy goes down, but GDP goes up in both cases.

Source: World Bank Database, accessed December 15, 2018 (latest available data)

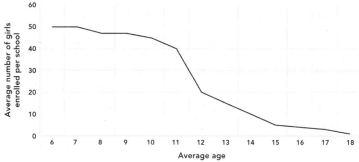

TYPICAL TRAJECTORY OF GIRLS' SCHOOL ENROLLMENT IN GHANA AND UGANDA, CIRCA 2008–2011

FIGURE 6. This line graph distills hundreds of photographs and field notes my colleagues and I took of school enrollment records in rural and peri-urban Ghana and, later, in Uganda (where the randomized trial of the intervention was done). As in this graph, the drop in girls' enrollment between primary and secondary school—when most girls were eleven to fourteen years old— always looked like a ski jump.

pads. Or they said the women used some ancient ritual device for the purpose, and it worked just fine. But these answers were made up—no one had ever actually broached the subject with the women themselves.

CARE International's office in Kumasi (a city in south-central Ghana) was our last chance to convince an NGO to help us. For the first twenty minutes of the meeting, my colleague, Paul Montgomery, and I were sure they were going to turn us down. Then suddenly, a big man walked into the room, breathless from running late. Conversation stopped; everyone turned in his direction. The man explained that when he heard we were coming to discuss sanitary care, he had decided to find out for himself whether there was an issue. He had gone out to the villages to ask the women and was just returning. "The problem is real," he said simply, adding as he sat down, "They just don't talk about it." A little later, Paul and I piled into the big man's truck and headed out to talk to the women and begin seeking approvals from community elders.

The big man, George Appiah, always called ahead to the chiefs, so each council was prepared to receive us. When we arrived, we would be greeted by women singing and dancing—a welcome ritual that I loved. But once we settled in for the meeting, only men were gathered for decision-making; we inevitably had to negotiate a way to include the women.

One particular village sticks in my mind. We were seated beneath a large tree, with an older, all-male council facing us. We asked whether some of the women could join us and were assured that was not necessary. We insisted. So they called to the women, who gathered under another tree, too far away for them to see or hear us and vice versa. We asked whether the women might sit with the rest of us, pointing out that our project was really a women's issue. The council gave the okay and the women moved over. As we explained the problem, I could see the men's eyes grow shocked, then uncomfortable, and finally a bit glassy as they decided this was not a matter they wanted to think or talk about. I suggested we might go with the women to a more private spot for discussion and agreement. The men were relieved to let that happen.

We went to an empty classroom in the school and, now able to speak candidly, explained our mission. The women were very interested, but since they had never seen a sanitary pad, they had trouble imagining what they would be approving. I had purchased pads at kiosks along the road to see what products were available and at what prices, so I had some with me. I then grabbed a half-full bottle of warm Coca-Cola sitting in a cup holder in the truck. With the women gathered close and straining to see, a young woman from CARE poured Coke across a pad, then lifted it up to show that the brown liquid did not leak through. "Aaaahhh!" the women breathed, all at once, then laughed. Their leader, called the "queen mother," shouted that they all approved the research.

Before we began the actual field test, though, we interviewed hundreds of people—teachers, nurses, school officials, parents, and students—all over Ghana. We found that girls did indeed miss school because they had only improvised sanitary materials. However, we also learned that they did not drop out of school from academic discouragement but because of forced marriage, pregnancy, or a decision to run away.

When a girl menstruated, we were told, she was considered "ripe" by the men in her community and therefore both marriageable and sexually available. Her father would want to marry her off quickly to get the "bride price," a significant payment that a groom makes to the father in exchange for his daughter. The going rate for a wife was about US$500, with which a father could buy a cow and still have US$150 left over. The girl's marriage also unburdened the parents of her education and upkeep. So marrying your daughter off early looked like a great deal.

The father usually chose the prospective husband who made the best offer or struck a bargain with someone to whom he owed a debt. I once asked a teacher in Ghana whether daughters had any choice over what man they married. "No!" he snapped. "When you are a woman, you do not choose!" I let it drop, unsure whether he was incensed by the practice or with me for asking an impertinent question.

After marrying, the daughter usually moved to live with her husband's family, often in a village some distance away, and was thereafter required to turn over any earnings she might have to him or his relatives. The birth parents, therefore, did not see any economic value in keeping their daughters in school; they were more likely to invest in their sons' education because the boys stay at home, gradually taking over farms and supporting their parents in old age. These cultural arrangements—common across the developing world—result in a strong preference for sons.

The girls in Ghana became pregnant out of wedlock for many reasons, including the usual one where passions and pleasure just ran away with them. But there was also a high incidence of "transactional sex" (sex in return for some favor, object, or payment) because the girls had few options to earn money. Girls being raised by a relative other than their parents—which was often the case, given the HIV/AIDS epidemic—sometimes had their economic support taken away from them when they began to menstruate. The relative would insist that the girl was a woman now and should be able to take care of herself. As we were told by mothers, aunts, and grandmothers, the common expectation was that the girl would "take a boyfriend" to support herself, especially if she wanted to stay in school. If she got pregnant, this boyfriend sometimes married her, but otherwise she and her child fell further into poverty.

Too often, pregnancy was the result of rape. I was shocked at how common forced sex was and how much it was tolerated. A 2012 study of fifty thousand schoolgirls in ten African countries showed that a third of sixteen-year-old girls had experienced forced sex, usually from about the age of twelve—probably on the arrival of puberty. Coercion was more likely when the community had a favorable attitude toward transactional sex, and many adults themselves had experienced forced sex.[2]

Once a community knew that a girl had menstruated, men would begin following her to and from school. This stalking behavior—euphemistically called "eve-teasing"—is common in developing countries. The "solution" to rape was for the attacker to marry the girl as a way of making things right with her father. Few seemed worried about the trauma suffered by the girl. Male sexual aggression was just an expected part of life. We saw lots of public health campaigns aimed at sexual abstinence, but it was plain that unwanted pregnancy and sexually transmitted diseases weren't going away with "just say no."

We could now see that many girls were indeed leaving school because of pregnancy, as conventional wisdom held, but it wasn't because girls wanted stylish clothes and cool cell phones. Instead, the overwhelming sexual pressure, much of it coercive, as well as a total absence of economic options, pushed the girls in that direction. However, if you could put the brakes on this pressure, GDP would undoubtedly go up, not only because of the better labor supply but also because the many social, health, and economic costs associated with adolescent fertility would go down. The World Bank estimates that keeping girls in school through the twelfth grade would save poor countries between US$15 trillion and US$30 trillion in lost lifetime productivity and earnings. Child marriage costs the world about 1.4 percent of GDP annually, an average of US$4 trillion a year.[3]

Keeping menstruation a secret was critically important to making the change. Unfortunately, the materials girls used in place of sanitary pads were a dead giveaway. They used "found" cloth, usually scraps from old garments, but sometimes stuffing from mattresses or anything else that might absorb fluid. However, the materials usually were *not* absorbent enough, so leaks were frequent; if that happened in a public place like school, they were "outed."

But it gets worse. Cloth has to be washed and dried, yet there was no plumbing, and often girls did not have soap or a private place where the materials could dry. They rinsed the cloth in river water (which is often unclean) and tried to dry it in a secret place, usually under a bed, where it was dark and dirty. Because cloth was scarce, they had to wear each scrap again, even while it was still damp. After a day or two, the cloth would emit a distinctive odor that everyone recognized, and some would comment openly. The health agencies taught girls to hang cloth to dry in sunlight, but putting the bloodstained rags in public view only made the girls more vulnerable. Men in northern Ghana once told my male colleagues that the sight of bloody cloth hanging to dry was arousing, because it meant the girl inside was "ready."

Inadequate infrastructure made the situation even worse. Schools were few and far apart. Roads were so badly eroded that crossing them could be akin to rock climbing. The improvised menstrual materials would shift in the girls' underwear as they moved, making leaks more likely. Schools frequently had no toilets at all, while other latrines were boarded up. Some schools had one toilet that was shared by boys and girls. There was never water for cleaning up.

Girls who did go to school during their periods worried all day about leaks. Their anxiety was particularly intense because of teaching methods in the schools. Instruction is done orally and performance by recitation. Students were expected to stand to respond to questions. Fear of blood on the back of a skirt discouraged girls' participation; the anxiety about it interfered with learning.

That's why girls who were menstruating at school would often run from the classroom and hide in the undergrowth while they changed—an awkward, messy business when you are using cloth scraps. While they were out there with their panties down, they were vulnerable to any men watching them in wait for an opportunity. So, existing practices increased the risk of discovery, with more serious consequences than mere embarrassment.

Disposable pads would offer a considerable advantage under these circumstances, but we knew there would be people in the West who would push for the use of cloth pads instead of disposables for environmental reasons. We did a short test of several cloth options at a big secondary school. We found that even when the cloth pads were given to the girls, they would purchase disposables if they had the money and the pads were available. In fact, they would go without food rather than without pads. But the disposable pads were not available in the most remote villages, which presented a distribution problem.[4] Menstrual cups and tampons were out of the question: putting a foreign object inside a virgin was a strong taboo.

These conditions led us to first test commercially made sanitary pads, not cloth, and we trucked them in ourselves. Here's why. Disposables are cleaner; we forget they are called *sanitary* pads for a reason. All cloth pads, regardless of how they are put together, have the same hygienic issues. Commercial pads are also infinitely more reliable; the sticky plastic strip not only protects from leakage but also secures the pads to panties and makes them changeable in seconds. The ones we eventually chose for the test could last for eight hours if necessary. Because of poor nutrition, menstrual flow was lighter than in the West; most could get by on one pad a day. That meant they could make do with one ten-pack a month, at a total cost of US$1, which was affordable even in very poor communities. The pads were also biodegradable except for the plastic strip on the underside. In any case, we found a better way to handle disposal: an incinerator invented by a Ugandan engineer, Moses Musaazi, could be attached to the wall of the restrooms, with a slot accessible from inside so that girls could dispose of pads privately. The pads could then be burned at medical-waste temperatures, with zero emissions, after girls simply lit a match.

The trade-off between using disposable pads for this purpose and allowing runaway adolescent fertility to continue was also something to consider: such population growth has a massive impact on the environment. Furthermore, girls in the West use four to six times the number of pads and have the means to keep cloth clean. Those girls can cope better; poor African schoolgirls should not have to pay for the sins of the rich countries.

There was no trouble persuading the girls of our purpose. They knew education was their best chance for a better life. Some with older sisters were already trying to hide their periods from their parents. With access to clean, effective, rip-and-stick disposable pads, they might maintain their privacy and possibly delay their first sexual encounter. Eventually, girls would show secondary sex characteristics and would no longer be able to hide, but if pads bought these girls even a few more years, it would make a huge difference to them, to their children, and to their society. If girls were to be in control of their own fate, however, they had to be warned about menarche in advance. As it was, few spoke of menstruation even within families, so girls would see their first blood, panic, and tell their mothers, who would inform the fathers that it was time to arrange a marriage. So, with the permission of parents and schools, we tested free pads and introduced "puberty education."

Our pilot results in Ghana showed that girls spent more days in school after getting pads and puberty education. The large randomized study that followed in Uganda showed modest evidence that the combination of pads and education would reduce dropout rates.[5] But we now knew the intervention would not stop the trajectory of sexual and economic pressures, though pads might slow the impact. To achieve freedom of choice for girls, the negative male behaviors—selling daughters to the highest bidder and eve-teasing—would have to be confronted and stopped.

Just after we completed the pilot in Ghana, I flew to Bangladesh with Catherine Dolan, my longtime research partner. There we were studying a "rural distribution system," which is a sales network that employs poor women in rural areas to distribute goods directly to households. Our NGO partner, CARE Bangladesh, had implemented the system; however, the people at CARE were also keen to assess other interventions and wanted to show some to us. One afternoon, as we were about to get on an "information boat"—a riverboat equipped with communications technology that could give women in rural villages internet access—we were asked if we would wait a bit to talk to someone driving a long way to ask about our sanitary pad work. We finally saw a car careening toward us, and a tall young man jumped out. As soon as he was within earshot, he began explaining that he ran a school sports program for girls, but that droves of them were dropping out when they reached puberty. He jumped on the boat so we could talk more as we proceeded downriver.

The situation he described was almost exactly what we had seen in Ghana, with only two differences. First, the consequences for a girl having sex outside wedlock were far more severe in Bangladesh. Fathers arranged marriages for girls there, too, but if a Bangladeshi girl had sex outside of what her father arranged for her—even if it was rape—she could no longer be married and was said to have "dishonored" the family. The girl's male kin sometimes murdered her, in what is called an honor killing, a shocking practice that is common throughout the Middle East as well. Girls who refused their father's choice were punished viciously, sometimes disfigured or blinded by acid thrown in their faces. Because eve-teasing was common in Bangladesh and the risks were frightening, more parents took their daughters out of school.

The second cultural difference was that Bangladeshis pay a dowry, rather than a bride price. In a dowry system, the family pays the groom to take the daughter. The price of dowry is exorbitant in Bangladesh and can represent months of a poor family's income. The dowry price is lower if girls are young, so there is a strong economic incentive to marry them off early. Especially in dowry cultures, girls are seen as such a financial liability that parents will sometimes kill a female infant at birth. Female infanticide, which is common in Bangladesh, has been so widespread in India and China that their populations have become dangerously skewed toward males.

As we listened to the young man's story, I looked in horror at Catherine, who returned the expression. We were shocked to realize that the circumstances in Ghana, which had seemed so specific and local, might be one instance of a global pattern. There were obvious cultural differences between African countries and Bangladesh, but the mechanisms—eve-teasing and fathers trading daughters—were the same, as was the outcome: the girl was pulled away from potential autonomy to be dependent on a man, or she was pushed out, disfigured, or even killed.

Ten years later, sanitary pad programs are common in economic development. NGOs and governments work to make sure girls have them, and a whole community of researchers has grown up around the effort. Local entrepreneurs produce affordable, eco-friendly versions, as well as better means of disposal. One day, the United Nations' water and sanitation group leader telephoned me to ask about pads for a policy discussion. As she explained the debate, she remarked that the committee felt the real issue was dignity, not education, and that access to pads should be a human right. I felt proud; we had accomplished a lot. But if we had proceeded based on the explanations for the macrodata from outside observers—that the girls sold themselves for cool clothes or became academically discouraged or went home to help their mothers—we would have been well off the mark and misguided in our solutions.

I am now conducting a study in Uganda to assess whether mobile banking accounts help rural women keep control of their earnings. Back in the 2000s, mothers we interviewed accepted that their daughters would marry instead of finishing school and blamed them if they got pregnant or ran away. Today, when I ask this new generation of mothers what they are saving for, they tell me they want to ensure their daughters can stay in school. I get this answer from women whether or not they went to school themselves—they hope their daughters' paths will be different from their own. By economically empowering these mothers, we can help them make that happen.

Now let's turn to the United States to see the same pitfall—where looking at only the quantitative data leads to a conclusion that unfairly denigrates the females and therefore leads to inappropriate practical steps—with another set of data, as well as surprising similarities between two very different situations.

People in developed countries have their own gender problems, of course. Some educated Westerners think they are above sex discrimination, but there are still extreme gender biases, even among the faculties of elite universities. In 2014, two stories about gender inequality in top business schools hit the U.S. press. One was about how independent reviews had found the UCLA business school "inhospitable to women faculty"; the other, about how Harvard Business School was giving itself a "gender makeover."[6]

At *Bloomberg*'s invitation, I wrote a blog post arguing that statistics presented a prima facie case for sex discrimination across all U.S. business schools. Data from the Association to Advance Collegiate Schools of Business showed there were fewer than 30 percent females among the faculties (Figure 7). The vast majority were in untenured posts, and the top ranks were wholly dominated by men. Women were underpaid, regardless of seniority. Attrition, not recruitment, was the main problem: females left faculty posts more quickly than they came in. The largest deficit was among finance faculties, which were 80 percent male nationwide, with 90 percent of full professors (the highest rank) being men. Finance also had the largest gender pay gap, and it hired, retained, and promoted fewer female faculty than any other discipline. I ended the blog by calling on the schools to face up to evidence of unequal treatment instead of glossing over it, as they usually did.[7]

HIRING, PROMOTION, AND TENURE OF WOMEN IN BUSINESS SCHOOLS, 2013

FIGURE 7. The graph shows the percentage of faculty that is female for the four most common business school departments. Note that finance takes in fewer female hires out of graduate school, retains fewer overall, and promotes fewer to the most senior rank than any other department.

Source: American Association of Collegiate Schools of Business

The finance faculties had a ready defense: females are not good enough at math to succeed in their field. One UCLA finance professor wrote a *Huffington Post* piece in response to my blog, claiming that special efforts to hire more women would drag down the quality of school faculties.[8] Other UCLA faculty, both women and men, got in touch with me privately, complaining that my blog normalized the gender problem by suggesting it applied to all business schools, when the situation at UCLA was uniquely dire. They were particularly disconcerted because the school was led by one of the only female business school deans in the United States. However, they felt she was not taking up the cause—a fear later confirmed by another independent report.[9]

I pulled the *Financial Times* stats for business school rankings. UCLA was indeed among the business schools with the poorest female representation, but it had prestigious company: the bottom of the gender list was dominated by top schools like Columbia, the University of Chicago, and Harvard. However, some highly ranked schools, such as Yale, U.C. Berkeley, and Northwestern, had more women faculty, showing it *was* possible to be both a good school and a more gender-balanced one.

The schools with a poor representation of female faculty had another thing in common: all had enormous finance faculties, most of whose members were nearing or past retirement age.[10] These older professors had begun teaching in the 1970s, during the early years of the women's movement, and would have felt the impact of the first "affirmative action" programs directly. Starting in 1972, the U.S. government's diversity policies put intense pressure on universities to hire women. Somehow, this handful of high-end business schools had come through four decades during which diversity had been powerfully prioritized— and had never changed. That would have been possible only if they had consciously mounted a resistance. These guys had learned how to stonewall gender equality, of that I was sure.

The 1970s women's movement had also cast a skeptical eye on the conventional American marriage, in which women stayed home and men paid the bills. I suspected most of these men had stay-at-home wives, because that was the norm in their time, and I later confirmed my hunch was correct. I wanted to know because research shows that

American men with stay-at-home wives are more likely to think organizations hurt themselves by hiring too many women, and therefore they make decisions that prevent qualified females from advancing. Such men want to draw a sharp line between home and work—and then insist that the women stay on the home side. One man at UCLA said: "I don't see it. If you're going to be working, you've got to work. We should not have different standards due to kids, parents, etc. That's for you to work out at home." Female faculty at UCLA said they were often trashed for family reasons: "I heard someone say, 'She must ignore her kids to be that productive.' I heard another say, 'She's a terrible mother.'"[11]

These older finance professors further grew up at a time when American women were almost completely excluded from the financial system. In those days, most shared bank accounts with their husbands or were given a cash "allowance." They couldn't get a mortgage or credit card in their own name. Many knew nothing about their family's finances—it was widely seen as insubordination for a wife to even ask her husband about such matters. So the notion that a woman could hold a tenured post in finance must have been laughable to these older men.

The older finance professors would have trained in economics departments because there were not then separate Ph.D. programs in finance. Economics was at that time enamored of a philosophy advanced by Milton Friedman, who later won a Nobel Prize and whose thinking was brought to the public through popular books and television. Friedman was against nearly any government intrusion into the economy—like affirmative action—and insisted markets treated everyone the same. If individuals didn't like their economic lot, they had no one to blame but themselves. The most irresponsible premise ever promoted by an economist also came from Friedman: the idea that businesses did not owe social responsibility to the communities in which they operated, but should concentrate exclusively on delivering profit to shareholders.

Harvard Business School also had a gender problem, but the school's administrators were owning it. A new dean, Nitin Nohria, had promised Harvard's first female president that he would lead a bold program to improve the gender situation at the business school. Even

Slate grudgingly acknowledged that Nohria seemed committed: "Open contrition is a new look for HBS, groomer of trading-floor kings and boardroom honchos. When a willingness to admit fault, to question tradition, comes from entitlement-and-privilege land, perhaps that's reason enough to celebrate."[12] Nohria confronted issues head-on: low female faculty representation, especially at tenured ranks; lower academic performance by female students, despite admissions qualifications equal to men's; a toxic student environment; and gender-biased teaching materials. So far, no one knew how Harvard Business School faculty, also dominated by finance, would respond.

The narrative setup was too much for me to resist. I decided to get "behind the numbers" by doing some interviews about gender in U.S. business schools. Interviewees speaking to me would be taking a genuine career risk, as there was a strict taboo against speaking out on gender matters. Therefore, Oxford's research ethics board insisted I keep identifying information confidential. That's why I will not name people or schools from the interviews here. I chose business professors from all over the United States, including six top-ranked schools, as well as state universities and a few less prestigious schools. I selected respondents who were both distinguished as scholars and experienced at teaching; all of them were full professors.

My respondents first blamed the belief system inside the schools, especially as proselytized by the finance professors. They said that the foundational premise of "extreme-market economics," as some called it, was that the market is perfect and inexorable, with no bias or irrationality. Whatever the market produced, no matter how unequal, was the right outcome. Whatever people needed would be automatically provided; anything that was not produced, people shouldn't have. "Heroic efforts" to change what the market did were doomed.

Most of my interviewees found the extreme-market stance contemptible. They said it had been fashionable fifty years ago, but was no longer valid among "real economists." They also said extreme-market adherents were too zealous to be reasoned with. "They won't really entertain any other explanation," said an alienated finance professor. "They view it as a religion . . . There's not much talking you can do to people who believe that way, so there's not much you can do about it." "They think they are not only objective, but infallible," said a labor economist with business school experience. "The arrogance is breathtaking." Interviewees pointed out that the extreme-market framework provides a swift rationale for inaction on diversity. If the market wasn't providing qualified females to become finance professors, the business schools should wait until the invisible hand gently deposited some on their doorstep.

To buy this argument, you had to believe that the extreme-market proponents could objectively judge whether someone was qualified. But that was exactly the problem: at UCLA, for instance, finance professors had a narrow view of what a qualified candidate was, and their colleagues did not agree with them. Even the top tenure committee of the university had been reversing the business school's tenure decisions on women. Universities rarely reverse tenure decisions made at the department level; this was a red flag suggesting that the most accomplished scholars thought there was systematic bias at the business school.

The evaluation of professors' qualifications—whether for hiring, tenure, or promotion—swings on the faculty's opinion of the candidate's research. In the extreme-market stance, good research must adhere to the premise that markets are right and fair. Only quantitative methods are acceptable. Sample sizes must be astronomical by the standards of other disciplines—millions, not hundreds or thousands, of data points. Only monetary data, like stock prices and earnings ratios, collected in the normal course of business, counts.

All research is slotted into two stereotypes. "Hard" is quantitative, has big samples, holds consistent with the belief system, and is objective, difficult, and done by men. "Soft" is qualitative, uses small samples, is critical of the belief system, and is subjective, easy, and attributed to women. The conventional wisdom was that women were rejected because they do "soft" work. Several said that if a female did "hard" research, she was scrutinized more closely, and suspected of getting male colleagues to do her math.

Like most divisions between "men's work" and "women's work," these categories fall apart in practice. Imagine, for instance, the extreme-market economist, who gets his data from secondary sources and never collects it himself, sitting at a computer in Boston or Los Angeles, sipping a latte and pushing buttons. Compare that with the studies I just described in Africa and Bangladesh. We updated our rabies and tetanus shots, started our antimalarial drugs, and packed up the antibiotics before getting on a ten- to thirty-hour flight. We then rode in a truck for many more hours, the last few off-road, and spent twelve-hour days with no clean place to go to the bathroom, wash our hands, or get a snack. Every project took months of planning, had complex budgets, required winning the cooperation of loads of people, and produced huge amounts of both qualitative and quantitative data. But in the eyes of extreme-market believers, the secondary data manipulated by the guy with the latte is "hard" and our research is "soft."

Research is judged in a ritual imported from economics: a research seminar in which potential hires, promotion candidates, or doctoral students present their work and then the male professors compete with one another to rip the candidates to shreds. A tenured woman at a top-five school recalled: "Sitting in the job talk, I felt the way this questioning was proceeding was unfair. It wasn't just because they were female but they were also young . . . Then you have these really senior faculty members being very condescending, which was a really horrible reaction . . . You have this hangover of all these male faculty who live in a different era."

The overall atmosphere at schools where female representation is low is disrespectful, sarcastic, and aggressive. One highly regarded woman at a top school characterized a faculty meeting this way: "So it's a room of sixty-five people, sixty men. It is surging waves of testosterone, alpha male after alpha male after alpha male." All-male lunch groups are common; sports outings and scotch-tasting parties are central in faculty culture. Even in a mixed-sex setting, the talk can turn ribald: "One of the junior faculty members who's gone and is now at [another good school] came to me and said the most depressing thing ever: 'It's not all the butt-fuck jokes that depress me, it's the more subtle sexual things.' The more subtle sexual stuff, she said, was that they would tell stories about other people and the moral of the stories was: 'There's no way you're going to get tenure unless you're a man in a traditional household with a wife supporting you.'" A group of "grown-up faculty" became concerned that the conversations were creating "an environment of sexual harassment" and called a meeting to try to put a stop to it. One of the perpetrators took offense, saying the request was an infringement on his intellectual freedom. "I mean it's like, 'No, butt jokes and intellectual freedom are not in the same category, dude.'"

Some women, after winning tenure, found themselves working in environments they felt were even more oppressive and unfriendly *because* they had won a fight. However, many had husbands who could or would not relocate because of their own jobs. In academia, changing jobs means changing schools, which nearly always implies a move. So these women felt trapped in a workplace where they were not valued. The male faculty realized this limitation, which seemed to assure them that they could continue their negative behavior without fear of reprisal.

Though the finance guys set the toxic tone, they are rewarded with the highest salaries, the best offices, and the most assistants. The higher-ups won't risk disciplining them. The power imbalance makes it hard for the good guys to resist—and there *are* good guys in all these schools—so they bend the knee rather than risk a fight. The women seldom speak up. A woman who worked in an 88 percent male school told me she never spoke in faculty meetings because the response was like "a pack of pit bulls charging your neck." Whether women or men bring up the gender problem in a faculty discussion, the alpha males become highly offended. They lash out angrily. A code of silence about gender grows up among the rest of the faculty to avoid dealing with their rage.

Several interviewees alluded to an outlier, a prestigious school in the Midwest that had been able to train, hire, and retain an unusually high number of female finance faculty. A woman there told me her school was so different because its first dean had insisted people be polite to one another. To me, it spoke volumes that ordinary courtesy would make such a huge difference.

Most female business school faculty also struggle with student aggression. Male primacy among MBAs is established by taking down a teacher. Believing that women are born bad with numbers, these students usually try to catch a female professor in a math error while teaching. In one story, a group of male MBAs made a pact to reduce their female teacher to tears before the end of the term. They reached their goal, with time to spare. The schools generally don't discipline MBA students, leaving female faculty without recourse.

Female students are undermined by the aggressive culture, too. A few top schools have seen that even though incoming females had the same qualifications, their performance declined during the first semester. Finance classes, in which teachers and male students alike were reported to be disdainful toward women, had a particularly negative impact. Women who planned finance careers switched to marketing, believing that they "must not have what it takes." Because the toxic behavior in the schools affects career choice, it is then carried out into the financial sector.

Harvard's most candid confession was that its famous case method of teaching yielded biased grades. In this method, students get a write-up of a real-life business problem and then are asked to argue the solution during class. Professors grade them on how often they participate, not on the substance of their contribution, assigning grades from memory after class. Females performed equally on exams, but not in class participation, which counted for 50 percent of their grade. Investigation showed professors called on men more frequently and remembered them more often. When the system changed to make professors call equally by gender, aided by a note taker to count the responses, the difference in grades reversed dramatically. More women received awards and recognitions that year than at any time in HBS history.

At the end of the Harvard gender experiment's first year, 70 percent of professors, students, and staff agreed in an internal survey that the gender initiative had improved the atmosphere. At UCLA, the results were less positive. The university commissioned yet another independent report, this one by management consultancy Korn Ferry. In its survey, faculty were asked whether the school would be a better place if there were greater gender diversity; 78 percent said it would. A small group of disgruntled men, about 20 percent of the faculty, was holding everyone else hostage, telling Korn Ferry they were experiencing "reverse discrimination." Pretty cheeky coming from a school where the faculty was nearly 90 percent male—and where these same men control the decision-making.[13]

Korn Ferry's report stated the problems clearly and called out the leadership, but recommended actions that were unlikely to have impact: mentorship for junior faculty, coaching for the leadership, faculty collaboration on diversity planning, and education on unconscious bias for everyone. None of these tactics addressed the main problem: the most powerful people were dead set against gender diversity, did not care what the rest of the faculty wanted, felt completely justified in their bias, and would turn efforts to treat women equally into a narrative of their own victimization. A couple of years later, the university reappointed the dean, despite her reported failure to lead on gender diversity, which effectively told the women at the business school that no one at the top really cared and gave the extreme-market guys permission to continue their vendetta.

In this business school example, you can see once again that the conventional explanation for the big graphs was wrong: you really have to believe a lot of backward balderdash to think that all the women in the world are so bad at math that none could live up to the standards required by a business school. But there is no hard data on those factors that support the alternative narrative: no measure of "job talk" bullying, offensive lunchtime jokes, resentful old men, disengaged administrators, absurd research requirements, and toxic manners exists to plot alongside the line showing females disappearing from business school faculties.

In both places, the local explanation rested on prejudices against females—that they are slutty, selfish, or stupid—rather than empirical evidence. So, in the African case, the shortsighted next step would be to try to instill better values in the girls by encouraging abstinence, turning "fallen" girls into pariahs, and venerating the ones who quietly allow themselves to be married. Since the girls have so little control over their own sexuality and are often forced by economic straits into transactional sex, however, a *Scarlet Letter* program like this will not work. Challenging the men's aggressive behavior or rethinking marital practices would address the real problem, but people everywhere are loath to challenge patriarchal norms, even when they are this destructive.

In the business schools, the problem was said to be that women simply were unable to do math, which meant they were incapable of doing the "hard" research required to succeed. If women *were* biologically bad at math, not much could be done about it. And that is exactly what the finance professors wanted done—nothing. But even when the women did do the math—and did it correctly—the finance guys changed the narrative to maintain their prejudice, saying they must have had help from a man. So, the actual problem here was the disrespect the alpha males had for women. These men are extremely unlikely to be convinced by anyone else that they are wrong.

In both cases, therefore, the actual propellant behind the numbers was coming not from the females, but from the males, who exerted their will through the institutions they dominated by monopolizing decision-making and control over resources. Research shows that aggressive male behavior will continue for as long as it is rewarded.[14] In business schools, the faculty aggressors are paid the most and command deference from everyone. Fathers in Africa get paid for selling their daughters and improve their standing with other men by doing so. Even the rapists get sex without consequences and assert an attitude of prowess that gives them status.

Other features typical of the Double X Economy are present in both instances. Patriarchs make decisions for everyone else in each place—imposing marital norms on females who would rather pursue education and autonomy than bow under an expectation of silent servitude and self-sacrifice; fertility is used as a blunt instrument on both continents, with the African girls being forced to bear children, and the American women being heavily pressured to give up motherhood for work, or work for motherhood. In both instances, females are being deprived of the fruits of education because of the patriarchy's ideas about the proper role for a wife.

In both settings, the women, regardless of how unwelcoming their environment is, are tied to their husband's choice of location and therefore cannot seek more positive conditions elsewhere. Silence further enables both of these negative situations to continue. In the sanitary pads study, we confronted a taboo evident worldwide against talking about menstruation. In the business schools, silence perpetuated the gender inequality by allowing the alpha males to avoid confrontation and blame. Prohibitions against speech about gender also allowed the business schools to avoid taking responsibility for their toxic organizational cultures. The code of silence in both instances made the topic of gender inequality a shameful one, further discouraging its address.

In 2014, the business school faculties I was studying were upwards of 80 percent male, a proportion that portends not only problems for the women but also autocracy and bullying among the men. Small groups of aggressive males unsympathetic to the women exerted disproportionate control over the other men, some of whom saw the treatment of females as unfair. The explosive males were heavily invested in rigid, traditional notions of how men and women are supposed to behave, especially in marriage, and would retaliate if pushed.

In psychology, this sensitivity to gender role conflict is called "precarious manhood" or "masculine gender role stress" (MGRS): men who are too tightly attached to traditional notions of masculinity react with outsize anger to any gender role challenge, even trivial or subtle ones.[15] Economic dominance is a particularly sensitive issue for them. Psychologists explain this behavior by pointing to a pervasive need among males to "earn manhood" continually throughout life; the never-ending pressure makes some men particularly sensitive to the constant risk of being found inadequate. When directly confronted, these men respond with a flash of disproportionate wrath and then need to reestablish their manhood in order to let go of that rage. In laboratory tests and field studies, they defuse their anger by punching things, engaging in risky behavior, spending money, or gambling. In real life, these men, as a group, tend to drink a lot, beat their wives, gamble, and do drugs. One thing precarious men consistently do under threat is to reject any proposition that implies or refers to gender equality. Crucially, however, precarious men appear to be a distinct minority; in the studies, the men who *did not* exhibit the response were between 60 and 80 percent of the sample.

In a situation where MGRS men are setting the tone, normal men also become stressed about the requirements for manhood and will behave in ways they usually would not, sometimes by acquiescing silently and others by becoming aggressive themselves. Importantly, their response is not about the women at all, but is a matter of signaling loyalty and worthiness of "manhood" to other guys. The end result is often that all the men close ranks against the women, blocking a more productive response. Going forward, I will be distinguishing between the angry individual reaction (precarious manhood) and the group response, which I will call the "band-of-brothers effect."

Notice how the older finance professors model exclusion for the younger men, in their hiring, training, management, promotions, and pay practices. These guys have had decades to teach incoming males that this is what it means *to be a man* in their brotherhood. One way they perpetuate the brotherhood is by elevating new members who are male while excluding females. With this backdrop, it becomes more difficult to promote a woman without seeming to cross the group.

According to research, the key to resolving this situation is to change the gender balance of the group by increasing the number of females. A practical rule of thumb is that, at about 30 percent female, the problem begins to diminish; at about 40 percent, it has nearly disappeared. The business schools, however, would face the same catch-22 that many other male-dominated organizations confront: they need to change the gender ratio to dissipate the toxic environment, but they can't get women to stay *because* of the toxic environment.

In the business schools, efforts similar in purpose to Dean Nitin Nohria's program at HBS have been undertaken since 2014. As a result, most schools have actually increased their percentage of women faculty pretty impressively in the past five years. A key strategy in softening school culture has been to accept equal numbers of males and females into the MBA programs instead of the 70-to-30 or worse skews that had been typical. According to my interviews, changing the gender mix of the students has an immediate positive impact on the culture by reducing MBA aggression—the faculty say they can feel the difference right away. The second strategy has been to reduce the number of finance classes the students take, especially in their first term. That way, the finance guys don't have as much opportunity to set the tone by rewarding male students for aggression and using it to diminish the female students. By requiring students to take a full slate of finance classes in the first term, the schools had also been holding up finance professors as models to be emulated; reducing the number of finance classes gave other faculty the chance to step forward as heroes, especially by teaching courses on leadership or business ethics, which have a positive effect in themselves. In essence, the business schools addressed their gender problem by addressing some of the *institutional* issues perpetuating it. And that approach produced progress.

Another extremely important lesson emerges about male behavior from both Africa and the United States: there were good guys in both cases, and some of them were resisting. The UCLA women definitely had male advocates, and there were men supportive of gender diversity at the other schools, too. HBS's Nohria really seemed to "get it." In the Africa case, there were George Appiah, Paul Montgomery, Moses Musaazi, the driver in Accra (whose name is Thomas Okyere), and many others I did not mention here, including several teachers and all the males working for CARE in the field. There were also a few fathers refusing to follow the prescribed path and instead supporting their daughters' education, including (as we later learned) buying sanitary pads, even if the packs had to be brought into the village from the city by relatives. In both cases, the actions of these good guys are a critical factor in the effort to effect change. But it is always important, in this work, to respect the considerable risk the good guys take for stepping outside what is expected of them as men.

Finally, there is one crucial difference between the women in rural Africa and the women in the United States. Female faculty in American business schools have money, education, and social mobility that dramatically overshadows what is possible in Africa. Those freedoms are a direct result of two hundred years of activism. The presence of a sisterhood makes a big difference when women want to stand up to the brotherhood.

The older men in the U.S. case, however, may still be reacting negatively to the memory of what's often called the "Second Wave" of the 1970s, the "First Wave" being the early twentieth-century suffrage effort.

The young women on these faculties were, literally, the daughters of the Second Wave, but it may never have occurred to them that they might be on the receiving end of a fifty-year grudge.

Without a historical perspective, it can be hard to make sense of what we see in the here and now. Next, I will show how hundreds of years of economic exclusion, applied on a grand scale, have left a mark so lasting that it now threatens something essential to us all: the food supply.

3 | CONTROLLED BY NECESSITIES

was standing idly in a rural Ugandan schoolyard. Our local research assistants were in the classrooms, trying to find out what happened to the girls on our roster who had disappeared from school. Since my foreignness always seemed an intrusion on these conversations, once the team deployed, I just waited outside.

From the corner of my eye, I saw an old woman approaching. I braced myself. Confused old women with angry looks sometimes haunt these schoolyards, and I am not very good with them. Sam, the driver from our NGO research partner, moved across the yard to intercept her, anticipating that she would beg for money. Global charities don't like begging when Westerners visit because the situation can become volatile. But before he reached her, the woman stopped, looked at me with unmistakable clarity, and said, in English, "Sister, can you help me?"

Sam put his arm gently around her shoulders and, whispering softly, walked her away. After a few seconds, she turned and said, "I do apologize. I didn't realize." The two headed toward a small thatched structure on the edge of the school's property.

As we drove to the next school, Sam explained that the woman, whose name was Agnes, had been born to a prosperous family and educated, then married a man from a similar background. When he died young, her husband's land passed to his brothers, as is customary in Uganda, leaving her nothing to live on. Then her father died and, as is the usual practice, his land passed to her brother, forcing Agnes to live on whatever generosity her sibling wished to bestow.

If the ending to Agnes's story were happy, it would read like a Jane Austen novel. Her brother speculated with the land and lost it. He and his family now lived in a small house near the school, while Agnes lived in the tiny structure behind it. Too small to stand in and big enough for sleeping only if you curled up, the shelter had no light or water. She served lunch at the school in exchange for food.

My encounter with Agnes crystalized something for me. Perhaps it was because I saw the common nature between this woman and myself more clearly than usual. We were about the same age and height; she looked me in the eye as she spoke in my language. There was also her manner of address, "*Sister*, can you help me?" I pondered this a long time, finally concluding that what bound Agnes and me, and also the girls forced to marry and the girls who ran away, as well as the wild-eyed "grannies" who peeped through the school windows, was that we were all characters at different times in the same narrative and not at all, in fact, worlds apart. In a single glance, there had been a still and perfect present where I could see that.

Agnes was reduced to begging, hunger, and quarters unfit for a human because, as a woman, she could not inherit land. The echo with Jane Austen—or, for that matter, *Downton Abbey*—suggested a historical link between land rights for women in the U.K. and in Uganda, a former British colony. That led me to wonder how common the prescription that only men could own and inherit land was elsewhere in the world, so I began searching for the answer.

I found that the *Downton Abbey* principle has been executed on a massive historical scale: in culture after culture, century after century, land could pass only from one male to the next.[1] Regardless of what statutes may have stipulated, customary practices, religious strictures, tribal councils, family norms, and gender roles have conspired to keep women landless. Even in matrilineal societies, though the land passes *through* the females, its control normally moves from one male to another.

Legal and religious codes that precluded female inheritance and property ownership swept across the world through trade and conquest. For instance, Islam's restrictions on female inheritance today were first spread along the path of seventh-century Arab conquest and trade, from West Africa to Indonesia. Europeans brought laws to their colonies that forbade women from owning property, but those strictures had been active in their own countries for centuries—since before written legal codes. British Common Law and the Napoleonic Code, which applied to North America, Australia, and much of Africa and Asia, denied property rights to married women entirely. Roman-Dutch Law, as well as the Iberian codes that were transferred from Spain to Latin America, sometimes did allow women to inherit, but other forces worked against any practical impact. For instance, where daughters were allowed to inherit, the allocation of assets usually gave land to the sons and possessions like jewelry and dishes to the female heirs. And if females did inherit land, they were pressured to turn it over to brothers or uncles.

In the Western countries today, women have property rights only because of a series of legal reforms taken between 1850 and 1980. However, history shows that whenever reforms have granted women land rights, the change has been only temporary. The Song dynasty in China (960–1275 C.E.), for example, awarded property rights to women, but the Yuan dynasty (1279–1368 C.E.) brought a resurgence of Confucian philosophy that caused those rights to be curtailed. The Ming dynasty (1368–1644) took back women's property rights altogether. Land was collectivized under Mao, but in today's China, the government has enacted laws that support the custom of transferring all property brought into a marriage to the husband.[2] Women won inheritance rights in the French Revolution, but lost them when the Napoleonic Code was enacted five years later. Women had extensive economic rights under the Ottoman Empire, including the ownership of land, but those rights were withdrawn after more than a century—and then reinstated under Atatürk in 1923. In short, no woman can assume that the property rights she enjoys are permanent. If watching *The Handmaid's Tale* makes you fear a massive overnight backslide for women's rights, it should.

The historical practices I uncovered were widespread and long-standing enough to explain the stark picture of land ownership in the world today. The United Nations Food and Agriculture Organization (FAO) has posted a reasonably complete nation-level data set showing that women are 18.3 percent of landholders across all regions of the world (Figure 8). Females also hold smaller and poorer plots than men do, so their share of the land is actually lower than 18 percent. In the developed countries, even after a century of equality laws and women's property rights, only 16 percent of landholders are female—fewer than the global average, a vestige of their having been forbidden to own land for centuries.[3]

More than 80 percent of the earth's farmable surface is therefore owned by men.[4] This single fact rolls up into a monopoly on power and wealth that is earth-shattering to contemplate. By cornering humanity's main source of material wealth, men have been able to retain power over the world's capital for hundreds, even thousands, of years.

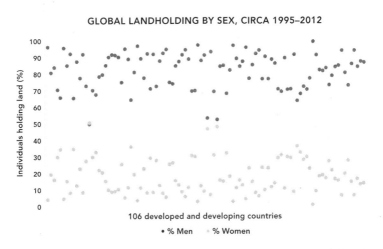

GLOBAL LANDHOLDING BY SEX, CIRCA 1995–2012

Individuals holding land (%)

106 developed and developing countries

● % Men　　● % Women

FIGURE 8. This scatterplot illustrates the vast gap between male and female ownership of land in a regionally balanced sample of about half the countries in the world. The black dots show that 70 to 90 percent of landholders in most countries, rich and poor, are men. Countries are shown alphabetically, starting with Algeria and ending with Zambia.

Source: Food and Agriculture Organization, "Gender and Land Rights Database," http://www.fao.org/gender-landrights-database/data-map/statistics/en/

My search revealed examples from all over the world where clan customs have kept women from controlling land prior to written statutes. Agnes's situation illustrates that customary practices make women vulnerable, regardless of formal property rights. In Uganda, national statutes give widows the right to inherit property, but in reality, there are three sets of laws—customary, religious, and statutory—and each differs on this question. Though the government insists on the primacy of statutory law, the customary and religious rules exert a much stronger influence, especially in the rural areas. By custom, males of a clan control all land under their family's power, with individual men given specific plots to cultivate and expand—or let run to ruin—during their lives. When a man dies, his property goes back to the males of his family, and most of it will then be bequeathed to the man's sons, if he had any, with the remainder redistributed among other men in the clan. Daughters may be allowed to live on their father's land until they marry, when the land goes back to the family's men. Clans go to great lengths to ensure that no property goes to a widow, because they fear she will marry again. The land would then be owned by a different tribe—because all clans have rules that attach land only to males—and lost to their family forever.[5]

East African custom holds that the widow herself *is* property and so cannot *own* property. Without property or income of her own, she would have no way to feed her children if she tried to take them away, so she is usually forced to submit to "wife inheritance," a practice whereby she becomes the wife of one of the tribe's other males. The question of which man the widow will marry is not for her to decide. The way it works is that the men who stand to inherit the deceased man's property have sex with her until *they* decide which one will take her as a wife. "That evening [after the funeral], many men come to her and there is no control," a Kenyan woman explained to Human Rights Watch. "She would have the ability to say no but for economic factors. If this man is giving you soap, this man is giving you meat, you cannot say no. It is only those women that are economically empowered that can say no to sex. This man comes with inducements, with inducements she needs."[6] Many communities in East Africa also practice "widow cleansing," by which a designated "cleanser," usually an outcast, rapes the widow;

his sperm removes her deceased husband's ghost, making her "clean" enough to be acceptable to her new keeper.

All this is done without a condom. As a widow cleanser in Kenya explains, "I don't use condoms with the women. It must be body to body . . . If no sperm comes out, she is not inherited . . . I don't do anything to stop pregnancy. Two widows have had my children. I don't act as the father or give assistance."[7] Uganda has one of the highest rates of HIV/AIDS in the world, and women there are twice as likely as men to have it.

Improbably, what I have so far described is the more orderly process. In a custom called "property grabbing," any male relative can come to the dead man's home, throw the widow and her children out, and plant himself as a claim on everything there. Others then make competitive claims, and violence often breaks out.

Why doesn't the widow go back to her birth family? Her parents were paid a bride price at the time of marriage. Her family cannot take her back unless they repay the husband's clan. The birth family would also have to take on the economic support of the widow and her children. Girls are married to distant clans in the first place because they are an economic burden. So, her own family may not allow the widow to return. The one stroke of luck Agnes had was that her family did take her back.

Why don't these widows just get a job? Formal employment is scarce in poor nations and almost nonexistent in rural areas. Where there is formal employment, it goes first to males. Husbands customarily take any money a wife earns—it is seen as their right, just as in the developed nations a century ago. Wives have few chances to save. Normally, a widow will not have the means to last even a few days. And, honestly, if her husband's predatory relatives learned she had money, they would take the cash by force and consider it their entitlement.

Claiming their rights under the law is therefore usually impossible for these women. You have to have money to hire a lawyer, as well as cash to take the bus to town, never mind an interval to pursue the complaint. The propensity for families to engage in violence is itself a barrier. You would have to post a twenty-four-hour police watch over a number of years to protect a widow who stood against customary practices—when literally everyone around her wants to take her property and feels they have a right to it. There aren't enough policemen in all of Uganda to pull off a national enforcement strategy like that. In the end, the best security a woman can have is a son to inherit land and so provide limited safety for her and her female children. The international community can be judgmental about this attitude, but son preference among women is rooted in real fears. The economics must change before the attitude can.

Religious rules also affect the administration of inheritance rights in Uganda. About 12 percent of the population is Muslim, and in the Ugandan interpretation of Islamic law, a widow with children may have one-eighth of her husband's property should he die. However, if the husband was polygamous, which is common in Uganda, that one-eighth must be divided among all the wives left behind. If a widow has no children, she might get nothing.

The upshot is that a Ugandan woman whose husband dies is at immediate risk of poverty and personal attack without recourse to anyone. Throughout sub-Saharan Africa, a similar narrative echoes, like this story from Kenya:

> Shortly after Emily Owino's husband died, her in-laws took all her possessions—including farm equipment, livestock, household goods, and clothing. The in-laws insisted that she be "cleansed" by having sex with a social outcast, a custom in her region, as a condition of staying in her home. They paid a herdsman to have sex with Owino, against her will and without a condom. They later took over her farmland. She sought help from the local elder and chief, who did nothing. Her in-laws forced her out of her home, and she and her children were homeless until someone offered her a small, leaky shack. No longer able to afford the school fees, her children dropped out of school.[8]

Multiply this story by millions of widows and their co-wives (and all the children they collectively have) and you can see why the number of souls in Africa living in poverty, infected by disease, and without an education keeps growing, making it nearly impossible to turn the region around economically. I once explained this situation to the owner of an international think tank that advises the G20. He was astonished. He had never thought the conditions of women should be considered in recommendations about how to bring Africa out of poverty.

Around the world, the advantage men hold through land ownership ripples out to give them command over equipment, technological know-how, and inputs like fertilizer and pesticides. Throughout the developing nations, banks accept only land as collateral against loans, so only men can own productive equipment, like tractors and threshers, as well as large animals.

The few women who do own land have smaller, less fertile plots and fewer means to develop them, so they also have a greater chance of losing whatever they have. Agriculture is a risky business, and when disaster hits, it is harder for women to bounce back. They have fewer assets they can liquidate and fewer opportunities to earn money another way. Their greater vulnerability makes them risk-averse, which the financial industry often attributes to cowardice. It never considers that women's risks are different from men's and their ability to recover more limited.

Agricultural field agents, who are virtually always male, tend to talk only to men about new practices and technologies. They see that males are better positioned to take advantage of innovations and assume any information will "trickle down" to females. Women are therefore less informed about new methods, as well as less equipped to take advantage of them. International planning for dissemination of new technologies usually assumes that the innovation will be equally available to men and women, when it is not.

Heavy agricultural equipment is designed for men, so if women can't use it, they have to hire men to do the work; the men usually resist working for a woman and will postpone the job until late in the season, reducing the woman's yield. The sum of the disadvantages women have in farming practices reduces their final production of food by 20 to 30 percent.[9] Having less access to productive resources also disadvantages women in a marketplace with many gender barriers.

One day in the mountains bordering Kenya, I talked about market challenges with a woman trying to turn a tiny triangle of land around her home into a coffee and banana business. Julia's husband ran a motorcycle taxi service, called in Uganda a *bodaboda*—after the sound of the bike. *Boda* drivers are killed or maimed every day in Uganda. Thinking of Agnes, I asked Julia whether her husband's brothers would take away her home if he died in an accident. "They wouldn't dare!" she said, laughing. I hope she is right.

Our conversation turned to the logistics of selling the produce. Julia could sell some of what she grew in the little village where she lived, but it is also a market town for smaller settlements up higher in the mountains. So once a week, there is a flood of bananas, coffee, tomatoes, or whatever happens to be in season. Prices are low, and not everything sells, so she was trying to sell in a larger town down in the valley, where I happened to be staying. Julia had no transportation of her own, however, and could not leave the children, so she had been hiring one of several men who drive the road between the mountain and the valley to take her produce to a friend who had a kiosk on the main highway. Because Julia had a small volume to carry, she was paying these guys through the nose. As I was chatting to her, I thought of Cristina, another woman I'd interviewed, who operated a kiosk on that same road. She barely made any profit because she bought inventory at a high price from the same guys who gouge Julia.

My mind tried to puzzle out solutions. There was no way Julia or any of the other women could afford a truck, but would it help if they had one? "Julia," I said, "if you woke up tomorrow morning and an angel had left you a truck, what would you do?" Quickly, she answered, "I would insist my husband learn to drive it!"

So the problem still nagged at me. That night, I asked around at Rose's Last Chance guesthouse, my favorite place to stay on the whole continent, to find out what the men did with their produce. Rose's place has no hot water and a rudimentary kitchen, but the food is good. There's a refrigerator with cold Coca-Cola and bottled beer, and there are flush toilets—all luxuries. Rose herself is a big deal in this very small town (with no post office, no bank), and she is great company.

In the evenings, people come in to sit and have a beer with her, as well as chat with whoever happens to be staying there. On that particular night, plenty of them knew the answer to my question about how men sold produce. They said groups of men organized into cooperatives to win regular contracts with food buyers from the city. The men's groups uniformly barred women from membership, as agricultural co-ops in developing countries usually do.

All over the world, food buyers award large contracts to males, even though the work is mostly done by women, whether as subcontractors, wage laborers, or unpaid family members. For example, FAO reports that 70 percent of the sugar contract farming in South Africa is done by women. Females put in longer hours than men do in vegetable contract farming in the Punjab, though the contracts are controlled by men. A large contract-farming scheme in China explicitly excluded women from signing the contracts, but thousands of women farmers did the bulk of the work. In Kenya, only 10 percent of all large farming contracts are held by women, while in Senegal the figure is 1 percent. Contractors avoid deals with female farmers because their hold over land is insecure, they don't produce large volumes, don't have the right equipment or transportation, don't have the stability that a credit line gives you, and just generally represent a supply risk.[10]

The folks gathered at Rose's told me that, on the same day each week, big trucks from the cities would roll into the valley and stop at a designated place to buy produce. The trucks were coming the next day, so I got up at dawn and went to see it for myself. Men brought in huge amounts of produce. They appeared to have their own pickup trucks or to be sharing them. They seemed to know the truck drivers and obviously had prearranged transactions. Once in a while, I saw a woman with a big bunch of bananas strapped to her back, and maybe a baby on her front, walking from truck to truck, looking bewildered. The women could not break into the routinized conversations and transactions. And the trucks were buying only in volume, not in bunches from someone's back.

Women are typically limited to squeezing income from a small plot close to home—graciously "given" by husbands—by growing a little produce or raising small animals. At the same time, they do most of the work on their husbands' land, for which they go unpaid, and they also take care of the house and children. Sometimes they try to sell handicrafts. Women typically do not share any income from their husbands' land, even though they provide most of the labor. So, in addition to being unable to join in the large contracts, they don't see money for themselves from their husbands' profit. Husbands will take produce that their wives have planted, cultivated, processed, and packaged, then sell it in the marketplace and pocket the money (see Figure 9).[11] Men then give their wives cash for what they deem to be necessities.

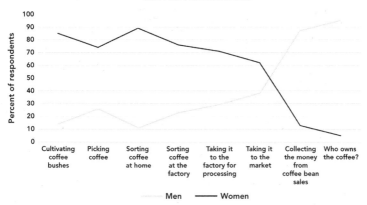

WHO IS RESPONSIBLE FOR EACH OF THE FOLLOWING ROLES IN COFFEE PRODUCTION?

Men — Women

FIGURE 9. The International Women's Coffee Alliance surveyed Kenyan women and men about the division of labor in coffee production. This line graph shows the results. On the horizontal axis are the steps taken to grow coffee, from planting to harvest to selling the yield. The vertical axis shows what percentage of men or women do the work in each step. The line from the beginning of the process to the end demonstrates that women do nearly all the work up until the product is taken to market, but they have very little participation in actually selling the coffee. The last measure shows that the men are deemed to own the coffee, even though women do most of the work to grow it.

Source: Mary Johnstone-Louis, *Case Study: International Women's Coffee Alliance*, Power Shift: The Oxford Forum for Women in the World Economy, 2013, https://www.doublexeconomy.com/wp-content/uploads/2019/09/Power-Shift-IWCA-Case.pdf

Maybe the women could form their own cooperative so they could sell to the big trucks each week, I thought. They would need transportation, so I started asking everyone the angel-leaves-a-truck question. Of all the women I asked, only one said she would learn to drive it. Why wouldn't the others try to drive? There were many excuses, but they all boiled down to the same reason: driving is a guy thing, and girls don't do it—like wearing a necktie or smoking a cigar. Even way out there beyond the reach of mass media, people are up to their ears in gender stereotypes.

My mind still would not let go of the problem. I turned next to the potential to add value. After all, that's what our grandmothers did, right? They made salsas and chutneys and jellies, letting the distinction achieved by their own recipe generate the profit. Up in the mountains again, I started looking closely at kitchens. Julia's kitchen was a few stones gathered in a circle behind the house, to which she brought wood every day for cooking. There was a canopy over this outdoor workspace, and the dirt under it was raked clean. I saw a few more substantial kitchens, but they were all open-air and fueled by stones-and-wood technology.

Producing the consistent taste required to build a reputation for a value-added product would be challenging using the unpredictable heat from such a fire. I wondered how much differentiation could be produced anyway, as meals in rural Africa tend to be the same every night and very bland. I asked about the spices available. They were ginger, onions, and a little sugar. It would be hard to create a distinctive product with those alone.

Selling outside the village would be the only way to make a salsa or chutney business worthwhile, which raised the vexing transportation question yet again. You would also need a standardized container that could withstand transport. I honestly did not know how someone like Julia would find, finance, move, and store such things. Sterilization and sealing would present a further obstacle. She would need capital, even if only a small amount, to start up. Where would that come from?

In the village where Julia lived, two women, Catherine and Alice, had businesses that also would be familiar to our grandmothers. Catherine had opened a restaurant that was more or less empty except on market day, when people came down from the mountain and needed a place to eat. By buying only what it took to make a meal and charging a little profit, Catherine earned enough to feed and school her kids. Alice had a tavern where she served beer that she brewed herself. Alice's brew, like other local beers, is made from maize and water and is served, without refrigeration, in a pot, from which men drink as a group through long rubber straws. There's local demand for beer every night because, in this village, like in others in rural Uganda, there is an entrenched evening ritual in which all the men treat each other to beer. On market day, however, Alice did a land-office business as the men from the surrounding hills finished their transactions and headed to her tavern to chill out. She was especially blessed because her husband let her keep her earnings, even though the beer was produced using ingredients that came off his land—he would be well within his rights to take from her anything his land produced. Alice and Catherine were serving freshly made food and beverages on-site in a market small enough for them to command. There was one other restaurant, right next to Catherine's, and I doubted the village could sustain another.

I concluded that, without better access to the larger agricultural market, the women in these mountains were severely constrained. The lack of transport, the inability to negotiate price or produce large volumes, the exclusion from co-ops, the restricted personal mobility, and their limited command over capital or technology all combined to form a massive barrier to economic viability.

The good news is that an external influence is emerging: some of the multinationals are taking steps to help the women, with assistance from the big NGOs, as well as governments. Coca-Cola and Walmart, for instance, teach new agricultural methods to female smallholders so that their yields are both larger and of better quality. Mondelēz International (the merged Cadbury, Nabisco, and Kraft) has let it be known that it much prefers to buy from co-ops that have at least 30 percent women. When the impact of these projects is assessed, the companies hope there will be more good food on local tables, more kids in school, and a decrease in domestic violence, which is what the research to date says will happen when you economically empower these women.[12]

The corporations participate in such projects for many reasons. These efforts have a positive impact on consumer attitudes as well as employee recruiting and retention. It's also increasingly recognized in the investment sector that gender friendliness, both internal and external, is good for stock prices, as I will explain later. But the most prominent reason companies work with women in agriculture is to ensure supply. Men are moving to cities and emigrating to other countries at increasing rates to look for work, but the women they leave behind to farm are still seriously disadvantaged. Manufacturers like Coca-Cola and Mondelēz, which need certain crops to produce their products, and retailers like Walmart and Marks & Spencer, which sell certain fruits and vegetables directly to consumers, are getting worried about the effect that leaving women—with their limited rights and resources—responsible for farming will have on supply. Already, the future supply of bananas, coffee, and cocoa has been jeopardized, and other crops seem likely to follow.[13]

We should all be concerned about the impact this inefficiency in agricultural markets has on world hunger and poverty. The United Nations says that 925 million people in the world are chronically hungry; of those, 150 million would be fed if we removed the disadvantages for women in food production. Research also shows that when the playing field is level, female farmers produce as much as men. For the many poor nations that rely on agriculture as their primary source of GDP, fixing this specific gender problem would cause an increase of about 2.5 to 4 percent per annum.[14]

The disadvantaging of women in agriculture also contributes to food insecurity. People fight when they are hungry, so food insecurity often causes friction at ground level. Local conflict damages resources, as well as people, and when conflict expands, so does disease. Because of the global media and dense connectivity of our times, any such conflict now holds the potential for global impact.

What are rich governments doing? Not anywhere near as much as they should be. The big donors in agricultural aid are the U.S. Agency for

International Development and the U.K.'s Department for International Development. Each has a number of programs for women in developing countries, but the percentage of their budgets going to women remains minute. Meanwhile, they give massive sums to men's programs, claiming their efforts are "gender-neutral," an obviously bogus assertion.

In a community where all the land and money is controlled by men, the only way women can access food or shelter is to be under a man's "protection"—and in his good graces—making them wholly dependent and alarmingly vulnerable. The course and quality of a woman's life is almost entirely determined by the character of the man she marries, a decision over which she probably had no control. Though they are persons in their own right, women are undermined by being bought and sold in marriage. Consequently, men will often see their wives as objects that they can use at will, as this man in the Democratic Republic of Congo described:

> I was a normal man, living with my family in a normal way. I behaved like every man within society. My wife was a slave to me, she had no rights and had to respect me absolutely. She was always in the home, and could not go out to meet other women. She belonged to me, because at our marriage, I paid a bride-price . . . which gave me all the authority to treat her as I wished. She was at my mercy for sexual activity, anytime, anyplace, anywhere. Refusal went with punishment. I was a complete tyrant in my home.[15]

Dependency often makes the person with the power hostile and punitive, so women who must rely on men for basic necessities suffer under the perpetual threat of domestic violence. A cross-national study by the World Health Organization determined the factors that predict domestic violence are (1) whether the man or woman observed such violence as a child, (2) whether the community tolerates such violence, and (3) whether there is a large economic gap between men and women.[16] In the rural parts of developing nations, all three factors tend to be present, combining to perpetuate violence from generation to generation. In poor countries, the community may even demand a beating if a woman gets "out of line." Violence within the home is often so normalized that women themselves will tell researchers a man is justified in beating his wife for infractions as small as burning the dinner.[17]

A more equal economic position, especially ownership of more productive assets like land and large animals, was found to significantly reduce intimate partner violence in a recent study of twenty-eight countries appearing in the *American Journal of Public Health*.[18] Everywhere, the most common reason a woman stays in an abusive home is that she doesn't have the means to live. What we in women's economic empowerment often see is that women will use the first cash they earn to leave a violent man.

Violence frequently takes the form of purposeful starvation. The displeased man will withhold food from the woman—and sometimes her children as well—until he sees fit to restore her right to eat. A 2011 University of Texas study, for instance, found that half of married women in rural Bangladesh had been physically abused by their partners in the previous year. In this culture, the women are not allowed to leave their residence, so everything that comes into the home must arrive in the hands of the head of household, making intentional starvation a convenient means of punishment. "They beat us so much but we don't go away," reported one. "They don't bring food when they are angry, not even for their children." Many of these respondents chose to go hungry rather than risk a beating by asking for more food. One woman gave her food to her daughters but would not mention her own hunger because, she said, "He will beat me at night."[19]

Male dominance over the allocation of food is most visible in the widespread practice of feeding females in a family last and least. Different dinnertimes, different rooms for eating, and different foods deemed "for women" are all ways in which unequal food allocation is ritualized and made "part of our culture." (In developed nations, we see the vestiges of this habit in larger food packages being touted as "man-sized.")

"In the morning when my father was given a bowl of cream with his tea, his sisters were given only tea," writes the Pakistani activist Malala

Yousafzai of her father's childhood among the Pashtuns. "If there were eggs, they would only be for the boys. When a chicken was slaughtered for dinner, the girls would get the wings and the neck, while the luscious breast meat was enjoyed by my father, his brother and my grandfather. 'From early on I could feel I was different from my sisters,' my father says."[20] Malala does not say what her grandmother ate, but if this tale is like others, her father's mother held back until everyone else was done and then ate whatever was left, sometimes going without food entirely. That is how it works out for women when food is scarce.

The "last and least" rule is now thought to be so widespread that international agencies are collecting data on its potential nutritional impact at the species level, and experts are developing a gender nutrition index.[21] One particularly worrisome bit of evidence shows the impact of feeding females last and least on newborn babies.

The International Fetal and Newborn Growth Consortium for the 21st Century—or INTERGROWTH-21st for short—is a consortium of obstetrics research scientists who recently carried out a global study of birth weights. Low birth weights are associated not only with many risks in infancy but also with diseases and weaknesses that persist throughout life; infants born of malnourished mothers are 20 percent more likely to die within their first five years.[22] For a long time, though, it was argued that countries where smaller babies were born simply had other cultural preferences. (Or something. "It's their culture" is a refrain that covers a lot of nonsense.) Anyway, INTERGROWTH-21st established definitively that birth weight is a function of how well the mother has been fed and cared for. The countries that have small babies are places where women are not treated well—and, in particular, are fed last and least.[23]

But that's not all. This research team says that the nutritional and health care of the woman, even before pregnancy, has an impact on the child; females must be cared for over the course of years before conceiving. Birth defects, some of them heritable, can be caused when a female is not fed well enough, even in childhood, because all the eggs a female will ever have are in her body when she is born. Whenever she sustains low nutrition, those ova are more likely to be damaged. So, the practice of feeding females less not only produces a whole train of people who are smaller than they should be, but also fits them out with a kit of diseases and hands them more birth defects.

I had a disturbing experience recently in which a group of feminist academics in New York, none of whom had ever been in a developing country, haughtily told me and my colleagues that international agencies should not interfere with the last-and-least practice because that would be a violation of culture by a "hegemon." These feminists seemed to think that the last-and-least rule was innocuous, even quaint. For us, it was a scary lesson in how important it is to tell the world the truth. Systematic starvation, accompanied by the threat of violence, is not harmless or picturesque. It is nobody's cultural prerogative. It is a violation of human rights and nothing less.

In addition to controlling the food, the male head of the household's control over land means he also controls the female's right to shelter. That gives him the power to dictate her whereabouts, not only via the tacit threat of being cast out, but by directly forbidding the woman to leave. Usually, such constraints are rationalized as an attempt to protect or maintain respectability, but restrictions on movement or communication effectively enforce female dependency.

In the many studies now being done internationally to assess women's level of empowerment, a set of standard survey questions is emerging. One of these asks whether the woman is allowed to leave home without her husband's permission. This question has proved to be an effective proxy for empowerment because it is so common for women to be forbidden from leaving the village, the family compound, or even the home. Occasionally, these restrictions are taken so seriously that a woman will die, especially in childbirth, because her husband is not there to give permission for her to seek medical care. An elderly woman in Uganda told me she had never left home without her husband's okay—nor had she ever in her life known another woman to do it.

Women in rural cultures suffer more from the burden of servitude than do women in developed nations. The absence of infrastructure such as plumbing and electricity, as well as the inaccessibility of labor-saving home appliances and products, makes their time spent in domestic duties much longer: the women spend hours every day searching for wood for stoves and carrying heavy containers of water. The time spent laundering is especially long and difficult because all clothing has to be washed by hand, often by a riverside or in a bucket. Cooking over wood-fueled stoves is a significant detriment to their health, and it occupies huge swaths of time. As a result of these disadvantages, women in developing countries suffer far more from time poverty than either local men or women in other countries, which in turn reduces their agricultural productivity. FAO recommends investments in both public goods and consumer durables to change this use of time; they estimate that in Tanzania, for example, investments in labor-saving assistance aimed at domestic duties would save 8 billion hours of unpaid work a year, which is the equivalent of 4.6 million full-time paid jobs.[24]

An around-the-clock, backbreaking workday is the tradition for women in the horticultural societies of Africa, as described by the Danish economist Ester Boserup in the 1970s. Wives were made to work their husbands' land, as well as doing all childcare and housework, unpaid, just as they do now.[25] They were also expected to make their own money by producing handicrafts and small garden crops to sell. The proceeds were to pay for each woman's own upkeep, as well as for any expenses her children had—so neither the wives nor the children commanded support from the husband. The women worked day and night. The men were a leisure class; they came to the fields only to "supervise." If they wanted to increase their income, the men bought more wives to work the land; since the women worked unpaid and were responsible for their own upkeep, the additional labor supply cost them only the upfront payment of the bride price. The women got nothing and owned nothing, not even their own bodies.

Today, women still try to make money by selling garden produce and handicrafts. They are still seen as responsible for the children, especially their education. They will approach your car with yams or tomatoes, even on a road you can barely see because it is so seldom traveled. You pass them standing by the side of the highways, their handicrafts arrayed on blankets, every item the same as those on the next woman's blanket because they are all products of traditional craft-making. The objects are clichéd even in the local setting; they would never sell online or in the West. But as the women are landless paupers working without pay, putting these old-fashioned goods into this inadequate market is the only way some have to make a living.

You needn't have read *Das Kapital* to realize that if men own the means of production, they are also more likely to be employers. Women participate in farmwork as paid workers as well as unpaid family laborers. FAO surveys show that women do about 43 percent of all farmwork, but the organization cautions that this number is too low—women do so much agricultural work alongside housework and childcare that they often do not consider themselves farmworkers, despite spending hours planting, cultivating, and harvesting. So, when FAO comes around with the survey, those women don't check that box and get left out of the count.[26]

Women working for wages in agriculture are more likely to be seasonal laborers, informal workers, and part-time help—in other words, they are concentrated in the lowest-paid and most insecure positions. Violence against female laborers in agriculture is also rife. Even in the United States, where one might expect more protection, farm supervisors attack women in the fields; in most cases, employers show no sympathy, nor do the courts.[27]

There is also a gender divide in the type of agricultural tasks that each sex takes on. All higher-paying jobs involving heavy equipment are seen as "men's work," whether it really takes a man to do what's required or not. What jobs are considered "men's work" changes with the level of pay. When wages for an agricultural task done primarily by women increase, the men move in and take that job over. That job then becomes "men's work," even if it was rationalized as women's work for years. When FAO equalizes its data for hours worked, qualification, and experience and then puts women and men side by side in a "same work" comparison, females, worldwide, are paid significantly less than males for agricultural work.[28]

For decades, feminists believed that doing housework caused women to be devalued and that the path to freedom was to do "important" work, like farming. Feminist scholars have also used the presumed dignity of farmwork to argue that industrial capitalism or European colonialism began the subordination of women. If this idea were true, we would expect cultures in which women do a lot of farmwork to be more gender equal.

So let's take a look at that. The Organisation for Economic Co-operation and Development calculates a score called the Social Institutions and Gender Index (SIGI), which is designed to assess the presence of the abuses I have described in this chapter: discriminatory family codes; violence against women; restricted resources, specifically access to land and capital; son preference; and the practice of female infanticide. SIGI scores show that the rights to safety, resources, equal treatment, and human respect are generally lowest in countries where more women are engaged in farmwork.[29]

My team in Uganda is now running psychological tests to try to assess the impact of these conditions on women. We find that they are at a significantly higher mental health risk than men, a finding that replicates other studies in countries where women's rights are so few.[30] The distracted old women I so often see haunting the schoolyards have endured a lifetime of economic insecurity and abuse—and it has likely affected their state of mind.

We, as a community of human beings, owe these women our compassion and our help by making efforts to remove the gender-specific economic obstacles to freedom and safety. Programs to help women get title to land are underway in various places, but they need to be expanded around the world. The same is true of assistance with technology and market access. Certainly, governments should be more evenhanded about their allocations of aid. Some interventions are fairly simple and can be done by small volunteer organizations, like local charities and church groups. For example, in her book *The Moment of Lift*, Melinda Gates tells a story of watching farmers and their families act out the last-and-least practice in skits. As the males in the audience saw their neighbors pretend to serve men food first while hungry women and children waited, they were ashamed. Powerfully moved, they vowed to change their behavior. Responses like that encourage me to think that if we all pull together, we can win economic freedom for women.

The hundreds of millions of women who live under the circumstances I have described are imprisoned by their economic exclusion. The consequence of the male monopoly over land has been their misery. Yes, there are cultural norms involved and religious practices brought to bear, but these are merely local window dressing. The pattern that crosses nation, time, and culture is the economic dependency that leads to restricted mobility, uncertain access to food or shelter, and the vulnerability to violence for which there is no accountability.

4 | INADEQUATE EXCUSES,
INEXCUSABLE TREATMENT

No excuse justifies the suffering endured by women, but that doesn't stop people from trying. To explain away such massive inequity takes an equally huge myth, so apologists make assertions about our animal nature or about humans of the ancient past. They claim that male dominance is natural and necessary, that human mothers should stay at home as animal mothers do, that men are meant to be providers, and that males are superior because they do work that is more dangerous, difficult, or important. They call on science, religion, and folktales—whatever works—and end by warning that any attempt to change the balance of power will bring about destruction of the species. Male dominance, they pronounce, is immutable.

If you accept the women's economic empowerment mission, this rubbish will be hurled at you sooner or later. Here are some responses to fire back.

MALE DOMINANCE IS NATURAL AND NECESSARY.

When presented with a 2013 Pew Research Center statistic showing that 40 percent of American women are primary breadwinners, the conservative media pundit Erick Erickson exploded:

I'm so used to liberals telling conservatives that they're anti-science. But liberals who defend this and say it is not a bad thing are *very* anti-science. When you look at biology—when you look at the natural world—the roles of a male and a female in society and in other animals, the male typically is the dominant role. The female, it's not antithesis, or it's not competing, it's a complementary role. We've lost the ability to have complementary relationships . . . and it's tearing us apart.[1]

Erickson's "scientific" justification for male dominance is misinformed. Here's why.

One of the primates closest to humans is female dominant. Bonobos look so much like chimpanzees that they were confirmed as a distinct species only in 2012.[2] Like chimpanzees, bonobos share with us 99 percent of our DNA. These two primates are also genetically nearly identical to each other, sharing 99.6 percent of their DNA between them. But despite their almost indistinguishable biological profiles, their social systems are total opposites.[3]

Chimpanzees are patriarchal. Their communities have an alpha male at the top and a hierarchy of other males underneath, with females at the bottom. The males constantly jockey for position but are a close-knit group that police their territory, invade the territory of others, and terrorize neighboring tribes as a team. Females are continually bullied and attacked. Both sexes hunt and gather, but males tend to share food with one another, apparently to build alliances among themselves, and don't normally form significant relationships with females or offspring.

By contrast, bonobos organize as matriarchies. Rather than have a single leader, the females govern as a collective. Males and females forage and hunt together, sharing food with one another, as well as with offspring. Males and females alike are merciless hunters, but bonobos avoid conflict with one another. When they see any potential for competition, they play or have sex to distract themselves and relieve tension, before settling down to share. Fights between bonobo communities are extremely rare. Unlike chimpanzees and humans, bonobos do not kill their own kind.

The basis for the bonobo matriarchy is an alliance built by young females as they join the troop. All primate adolescents migrate to a different troop to breed, but in some species, the males leave their birth troop, while in others the females do. Species in which the females migrate usually exhibit pronounced male dominance and aggression. Scientists speculate that the males in the destination troop can dominate because they are already bonded by kinship, while the females are strangers and so have less basis for solidarity. But when female bonobos join a new troop, they immediately establish bonds with multiple females already there, especially by having sex with them, and they continue to cultivate these relationships throughout their lives. The behavior builds a female coalition strong enough to stand up to the males. Scientists don't know why bonobos do this and other primates don't.

Scientists describe bonobos as "egalitarian." Humans often equate leadership with dominance; bonobos demonstrate a different truth—social order can exist without tyranny based on violence. I do not advocate female dominance because I believe gender injustice is rooted in an escalating desire to *dominate* among human males. The impulse to dominate is unnecessary, destructive, oppressive to all, and utterly changeable.

Bonobos do have one actively policed limit: the matriarchs don't tolerate male sexual aggression. Among chimpanzees, aggressive males are more often fathers because they force sex during estrus, the time when females are receptive to males, as well as when the females are not receptive. The scientist Barbara Smuts observed the following interchange in Tanzania's Gombe National Park:

> It's a disturbing scene: a full-grown male chimpanzee, heavily muscled and with hair standing on end, crashes through the forest undergrowth, running partially erect and noisily flinging branches. Other chimpanzees scatter, screaming or making submissive grunts. His target, a smaller female, cowers and bares her teeth in a fear grimace as he concludes his rampage by kicking her and stomping on her back with his full weight. It may

be over in a few seconds—she can provide little resistance—but the victim is clearly traumatized, emitting rasping, strangled screams long after the male has returned to his normal routine.[4]

To pacify the aggressor and avoid violent encounters in the future, female chimps in estrus will offer themselves first to a male who has bullied them. However, the females also pointedly copulate with every unrelated male during each estrus, in an apparent attempt to confuse paternity. Scientists believe the females do this because male chimpanzees often kill newborns, even sometimes eating them in front of the mother and the rest of the community. They speculate that males will not kill their own offspring, so, by having sex with everybody, the mother muddles the question, thereby protecting the life of her future infant.

There is normally no way for male chimpanzees to know their own offspring, however. In fact, the only way for scientists observing chimps to discern paternity is to run DNA tests on feces. There are two rare occurrences that might allow a male to know which infant is his. Occasionally, an alpha male will guard a female in estrus, fending off other males during the whole period. Even then, however, the female may not conceive. To be certain that only his offspring are born of a given female, a male would have to guard her repeatedly for a long time, which would be impractical in the wild.

Another rare opportunity to know paternity is when the female chooses her mate. Occasionally, a male and a female will have a courtship in which they share food, groom each other, and then sneak into the forest when estrus comes. In controlled tests female chimps prefer this "nice guy" type, but that outcome is rare in the wild because aggressive males overpower the females *and* dominate the other males.

Because female chimps can't choose their mates, and would pick a different kind of mate if they could, we cannot default to the usual evolutionary narrative where the best characteristics are passed on because the females like those males the most. Instead, chimp rapists are essentially forcing violence into the gene pool, as well as reinforcing it through their behavior.

A group culture of aggression is rooted in both behavior and biology.

Testosterone, for instance, fuels a drive to dominate and stimulates status competition. In a situation where a male primate's status is threatened, testosterone rises, often resulting in aggression. Unfortunately, climbing testosterone and increasing violence work in a mutually escalating fashion to foster an aggressive social environment: rising individual testosterone spurs violent action, which increases group testosterone, in turn ratcheting up the aggression in the environment, further encouraging defensive response, and so on. In this way, groups of males in a competitive situation can feed each other's insecurities and aggressive impulses, spiraling into a cycle of ever-escalating conflict. Unfortunately, this group dynamic pushes to the top those males who are the most obsessed with status, the most reactive to challenge, the most aggressive in their response, and the best able to bully the other males—not the wisest leaders, but the most vainglorious ones.

If this group behavior is sustained, the result can be to permanently increase overall aggression among the members. While testosterone rises and falls in response to social circumstances, high testosterone can also become trait-like in individuals. In laboratory experiments with human males, high testosterone in individuals has been linked to greed and corruption as well as violence and dominance—and it consistently produces unwise risk-taking. High-testosterone human males punish those who cross them more harshly and reward those who assist them more lavishly. Such males are more likely than normal men to be violent criminals *and* to be CEOs. Elevated testosterone levels and a propensity to aggression are both heritable in human males.

While it was once widely believed that genes simply dictated everything about an organism, from its appearance to its habits, scientists now view genes, behaviors, and biological processes—like hormone levels—as interdependent influences on both the creature and its progeny. So a culture in which male aggression is constantly rewarded, especially through coerced reproduction (rape), might replicate violence, with increasing intensity, in subsequent generations. But even among scientists, there remains a default assumption that whoever and whatever survives from one generation to the next represents the best outcome for the species. In truth, however, what features are adaptive for a species can be judged only after many generations—for primates, over hundreds or thousands of years—and evaluated in the context of the larger habitat. Viewed in the long run, what survives today may produce an unfortunate tomorrow.

"Warrior chimps" demonstrate that possibility. In 1995, a community of chimps even more warlike than usual was sighted in the Ngogo research section of Kibale National Park in Uganda. They are larger and stronger than other chimpanzees, and they live longer. They are also multiplying faster and form communities three times the usual size. These "gangster chimps" wage wars on other communities, killing to gain territory and to steal mates. After twenty-five years of study, the scientists are unable to decide whether annexing territory or stealing females is the primary motive.[5]

According to the primatologists studying this tribe, the environment is heavily stacked in the warriors' favor. Fruit in Ngogo is abundant year-round. There are no predators, and no disease has threatened this group in the time they have been observed. This generous habitat might have sustained these warriors, despite any maladaptive behavior. Life is so easy, they have nearly killed off their favorite animal protein, the red colobus monkey. Since these gangsters will eventually vanquish the other chimps in their habitat, we might assume they're the "fittest" for survival. Unless we take the long view.

Once the aggressors have conquered all of Kibale Park, they will have no place to go. Unless there is a significant change in their behavior, the warriors will deplete their food supply and probably destroy one another over it. Their only hope is to begin selecting for sharing instead of fighting. Otherwise, their aggressive behavior will not have been adaptive at all.

Homo sapiens faced a similar challenge about seventy thousand years ago, but responded by leaving their habitat entirely, traveling north out of Africa into eastern Europe, central Asia, and the Middle East, as well as southeast to Australia, apparently by boat. Since then, humans have colonized every habitat on the planet, including deserts, mountains, and even arctic zones. Adapting to these places required intentional changes in foods eaten and shelter taken. As we developed these flexible behaviors, our brain enlarged, changed shape, and grew more complex.[6]

Though human brains are structurally similar to those of both bonobos and chimps, the comparison to our peaceful relative raises important possibilities for our mission. Bonobos have remarkable empathy. Their ability to "read" each other's emotions arises from the limbic system in their brains, which is very similar to ours, except that the human limbic system is dramatically more developed. Like humans, bonobos know when they are causing distress in others and can adjust their behavior accordingly. Bonobos are quite cooperative and communicative, but humans are so to a far greater extent. Humans and bonobos are also among very few species that have sex for fun, rather than only for procreation, and both will couple with the same sex or the opposite sex for the sake of pleasure and affection. Bonobos frequently copulate face-to-face and they kiss on the mouth, both rare behaviors. Their playfulness has remarkable range, as does ours. The brain structures of both humans and bonobos allow them to control aggressive impulses in a way that chimps can't.

Chimpanzees, however, mirror our own patriarchal social systems; their rape culture, their obsession with status, and their drive to dominate are echoed in humans. As I have suggested, chimpanzee violence may have evolved *with* them, rather than being essential to their original nature.

The same may be true of humans. According to evolutionary scientists, the human mind evolved in a setting of violent conflict wherein coalitions of males struggled to gain dominance over one another. Current scientific thinking holds that testosterone itself is most properly understood as an expression of the impulse to dominate. The appetite for dominance further translates into a personality trait, social dominance orientation (SDO). People with high SDO prefer a rigid hierarchy that their own group dominates and approve of violence to maintain their power. High SDOs are more likely to be male, sexist, homophobic, and racist. They prefer authoritarian, male-dominant social structures. Some evidence suggests that SDO may be inherited. Decision-making and discipline in any organization where there is a higher proportion of SDO people than those with egalitarian values would profoundly affect the daily experience of each individual—and would certainly reduce inclusivity toward women. This would be particularly true in groups where the SDOs hold the top posts.[7]

Evolutionary scientists therefore emphasize that, even though we have had a long history of violent social dominance by males, the human orientation to dominance is *highly malleable*. This is true in part because the human brain gives our species a special ability to assess situations and then to change radically and rapidly in response. This ability is one reason that *Homo sapiens* now covers the world, while our cousins still live solely in Africa.

Soon after leaving Africa, however, *Homo sapiens* exhibited the behaviors that would ultimately make humans the most violent and destructive species on earth.[8] Though it was once believed that prehuman species lived and died before *Homo sapiens* appeared, new archaeological discoveries suggest that humans, as they migrated through Europe and Asia, killed off all the other *Homo* species. Furthermore, when humanity expanded across land and sea, an astonishing number of other mammals—huge rats, giant wombats, mammoths, mastodons, giant lions, and giant sloths—also disappeared. In North America, thirty-four of forty-seven types of large animals were driven into extinction. In South America, it was fifty out of sixty. In Australia, of twenty-four species weighing at least one hundred pounds, humans killed off twenty-three.[9]

So humans have been scorching the planet for thousands of years. We have finally reached the point that warrior chimps will eventually confront: we've pushed the limits of habitat until our survival is threatened. Having adopted a "survival of the fittest" philosophy, even in our economics, to justify raiding and pillaging, we now need to select for sharing, or we will die. Male dominance has proved to be a disaster.

MEN ARE THE PROVIDERS.

Men have controlled economic resources for thousands of years, but that does not mean they have been good providers.

The first human economy was the hunter-gatherer system. The myth says men hunted while women gathered, working close to home so they could watch the children. Heterosexual mating combinations therefore guaranteed balanced diets for couples and their children. This "gender division of labor" is now the archetype for all roles in the economy, since most cultures separate "men's work" from "women's work."

This is a neat myth, but it doesn't fit the facts. We can infer something about ancient hunter-gatherer societies by looking at the few "forager" societies observed by modern anthropologists. Women often hunt in these societies. They normally kill small animals, close to home, as do men. Men hunt big game, but such expeditions don't occur often. Indeed, hunting big game is actually an inefficient means of getting food, and meat is not usually a big part of the diet; rather, most groups subsist mainly on plant foods. The men nevertheless recount elaborate stories of big-game hunting—apparently endlessly—so meat becomes solidly identified with masculinity. Some anthropologists suggest that the function of hunting is better understood as "status signaling" among the men, rather than as a quest for nutrients.[10]

The earliest humans did not form nuclear families. Like chimps and bonobos, humans were originally "fission-fusion" animals who went out to forage in small, ever-changing groups, before returning to a larger community to sleep or share food. It was once believed that this food-sharing practice among foragers made nutrition equal among all members, but later research has revealed that the organization of sharing is unequal between the sexes.[11]

Anthropologists analyzing twentieth-century dental records among hunter-gatherers have found that the females are consistently undernourished, having had less access to meat and fat. This inequality occurs for several reasons. First, when men do go out to hunt, they eat the most nutritious and fattiest parts of the carcass at the site of the kill, before taking the remaining meat back to the group. Once they return, food-sharing rituals determine who gets fed first and which parts of the animal they are given, and these often disadvantage women. One anthropologist remarked that "the order of precedence of food distribution—

old men, hunting men, children, dogs, and women—suggests females are the most likely to develop malnutrition."[12] Taboos further stipulate that certain foods are forbidden to particular recipients at specific times, and these, too, tend to disadvantage females. The pattern of gender inequality in food sharing among foragers is often severe enough that it leads to chronic malnutrition among females, causing low fertility rates and birth weights, as well as high infant and maternal mortality—hardly an adaptive outcome.[13]

The hunters' practice of eating the best parts of an animal before returning to camp ensures their nutrition will be better than anyone else's, making them bigger, stronger, and more admired than other men. Food-sharing habits confer prestige and power, establishing a hierarchy with tribal elders at the top, followed by hunters. These practices are clearly more about male status than about providing for women and children, who both get only the scraps.

Evidence of unequal allocation of food can also be seen in the skeletal remains of prehistoric peoples. One study, published in 2008, assessed all the viable records of teeth from all the digs in the world. The researchers found that, on every continent, the women had more dental decay than the men.[14] The most likely explanation is that women ate more carbohydrates and men ate more meat, which is consistent with the ethnographic data. But archaeologists suggest that some of the malnutrition visible in the remains of women occurred in part because their caloric intake was insufficient to offset the hard labor they were doing. In some sites, stress on the bones of females indicates they did work requiring considerable physical effort.[15]

At least as early as the Upper Paleolithic period, or Stone Age, the rudiments of organized patriarchy began to appear.[16] Small groups of men coalesced to exert power over others, especially females, often organizing around an alpha male. The rules and practices they created eventually evolved into the laws and institutions that allowed larger societies to hold patriarchal dominance in place. For example, forager men formed fraternal groups that met in hidden places and guarded mystical secrets. Women were so emphatically excluded from these brotherhoods that if one of them happened upon a ritual or observed any mystery, she was brutally punished, usually killed. Exclusively male organizations have been common throughout history, as has the practice of withholding important information from females.

Aggressive male behavior also scaled up over time. Hunter-gatherers fight with other clan members, sometimes to death, and the males beat and kill the females. What distinguishes human aggression from that of other primates, however, is the greater belligerence that clans show toward outside groups. Women are used as tokens for negotiation between warring tribes. A leading evolutionary scientist, Richard Wrangham, described the way women were used in intertribal aggression among the Australian Aborigines: "Women could be sent on sexual missions into dangerous situations. When potential attackers were seen approaching a group, one response was to send women out to greet them. If the strange men were willing to forgo their attack, they signaled their intent by having sexual intercourse with the female emissaries. If not, they sent the women back and then attacked. The final stage of peacemaking between two tribes almost always involved an exchange of wives."[17] Women have been the pawns of war, the booty for soldiers, and the means of creating alliances since the dawn of history. How terrifying that must have been for them.

Once humans began forming settlements, the fighting between groups led to raiding, establishing a new basis for subsistence: goods taken by violence. As the most aggressive raiders wiped out settlements—in the same way gangster chimps destroy others—the human way of life became even more violent. As with the warrior chimps, the destruction of more peaceful communities and the capture of females for breeding would have skewed our species further toward violent domination. Eventually, hunting and raiding grew into a phenomenon that encircled the globe: the warrior economy.

From there, human history marched on like four thousand seasons of *Game of Thrones*. Warrior societies built vast stores through conquest.[18] Kings and emperors, as well as their circles of sycophants, controlled the wealth and distributed it among the best warriors, so, like hunters, they had material advantages as well as prestige. These men, the most violent in the society, were also rewarded with multiple wives, so they had more opportunities to leave their mark on the gene pool than less warlike males did—possibly pushing humanity further down the path of selecting for dominance.

Human societies have strongly discouraged women from having weapons or knowing how to use them. Generally, females have neither been taught to fight nor been allowed to participate in activities, like sports, that would develop strength and skill. Since size and strength are a function of adequate nutrition and exercise, norms that kept women inside and underfed would have led to their being smaller and weaker.

Nutritional inequality between the sexes may have widened. For example, in two sites from the first millennium in what is now Peru—both home to warrior cultures, with dominant alpha males, strict hierarchies, and elite holy men—women's remains show signs of nutritional inequality across all social classes, including the unmistakable marks of prolonged malnutrition during child development.[19] Malnutrition during childhood stunts growth and impairs cognitive development, so the withholding of food by males would have made the females both smaller and less able to think. Those effects just gave the patriarchy new excuses to justify their own dominance.

With the rise of warrior economies, patriarchy became a beast with two horns, violence *and* greed. The patriarchs' attitudes toward other peoples, whether at home or at war, foreshadows the economic philosophy of our own time. The conqueror had the right to destroy or expropriate everything in his path simply because he had the strength to do it. It was winner take all; might is right. Military leaders subjected whole populations to their rule, enforcing their rights as "master" to everyone else's "slave," often with religious beliefs that justified it all as some kind of divine plan.[20]

Agriculture grew alongside warfare; land possession often drove conflict. As we have seen, agricultural economies are no party for women and certainly don't provide for them well. But there is no reason to believe that women's subordination grew out of farming, as some have argued. There is too much evidence that women had been mistreated for a long time before agriculture appeared. Furthermore, non-agricultural economies, such as pastoral societies, are also warlike and subordinate women.

When industrialization arrived in the Western countries, households began using cash to purchase food and other necessities. Males still controlled these resources because they monopolized paid work. So, it was in the industrial period that the nuclear family with a single male breadwinner first came to the fore. But even in postindustrial societies today, the powerful male provider sometimes denies food and other essentials to punish "his" woman and children, just as in poor nations.

By the middle of the twentieth century in the Western countries, the self-contained nuclear family had become a widely held social ideal. The demise of this gender role divide since 1970 has distressed conservatives—because they think this arrangement is natural and must be sustained. But the "traditional" nuclear family with a single male provider has been the standard for only about 150 years out of humanity's 200,000-year history.[21] Since that family form appears to be on its way out, it may ultimately become a small blip on the timeline of human development.

Nature did not award men the beneficent role of providing for women and children. Instead, throughout human history, men have controlled the distribution of resources, which gave them the power to *withhold* necessities, sometimes to an extreme degree.

WOMEN SHOULD STAY HOME TO CARE FOR THEIR CHILDREN, AS NATURE INTENDED.

"That women, on average, earn less than men is true," wrote Tim Worstall in *Forbes* in 2015. "That this is the result of discrimination seems not to be true. Rather, it appears to be down to the different reactions of men and women to becoming a parent. Which, given that being a mammalian and viviparous species is pretty much central to the experience of being human means that the gender pay gap just might be one of those things not amenable to having a solution."[22]

In recent years, apologists like Worstall have increasingly focused on motherhood as a reason to chase women back home, invoking our animal nature to justify the demand that women with children should stop working or be paid less if they don't. There are, however, variations in nurturing practices, even among mammals. Primates, for instance, adopt one of two modes of parenting: in one, the mother does everything; in the other, care is shared among members of the group, males and females. In the second case, the mother is still the primary provider, but others watch her baby while she forages and assist her in other ways. The term for this shared care is *allomothering*, which means "other than the mother."

Chimpanzee mothers often disappear from the troop at the time of birth, sometimes staying away for as long as a month, and afterward will not allow others to touch their babies. For the first two years, the infant clings to the body of its mother. Until the offspring are five years old, they stay within a few feet of her, going along to forage and hunt and learning how to provide for themselves by watching her. But the mother is guarding her offspring from predatory male chimps, rather than just "doing what comes naturally." Bonobos, by contrast, are an allomothering species. Mothers not only share care with other females but also allow males to hold their offspring, play with them, and share food and shelter.

In both the species closest to us, therefore, the mother is the main provider for the offspring. In fact, mothers are the providers among all primates, as well as other mammals.[23] As the sex that makes the greatest parental investment in offspring, mothers are more central to the survival of species than fathers are, but can provide only if they are able to go out, with or without the children, to forage and return with food.

Humans are an allomothering species. Forager mothers take children and babies with them to gather and hunt, but also share childcare communally. In fact, shared care has been the norm through nearly all human history. Fostering and adoption have always occurred; day care is nothing new to our species. Another distinctive human feature is that males, except for breastfeeding, are just as able to care for children as females are.[24] Allomothering is thought to be one of humanity's most favorable adaptive traits, so a society structured to prevent mothers from providing and to keep fathers away, as the postindustrial economy is, undermines humanity's evolutionary advantages.

MEN DO HARDER, MORE DANGEROUS, AND MORE IMPORTANT WORK THAN WOMEN DO.

After a 2011 White House report said that women were paid seventy-five cents for every dollar earned by men, Steve Tobak wrote an enraged piece for CBS News online in which he tried to justify the pay gap. Men choose to do dangerous jobs, he asserted, which "naturally pay more." He then listed the following occupations as dangerous: "fishers, loggers, aircraft pilots, farmers and ranchers, roofers, iron and steel workers, refuse and recyclable material collectors, industrial machinery installation and repair, truck drivers, construction laborers."[25]

You will notice that several occupations on this list are not particularly dangerous and that some, like fishing and farming, employ a lot of women worldwide. But Tobak insists that women *choose* not to do these jobs, implying they are too cowardly. By dividing jobs in this stereotypical way, he is parroting a common strategy for justifying economic inequality.

Men do engage in risky behavior substantially more often than women. We should not necessarily attach such positive value to danger-seeking, however. The male fascination with risk manifests as a greater propensity for substance abuse and vulnerability to accidents, for instance. Being in risky circumstances elevates testosterone, which in turn causes men to underestimate threats and act recklessly—not particularly good attributes to bring to dangerous work.

Crimes of all sorts, but especially those involving violence, are committed by men vastly more often than by women, in part because of male danger-seeking. In every country for which there is data—about a hundred nations—men are 90 percent or more of the prison population and commit close to all the violent crimes. Most violent attacks are not male-on-female, but male-on-male. By far the most frequent scenario is two men having a heated argument over status that ends when one of them attacks, and kills, the other. The United Nations Office on Drugs and Crime reports that, globally, 96 percent of all murderers are men and 70 percent of their victims are male. Those who have the strongest attachment to traditional masculinity are most likely to perpetrate crimes. Their behavior is costly. In the United States, there are 23 billion crimes committed each year, resulting in $15 billion in losses to victims and $179 billion in costs for police and prisons.[26]

Because men so often fall victim to the consequences of unwise risk-taking, discouraging mothers from providing for children produces unacceptable uncertainty for our offspring: there is a much higher probability that children will lose their fathers than their mothers. It doesn't make sense, in the bigger picture, if we are paying more to the ones who take foolish risks while paying less to those most likely to be left behind to provide.

People making this "paid for danger" argument often go back to the hunter-gatherer myth. Hunting is said not only to be more dangerous but also to require "masculine" abilities like running fast or seeing long distances, as well as "manly" skills, like using guns or setting traps.[27] Hunting is also said to be the original reason men worked away from home, while women stayed put. But since hunting has also been a sport, even a leisure activity of the privileged, for a few thousand years, we should think twice about categorizing it as "work" at all.

Mythical male-hunting history is sometimes even ramped up to make claims that men are more aggressive at work today, whether in seeking new customers or asking for a pay increase, and to argue that men will move to take better jobs, while women often will not. The "original" gender division of labor is also used to excuse male aggression against women at work: it's "just how men are," and women must learn to cope with it by developing a "thicker skin."

This kind of talk also draws on an archaeological theory of human origins widely popularized during the 1960s.[28] You can still see the impact of this "Man the Hunter" narrative in caveman cartoons or tableaux in museums where men dressed in fur threaten a large animal with clubs. Rebecca Solnit, writing in *Harper's* in 2015, recaps this myth succinctly:

> Sooner or later in conversations about who we are, who we have been, and who we can be, someone will tell a story about Man the Hunter. It's a story not just about Man but about Woman and

Child too. There are countless variants, but all of them go something like this: In primordial times men went out and hunted
and brought home meat to feed women and children, who sat
around being dependent on them. In most versions, the story
is set in nuclear units, such that men provide only for their own
family, and women have no community to help with the kids. In
every version, women are baggage that breeds.[29]

Man the Hunter, said mid-twentieth-century archaeologists, was a
carnivore with a killer instinct that female humans did not have. He
was tall and walked upright to see large game across the savanna. His
big brain gave him the idea that first separated humans from animals:
tools, especially for killing prey. Man the Hunter traveled in all-male
groups and was often gone from home for a long time.

This scenario has been completely debunked. We don't have the
teeth of a carnivore, nor do the remains of our predecessors. Proto-
humans were not tall, did not live on the savanna, did not hunt large
game, lived in trees rather than caves, ate mostly plants, and had brains
the size of chimps'. They were more likely to be prey than predator.[30]
No one knows whether men or women invented tools. Yet Man the
Hunter continues to enforce gender roles in the economy.

Those trying to justify economic gender inequality also argue that
men's work is "heavy" and "hard," compared with women's. Since
women are just too weak to do things men do, these people seem to be
saying, paying them less and treating them badly is justified. In economic development and international policy, the germ for this idea
is attributed to Ester Boserup, the Danish economist, who claimed
that women's economic subordination began because they were too
weak to plow. Boserup made a huge impact with this argument in
1970, but its power can still be seen.[31] *The Economist*, for instance,
published a 2011 piece called "The Plough and the Now: Deep-Seated
Attitudes to Women Have Roots in Ancient Agriculture," featuring
a new study claiming to have proved that women were equal before
the plow and that the impact made them unequal for the next five
thousand years.[32] This study, by Alberto Alesina and Nathan Nunn

of Harvard and Paola Giuliano of UCLA, is now required reading in many colleges and has formed another meme that justifies economic gender inequality.

Women's economic subordination is too cruel, too widespread, and too lasting to be blamed on a five-thousand-year-old farming technology. Furthermore, plows are not usually pushed or pulled by people, but instead are harnessed to large draft animals. Plows had wheels early on, and then seats to sit on while the animals worked. How much upper-body strength one really needed is questionable.

As with hunting, it's not so much that women can't plow but that no one notices when they do. Through history, women have plowed whenever a husband or father died or became incapacitated. They have also plowed when men went off to war—and continued to do so if their men didn't return. For instance, in the U.K. and the United States during both world wars, women were recruited by the government to farm—and to plow, as can plainly be seen in recruiting materials from the period (Figure 10).[33]

Not only are women strong enough to push a plow; they can pull it in place of draft animals. I found a travelogue written in 1870 in

FIGURE 10. On the left, British Women's Land Army recruiting poster from World War I; on the right, an American "farmerette" in wartime.

Sources: Land Army photo by Hulton-Deutsch Collection / Corbis Historical / Getty Images; farmerette photo by Bain News Service / Buyenlarge / Getty Images

which an American describes a scene said to be common in Germany. A man would harness his wife to a plow, then drive the woman like an animal while he himself sat on the little seat and smoked. The American claimed that German women were proud to do this for their men (though he did not actually talk to any of them). He chastised American women, who were then organizing for the first time, as selfish, lazy whiners who didn't really care about their men.[34]

I thought this story might be apocryphal until I found another photograph, this one from the early 1900s in Canada. In it, twelve Russian immigrant women are hitched to a plow, while a man seems poised to push. I think this picture says it all. Gender inequality can't be justified by some fairy tale about plows, nor with lame taxonomies about men's work being more demanding. The bottom line is that women's economic subordination comes from the power men have to make women work, in service to them, for less or no pay. The cause is male aggression and control of resources rather than men's natural superiority as stronger, braver, more important beings.

Women's work has always been important to the development of national economies, but it is seldom noticed in practice and is usually ignored by historians. A striking example is the production of Chinese silk at the time of the ancient trade routes. In 130 B.C.E., the Han dynasty opened to trade with the West, joining a trade network that linked China to the Mediterranean, western Asia, and the Indian subcontinent. The route came to be known as the Silk Road because of the trade in silks that made China rich. But you can read histories of the Silk Road until your eyes burn and never see mention that women made the luxury fabric that built China.[35]

The production of silk in China was brutally hard work that gave us foot-binding, an iconic emblem of women's subordination. Early in the twenty-first century, Laurel Bossen and Hill Gates traveled to interview the last surviving women who'd had their feet bound. Bossen and Gates established that the purpose of foot-binding was not sexual, as had previously been thought. Instead, this crippling act was performed on three- to five-year-old girls to immobilize them so they would sit still for the long hours required to spin. Somewhere in the past, demand for fabric became so great that women worked day and night, struggling to keep up with quotas. The pressure was so intense that mothers would perform this mutilation on their own daughters. It had been going on for centuries.[36] Does *this* count as hard, dangerous, and important work?

MALE DOMINANCE IS UNIVERSAL AND UNCHANGEABLE.

Male dominance *is* universal in human experience, as are war and disease.[37] But we don't let conflict and infection go unchecked, and we should approach patriarchy the same way. Rule by violent, greedy men is what we have always had, but it causes great harm. Can we change it?

To suggest an answer, let me give you a story to think about. Robert Sapolsky, a neuroscientist and leading primatologist, has been observing the same group of baboons since the late 1970s, to learn about stress. Scientists interested in the health effects of stress on humans study baboons, not so much because they share genetic material with us (94 percent), but because their social structure and behaviors are so similar.

Baboon hierarchy has a single alpha male at the top who acquires and maintains his rank by beating any challenger in a fight. The alpha spends most of his time intimidating the other baboons and sticking his nose in everybody's business. He does not find food, but waits for the females to do it, and when the group is attacked, he finds a safe place to hide and lets the other males do the fighting.[38] In other words, he is a freeloader and a coward, as well as a bully.

All the other males are stratified into ranks beneath the alpha, with each having the right to dominate the ones beneath. All males can bully the females. Since baboons don't have to spend much time searching for food, they occupy the rest of each day harassing each other. They appear to be miserable, as well as unhealthy.

Over the years, Sapolsky collected blood samples from all the males in this particular troop, and once he was back at Stanford, he tested the samples and arranged them in the order of the baboons' hierarchy. He found that the blood of the ones at the top was clear of stress hormones such as adrenaline, cortisol, and norepinephrine, while the further he went down the ranks, the level of stress-related substances rose.[39] The increased presence of these substances, in humans as well as baboons, is a real and present threat to life.

Then a dramatic change occurred among Sapolsky's troop. Meat was left in the garbage bin of a tourist lodge nearby, and the baboons discovered it. The top-ranking males ate it all, refusing to share it with the downscale males or any females. Suddenly, the alpha male and his stooges were dead; the meat had been infected with bovine tuberculosis.

We might predict that a new contingent of bullies would rise to the top, but that's not what happened. The deaths left behind a population with a higher percentage of females, as well as males both lower in rank and previously identified by Sapolsky as affiliative and cooperative. The good guys and the females devised a culture that was less abusive, more cooperative, more egalitarian, and healthier.

Even after this generation passed and another came in, even after the sex ratio went back to normal, the community was still living under the new order. Among baboons, males migrate to mate, but this newly gentle tribe maintained its ethic despite the periodic infusion of outsiders. The peaceful group insisted that new males behave. In particular, the females refused to mate with any males who did not adopt the new ethos— and their homeboys backed them up.[40]

If baboons can change, we can, too. We are far more adaptive than our primate cousins. The ability to know when we are in trouble, diagnose the situation, plan practical steps, and then execute that plan is a preeminently human talent. More than any jaw shape, skull cavity, or mating dance, the ability to create change is in our nature.

The question now is whether we have the discipline and commitment to change our self-seeking, status-obsessed, warrior-chimp economy and create a different kind of future. Male dominance has led us to the brink of humanity's destruction. If we intend to act against it by lifting the economic constraints on women, the best first step should be to understand how and why those restrictions appeared in the first place. If the economic patriarchy didn't start with hunting or the plow, then when was the Double X Economy born?

5 | FOR LOVE, NOT MONEY

A woman cannot *own* property, because she *is* property. A father gets a better price for his daughter if she is young. A widow must submit to wife inheritance if she wants to be near her children. A man must pay the father and marry his daughter if he rapes her. If a man wants to increase his production, he can just get more wives.

All these prescriptions circled through my mind; each of them was a rule governing an economic exchange, but also a stipulation about marriage. In each principle, the female does not *make* the exchange but *is* exchanged for money or goods of value, without being asked for consent under any of them. As the teacher in Ghana told me sharply, "When you are a woman, you do not choose!"

I had observed these rules being followed in Africa, but I knew they were not unique, because I had seen some of them in force elsewhere. I had also read histories in which the same rules appeared in other times and places. And I was haunted by an essay that had once puzzled me but that described what I now saw with my own eyes.

I first read Gayle Rubin's "The Traffic in Women" when I was studying for my Ph.D.[1] It initially appeared in a book-length anthropology collection, Rayna Reiter's *Toward an Anthropology of Women*, the first such work ever to concentrate on women, published in the early 1980s. Rubin's premise was that the subordination of females originated in the apparently universal hunter-gatherer practice of exchanging women in trade. Rubin emphasized that women did not choose to comply with these exchanges, but were forced by male violence to do so. Since forager systems account for 99 percent of human history, Rubin's insight had profound implications.

Given the echoes in contemporary Africa, I now thought there might be a thread running from hunter-gatherers to industrializing countries that would answer the question of how the Double X Economy we see today came into being. So I began working from Rubin's starting point all the way to economic arrangements in the present. I read widely, covering many societies in many places, just as I had done to investigate property rights. I did not attempt to investigate every group of humans who have ever existed, but worked instead to determine whether there was a preponderance of evidence that could explain the widely consistent patterns in the Double X Economy today.

In 90 percent of human forager societies, it's the females who migrate—and they apparently go with the flow of goods in trade. Female migration, male aggression, and patriarchy are also associated with polygamy in primates—and 85 percent of human forager societies are polygamous. Indeed, most of the historical world was polygamous until the mid-twentieth century. Of the world's major religions, Hinduism, Buddhism, and Judaism do not forbid polygamy; wherever one of those religions was practiced, polygamy has been common. Islam allows polygamy. Confucian culture considered the experience of managing multiple wives part of a man's spiritual development. Christianity is the only one of humanity's main religions that has explicitly forbidden polygamy.[2]

Polygamy has been common more recently than you might think. Having multiple wives or concubines was legal in China until the People's Republic was established in 1949. Hindu men in India were allowed to take multiple wives until the Hindu Marriage Act of 1955. Though a few Muslim-majority states, like Tunisia and Turkey, have outlawed polygamy, most Islamic states still allow it—and India, home to one of the world's largest Muslim populations, makes an exception to allow Muslim men to have multiple wives. Today, polygamy is still accepted in fifty-eight states scattered through Africa, the Middle East, Central and South Asia, and the Malay Archipelago.

Having many wives has been a way for men to display wealth and status in all polygamous societies. "Common" men have often been limited by law or religion to one wife, while higher-ranking men could have many. For example, in Indian history, the number of wives a man could have was determined by caste.

Until Rubin's essay, however, few scholars had stopped to consider the effect of this widespread trafficking on women. In fact, anthropologists had romanticized the trade of women at least since the first economic anthropology, Marcel Mauss's *The Gift: The Form and Reason for Exchange in Archaic Societies*, appeared in 1925. Mauss's book built upon all existing accounts of pre-monetized economies, in a sweeping analysis that reached from the Northwest of the Americas to the Trobriand Islands of Oceania, as well as covering everything known about the economic practices of ancient societies.

Premodern societies conduct trade through exchange ceremonies that occur between tribes. The ceremonies and the goods traded are consistently controlled by men; the patriarchal economy clearly has roots in the earliest forms of exchange. Mauss, however, argued that these rituals had a reciprocal ethic that stood in contrast to the self-seeking of capitalist life:

> All these institutions express one fact alone, one social system, one precise state of mind: everything—food, women, children, property, talismans, land, labour services, priestly functions, and ranks—is there for passing on, and for balancing accounts. Everything passes to and fro as if there were a constant exchange of a spiritual matter, including things and men, between class and individuals, distributed between social ranks, the sexes, and the generations.[3]

Mauss's assessment of these ceremonies—shared by many anthropologists for decades—was pretty rosy: this ceremonial trade allegedly benefited the whole group by weaving a web of human solidarity unrivaled in the modern world. No one recognized, it seems, that the hunter-gatherer economy could just as easily have been called a "human trafficking economy." The implicit assumption was that what was good for the men was good for the women—and that the females willingly allowed themselves to become the objects of trade.

But even as *The Gift* was translated into multiple languages, the ethnographic record held evidence that forager societies' exchange of women was something far more sinister than Mauss's account allowed. Writing in 2019, Richard Wrangham summarized Australian Aboriginal practices first recounted in a 1938 ethnography as an argument against the long-standing belief that hunter-gatherer morality benefits the *whole* group: "Wives could be required to have sex with multiple men at special ceremonies. They could also be lent to a visiting man, or given sexually by a husband to a man with whom the husband had quarreled, in order to erase a debt or make peace." The women, far from being the willing markers of kinder, gentler exchange systems, saw these experiences as acts of violence. "Apparently," he adds, "women did not enjoy these coercive encounters . . . Australian Aboriginal women would live in terror of the use that was made of them at ceremonial times." Wrangham concludes that the Aboriginal behaviors described were the "moral practice of ordinary men" and reflected the widespread reality that allegedly prosocial behaviors among such groups were beneficial for the men but damaging to the women.[4]

Historians have had a similar blind spot. As they documented the use of females to forge alliances, settle disputes, solidify contracts, and compensate warriors, the authors of history have consistently ignored the effect of the transactions on women. In fact, they frequently assert that being chosen for such an exchange was "an honor." For instance, Gordon McEwan, in his account of the Incan Empire, claims that women felt privileged to be pressed into that culture's extraordinary use of females as forced labor and even as a kind of currency.[5]

The Incan emperor lavishly rewarded loyal nobles and successful warriors by giving them wives—sometimes many of them—in recognition of service. The ruler's inventory of women came through a tribute system. Each province paid annual taxes in ten- to twelve-year-old girls, selected for their beauty. Upon their arrival in the capital, the girls were ranked on appearance, then sorted into classes. The highest class became priestesses, the next became secondary wives of the emperor, while girls among the third class were awarded to nobles and warriors. The least beautiful became servants. A fifth group were employed as court entertainers and spent their days weaving cloth. And, according to McEwan, all these little girls were thrilled just to be there.

As unsavory as the Incan example is, I found here the most compelling link in my effort to trace a long-standing and worldwide practice of trading women as goods. Consider this: The humans who populated the Western Hemisphere had been separated from other *Homo sapiens* populations for twenty-five thousand years after they left Siberia. Yet when the Spanish arrived in what is now Peru during the sixteenth century, polygamy, patriarchy, male aggression, and trade in women were entrenched in the Incan culture they found—just as they were in Eurasia, where these phenomena can be documented going back at least four thousand years. That connection suggests strongly that patriarchy, polygamy, and the trade in women were already present among Eurasian populations when the forager ancestors of the Incas left.

There are many similarities between the practices of the Incas and those of other societies elsewhere in the world. Organizing women into classes on the basis of their service to men was common once complex societies emerged. Virtually every ancient Eurasian society, including the Greeks and Romans, thought captured women were appropriate compensation for soldiers.

I found the practices I was tracing echoed in the broader cultural record, sometimes in disturbingly familiar ways and places. Kings have given away daughters to perfect strangers in venues from fairy tales to history books, usually without mention of the young women's wishes. Oral scriptures, songs, and sagas, like the Old Testament, the Vedas, and the Old Norse tales, refer variously to the trade of women, the rights of fathers over daughters, the absence of female consent, polygamy, wife inheritance, and marriage as a solution for rape.[6]

When writing technology emerged in Mesopotamia, records were created that illuminate the economic consequences of the trafficking for the women themselves.[7] The first set of written laws we have is the Code of Ur-Nammu (circa 2100 B.C.E.), an incomplete list of forty statutes inscribed on fragments of a stone. In it, property rights are awarded to men. Marriage was a formal contract that primarily served to give the husband exclusive sexual services and to protect him from incursion on his rights by other men. Since the statutes include fines as punishment, we can infer a woman's value from the measure of silver demanded as compensation from another man who had sex with her; the fines show an escalating price list, from slaves at the bottom to virgin daughters at the top.

The laws of Ur-Nammu stipulate or suggest strongly that men controlled wealth; women were owned and their value inhered in their sexual services rather than in procreation or housekeeping; husbands gave material support to their wives in exchange for sexual exclusivity; women did not have economic means other than through men; brides were bought under a contract between a prospective husband and her father; husbands were free to have sex outside of marriage, but wives could be punished by death if they did the same; and, finally, divorce was easy for husbands but impossible for wives.

Similar arrangements appear with more detail and cruelty in the Code of Hammurabi, which was written in Mesopotamia about 350 years later. Hammurabi's code shows that polygamy was the norm, females were traded by fathers, and women were rigidly stratified according to their relationship to men. The punishments listed also make clear that though the state issued the rules and would enforce them when necessary, enforcement rested primarily on the head of household's authority to mete out physical punishment, to control all material goods or money, and to trade away any woman at will.

Hammurabi's rules for handling the rape of a man's daughter are familiar, but add a dark twist. The rapist compensates the father by paying a fine and marrying the daughter, as she is no longer valuable to the father. However, it is up to the father to either accept the marriage or dispose of her in some other way—for instance, by putting his daughter out as a prostitute or by having her killed as "an adulteress."

Notice that adultery includes not only a wife being unfaithful to a man to whom she is married, but also a daughter having sex outside the arrangements made by her father. For thousands of years going forward, the most common sentence for a woman committing adultery of any kind would be death. The honor killings in Bangladesh, Pakistan, and the Middle East are the end of a very long line. And even now it is the law in Angola, Bahrain, Cameroon, Equatorial Guinea, Eritrea, Iraq, Jordan, Kuwait, Lebanon, Libya, Malaysia, the Philippines, and Tajikistan that a rapist must marry his victim to compensate for the economic loss sustained by the victim's father.

Though activists currently claim that marriage-by-rape regulations grew out of European colonial law, the practice, as we can see, actually appeared at least three thousand years ago. It is also not a Muslim custom, as many in the West would assume from the geography; the rule even appears in the Old Testament: "If a man happens to meet a virgin who is not pledged to be married and rapes her and they are discovered, he shall pay her father fifty shekels of silver. He must marry the young woman, for he has violated her. He can never divorce her as long as he lives."[8]

No mention is made of restitution to the victim in any ancient legal code—her welfare appears to be of no concern.

In the Middle Assyrian code that followed Hammurabi's by about five hundred years, we can see economic restrictions on women that are present in today's Double X Economy. In addition to women's total economic dependence on men and the male monopoly on property ownership, there now appear constraints on mobility, exclusion from the exchange system, and barriers to participating in commerce on your own behalf. We also know that women were not allowed to learn to read and write, which would have excluded them from the financial system.

Though the Ur-Nammu and Hammurabi laws allude to inheritance rights, the emphasis on passing wealth from father to son—or at least keeping it in the hands of male kin—comes forward more emphatically in the Middle Assyrian code. Widows, in this society, were left destitute when their husbands died, just as they are in developing countries today. (There are 40 million such widows in India alone.)

Under the Middle Assyrian code, wives do not appear to have shared ownership of even ordinary household objects. The Middle Assyrian laws stipulate that if a wife takes something from her husband's home, it is theft—and recommends cutting off her ears as a punishment. If the husband is not able to punish the wife, because of his death or incapacitation, the law says the state will kill her.

Middle Assyrian law dictates specific practices that deny women mobility and privacy, thereby blocking their ability to participate freely in the economy. The codes stipulate that women who belong to one man must wear veils when outside the home to announce to others that they are under male control. When these women went out, they were accompanied by a chaperone.[9] So, except for excursions under guard, these women were housebound. That level of control allowed the husband to be sure each gave birth to only his children, something that does not seem to matter to hunter-gatherers, given the heedless way they pass women around. The male obsession with paternity, it appears, is not "natural," as some claim. The almost pathological desire men came to have about maintaining sexual exclusivity over wives may have emerged with the invention of these means to control who had access to them (by fines or by restricting movement).

For the women, the economic consequences of being unable to leave home unmarked and unaccompanied are significant. These restrictions would have made it impossible to earn outside the home without a husband's knowledge. If the women did not own even the things in their homes, they were utterly dependent on the men who owned *them*. If they wove or sewed, the proceeds from things they made probably belonged to the male heads of household, just as married women who farm in Africa don't own the products of their work. That's because, in addition to owning the female workers, the men would also own the land, the buildings, the looms, and the thread—all the capital equipment and materials.

The practices of veiling, seclusion, and chaperonage seem to have been spread around the world by trade and conquest, just as other beliefs, practices, and objects were. If we take veiling and seclusion as markers for a system that excluded women from economic participation, we can trace the Double X Economy, going east from the ancient Middle East into India, west into North Africa, north across the Mediterranean, and eventually into Europe. In some societies, such as in ancient Greece, women were so secluded they went from their father's home directly to their husband's, never interacting with the outside world at all.

In the Mediterranean cultures from which European history is normally traced, veiling, seclusion, male arrangement of marriage, male control of property, and exclusion from inheritance were generally present. In medieval Europe, there was some veiling and seclusion, as well as male control over all property, arranged marriage, and restrictions on female inheritance. The Spanish carried many of these practices to the New World, having themselves been influenced by the rules of Islam coming north from the Middle East. Indeed, some form of veiling, seclusion, or chaperonage has been practiced in most of the world, and seclusion is still practiced today, from Africa to the Middle East and into the Indian subcontinent.[10]

While it is commonly accepted that women have always worked in the home because of children, there is an equally strong case to be made that women worked at home because they were not allowed to leave. We have many names—*purdah* and *cloister*, *hijab* and *wimple*, *mantilla* and *sheitel*, *harem* and *convent*—for items and practices that derive from the same intent.[11]

As we have seen, many of the rules found in these ancient legal systems are still in force around the world. The restrictions do seem to spring from a huge historical root system with a global reach. It's commonplace to try to excuse or protect the worst of these practices—like child marriage or female genital cutting—by saying, "It's their culture." But the truth is that this tragic system of exploitation and control is *everyone's* cultural history.

Furthermore, wherever the most restrictive practices are still in place, the people of that culture don't necessarily agree that they should continue. *Understanding Masculinities*, a recent study of Middle Eastern men's and women's attitudes toward the vestiges of these ancient practices, shows the divide.[12] The men and women disagree on lots of these issues—but on virtually every item, the men disagree with each other. Large majorities of both sexes agree that their culture, though it does have these restrictive practices, should do more to achieve equality for women. So we should not assume that, just because these practices appear in a place, the local citizens don't want them changed.

The ancient laws did not stop at restraining married women, however. The veiling that excluded wives in Assyria was turned into a weapon against women who were not "under the protection" of men and that, too, has spread around the world. The Middle Assyrian code says that women who *are not* owned by one man may not wear a veil, so it will be known by everyone that they have no protection. In *The Creation of Patriarchy*, the first attempt at an ancient history of women, published in 1986, Gerda Lerner argues that this provision was aimed at making clear when a woman belonged to *all* men by virtue of being under the wing of no *one* man, and so invited sexual assault. The Middle Assyrian rules therefore made it unsafe for a woman to remain single or to work outside the home and thus pushed females toward marriage in order to avoid violence. As a consequence, they would have been blocked from economic independence.

Treating unattached working women as shameful exemplars, even "sluts" who deserve sexual assault, is a phenomenon that reached around the world. This attitude prevailed in North America and Western Europe until at least the second half of the twentieth century and, as we shall see, working women in the developing world today are reviled for their presumed immorality and subject to unending harassment and violence.

The punishments for breaking the veiling laws in Mesopotamia were severe: citizens were exhorted to take any prostitute wearing a veil to the palace gates, strip her, strike her fifty times, and pour hot pitch over her head. When slave women committed the same crime, citizens were instructed to cut off their ears and take their clothing. However, men who assisted a woman who had broken with the code also received a severe punishment: if a man seeing such a woman did not seize her, he was to receive "50 blows with rods," be relieved of his clothing, and have his ears pierced and threaded on a cord that was tied behind his back.

The penalty for men would not have been necessary if the patriarchs hadn't thought *some* men would choose to assist the unveiled women.

The societies of Mesopotamia were autocratic, complex states with formalized economies and agricultural technology. They traded various goods over long distances and conducted large-scale warfare. The first standing army, the first war of conquest, and multiple weapons innovations designed to increase the range and impact of attack appeared in this empire. Capture during war brought an influx of female slaves, as is clear from the many regulations regarding their treatment. And, of course, warriors having more wives just shot that much more violence into the gene pool.

In *Sex and War*, Malcolm Potts and Thomas Hayden argue that the reproductive success of violent human males created an ever-escalating situation wherein destructive genes fueled a culture of war. Potts went to Bangladesh in 1971 to provide relief immediately following the Bangladesh Liberation War. A doctor of obstetrics and gynecology, he treated Bangladeshi women who had been victims of the largest systematic rape in world history. Since then, he has volunteered in Vietnam, Cambodia, Afghanistan, Egypt, the Gaza Strip, Liberia, and Angola, dealing with rape each time. *Sex and War* was the result of these experiences.[13]

In their book, Potts and Hayden, a journalist, exhaustively document male violence against women during conflict, starting with the behavior of chimpanzees and examining what seems like every war in human history. These authors point to the fact that warfare is normally organized into squads of about eight men, who work very closely to effect what Potts and Hayden call "team aggression." The teams strategize attacks, using rape as part of the offense, and bond over the violence they commit against females. The combination of rising testosterone, adrenaline produced by danger, and band-of-brothers bonding transports them beyond the confines of their usual behavior and personalities. Potts and Hayden argue that under such circumstances all men, including themselves, are capable of rape. The evidence they give for how successful warrior males have been is in our history *and* in our genetic material: 8 percent of the male population of Central Asia still carries the DNA of Genghis Khan, the inveterate rapist who led the

Mongol invasions of the thirteenth century. In fact, 16 million men alive today still carry his genes through an identifiable Y chromosome. But we must not conclude this violence lasts forever: the Vikings were among the most brutal warriors in history, but today the Scandinavians are seen as exemplars of peacefulness and gender equality.

Warrior culture prepared males for fighting from an early age. As in forager societies, the rite of passage to manhood usually involved a painful or terrifying ordeal, and some cultures killed boys who tried to run away. Here is where the extreme pressure to "earn manhood" starts. Throughout history, males have been expected to justify their masculinity continuously, enduring pain without complaint, hiding their emotions, and killing or torturing without compunction.

This is a horrible thing to do to a creature whose brain is literally wired for empathy. In 2019, the American Psychological Association recognized the hallmarks of "toxic masculinity," a harmful condition rooted in negative versions of manhood being forced on little boys—and something that requires special guidelines to be treated. APA announced that its decision drew "on more than 40 years of research showing that traditional masculinity is psychologically harmful and that socializing boys to suppress their emotions causes damage that echoes both inwardly and outwardly."[14]

Those the warrior societies groomed for war often lived together, at a remove from women. When males reside in a separate space, there is no counterbalance to the influence of competition and aggression. What typically emerges is a rigid, autocratic hierarchy, enforced by bullying and expressed in contemptuous behavior toward women.

We must recognize that males were conscripted for battle just as surely as females were forcibly expropriated for trade. They were commanded to fight and given no choice about where, when, and for whom. Desertion was nearly always punished by death. Archaeologists today emphasize that we must not glamorize the warriors of the past. Soldiers were human, no matter how toughened they were. They must have felt fear and pain. Just because these peoples did not use the term *post-traumatic stress disorder* does not mean they did not experience it.

The alpha males of ancient societies also commanded huge groups of male slaves to build elaborate irrigation systems and roads to connect their empires. And, of course, the emperors, kings, Caesars, and pharaohs wanted monuments to themselves built by the men they dominated. These ancient patriarchies brutally dominated and exploited men as well as women.

Stepping back, we can see in this history the point of origin for today's Double X Economy. As far back in written history as you can go, "wives" were bought and sold, forced into nonconsensual contracts with no end date, with owners who could trade them to one another on impulse. They received no payment, owned no property, and had no money. They were punished physically, even disfigured or killed, for the slightest infraction. They were underfed, weakened. They were captives under the threat of violence if they resisted. They were virtually always forbidden weapons and so had no way to defend themselves and no means of escape. Their access to information was severely limited and their communication with the outside world controlled. Today, when these things appear all at once, international policy calls it "slavery."

The darkest aspect of the Double X Economy is still slavery. Human trafficking preys disproportionately on women and targets those who are most economically disenfranchised. The International Labour Organization estimates there are 40 million slaves in the world today, of whom 71 percent are female and 15.4 million are women forced into marriage.[15]

The exchange of goods for a bride continues in the form of dowry and bride price. In India, dowry has become a life-and-death matter, even though the government has outlawed it. The Indian marriage exchange is subject to long negotiation, but sometimes the groom and his family protest afterward that they weren't paid enough or that they were promised something that hasn't been delivered. They continue to ratchet up their demands, as the bride's family keeps trying to come up with funds to pay. Eventually, it's just extortion, with the bride as a hostage. When the bride's family can no longer afford to pay, the groom and his family murder her. The typical method is to douse the wife with kerosene and set her on fire. The groom and his kin provide alibis for one another, so the police can seldom make a homicide charge stick.

Bride burning is extremely common, with officials estimating that one Indian woman dies this way every hour. Women's rights groups say it's more like every fifteen minutes.

Another current echo of the marriage practices of the past is "marriage by rape" or "bride kidnapping," in which the objective is to claim a bride without paying the father. The crime is committed by poor men, but also by men who would be unacceptable to families for other reasons, like drug addiction or a criminal record. A man kidnaps a woman, sometimes with the assistance of other men or family. He takes her to a secure place and rapes her repeatedly, to make her unacceptable to another man. Then he goes to the woman's father and offers to marry her. The families are so ashamed of their daughter losing her virginity that they usually pressure her to agree. Though marriage by rape occurs in every region of the world, it is probably most prevalent in Central Asia, where the crime has increased since the fall of the Soviet Union. In Kyrgyzstan, for instance, about a third of all marriages occur this way.[16]

You might now be asking yourself why and how Western marriages came to differ so dramatically from those in the rest of the world. The change began in Europe with the priests who brought their religion north from the Christian Roman Empire.[17] These evangelists stopped many cultural practices they saw as incompatible with their faith. Their efforts to change the basis for marriage eventually had a massive impact on the Double X Economy.

The Christian stance was that, based on Jesus's teachings as interpreted by Paul the Apostle, each man should have only one wife. The leaders of the early church in Europe also advocated monogamy in order to minimize sexual activity—they believed sex to be sinful and thought they could limit its occurrence if couples had only one partner. They also insisted that no marriage could occur without the bride's consent. These priests were not particularly friendly to women, but since there are several places in the Gospel where Jesus treats women in a way that implies they are human—even equal—in the eyes of God, it followed that they should have the right to give or withhold consent. Catholic priests therefore came into Europe demanding that all unions be monogamous and that no marriage could be made without the consent of the bride.

By 700 C.E. both England and France were officially Christian, but the progress was slower among the Germanic tribes. The last region to convert was Scandinavia, in roughly 1100 C.E. The contact between the Norsemen and Catholic priests demonstrates the transition from "pagan" marriage to Christian matrimony. The Norse sagas described a culture in which fathers sold daughters without their consent and men had multiple wives, conditions that were mirrored in the practices the Catholics found when they arrived. The priests left written records about their efforts to stop the trade in women and polygamy. We know now that the priests got their way, in the Nordic region as well as everywhere else that became part of "Christendom." The whole of Europe became monogamous, the first region of the world to make this change across such a large swath of geography and among so many diverse peoples.

We should be clear that the nascent Catholic Church was by no means trying to free women; its policies were often cruel to females, and the marriage reforms were frequently applied superficially, sabotaged, and twisted. However, the change was still a profound one because it formally recognized the *personhood* of women and implied that a wife was a partner in the household economy, rather than a possession.

Economic subordination, however, continued for centuries.[18] Common practice and, eventually, written law gave husbands control over all household assets, regardless of provenance, as well as any income that a person under his roof earned. Veiling and seclusion continued. Some women worked outside the home, but they were lower-class, considered "disreputable," and often subject to male sexual aggression.

Economic vulnerability kept women in bad marriages, but so did the near impossibility of divorce. The ecclesiastical courts would, on rare occasions, allow a divorce on the basis of desertion, extreme cruelty, or adultery, which was harshly punished, though not by death. Domestic violence, however, was rampant; it was legal under both customary and canonical law for a man to beat his wife, as this statute from France indicates: "It is licit for the man to beat his wife, without bringing about death or disablement, when she refuses her husband anything."[19]

Desertion was common. Men would leave home to go where there was said to be work. Long-distance trade also often required them to be away. Women, because they were obliged by custom to remain at home, were excluded from these opportunities and transactions. As shipping developed, men went off to sea, and they also marched off to the many wars Europe endured. Men could be killed on any of these trips. Nevertheless, abandoned wives had to wait interminable periods for the Church to recognize a husband's protracted absence as death, and only when he was declared dead could a woman marry again, rescuing herself and her children from destitution. Deserted wives and widows, as well as their children, became the most visible group among the poor.[20]

The economic vulnerability of women was eventually set by formal statute in Europe. In Britain, a common-law concept called *coverture* became written law. This legal principle said that a married woman was "covered" by her husband, such that she had no legal or economic identity of her own. Under coverture, women handed over control of all their assets to their husbands when they married. Britain eventually exported this rule to Canada, Australia, and the United States, and the same concept appeared under Roman-Dutch law. Other European countries achieved the same ends by legally making wives minors.

Quite a few historians take pains to argue that some women were able to own property in the Middle Ages, the Renaissance, and the Age of Discovery, though these are usually presented as singular cases—in essence, exceptions that prove the rule. It is hard to assess how many European women ever actually owned property in this period; in the majority of cases, it appears that what women had, even in dowry and inheritance, was only usufruct—rights of use, not ownership, until they married or died, or their sons reached majority.

The test for whether someone really owns land is whether they can sell, destroy, mortgage, or give away the asset. I doubt many women had true ownership, at least of real property. The graph in Figure 11 illustrates the problem of generalizing from exceptional cases, as well as conflating use rights and property rights. The figure shows the land "alienated" (by sale, donation, etc.) by men and women over four centuries in Italy, Spain, Southern France, Northern France, and Germany. There is simply no avoiding that, between 800 and 2000 C.E., men were in control of European wealth and productive resources.[21]

The common European farm was a tight economic unit that required at least two able-bodied adults to work it. People married more to get help with their work than for affection. However, historians are a bit too quick to conclude that the women in these homes were valued as "helpmeets" because their work was important and necessary. We have already seen that the assumed link between essential work and cultural respect does not exist, and given the other circumstances that married women faced, including a very high level of domestic violence, I think a respectful relationship would have been enjoyed by few.[22]

When the household economy was based on a business instead of a farm, women still had little economic power. For instance, a woman often became a valuable helper in a skilled craftsman's shop, sometimes

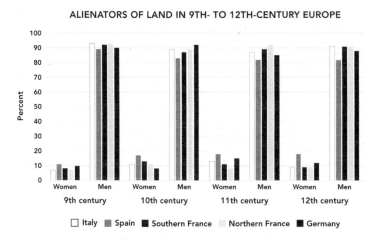

ALIENATORS OF LAND IN 9TH- TO 12TH-CENTURY EUROPE

☐ Italy ▨ Spain ■ Southern France ▨ Northern France ■ Germany

FIGURE 11. Historical sources sometimes imply that women owned land, when in fact they had only use rights. This graph shows how much land was dispensed with ("alienated") by men and women over a four-hundred-year period in four European countries.

Source: David Herlihy, "Land, Family, and Women in Continental Europe, 701–1200," in *Women in Medieval Society*, ed. Susan Mosher Stuard (Philadelphia: University of Pennsylvania Press, 1976), 28

learning the craft herself, but she could not walk away and set up her own business, because the guilds did not accept women as members. Sometimes a widow would be allowed to continue operating a shop if her husband died, but only until she married again. The default was always that the married woman was dependent on her husband. These European women were still economic captives, even if they were not behind veils and screens.

A disturbing story of a fourteenth-century European woman illustrates how captivity was effected in the Middle Ages. Susan Mosher Stuard, in an essay in *Women in Medieval Society*, explains that among aristocrats in Ragusa (now Dubrovnik), women were "legally defined by the extensive and highly specific laws governing dowries."[23] She remarks that a woman passed from her father's household to her husband's custody, "insuring that she would be a private rather than a public person all her life." She observes that the role of aristocratic women was to be beautiful displays of their husband's wealth, and the women of Ragusa seemed happy to conform to that expectation. But that is what makes the story of Nicoleta de Mence so mysterious.

The historical record doesn't say why Nicoleta suddenly took herself and all her goods from the home of her husband, Jache de Sorgo, in 1390, but something awful must have happened. When Nicoleta left, Jache complained to the "Small Council," the merchants who administered the law. As "few women behaved in a manner contrary to the spirit and provisions of the law," the council was unprepared for Nicoleta's situation. First, they sent representatives to persuade Nicoleta to return, but she refused. Next they gave her an ultimatum: be home in fourteen hours, or else. When she refused again, they enlisted her "old mother" to persuade her, but it did no good. Jache continued to press until the council imprisoned Nicoleta and put her under guard. When she still refused to return, and since her husband would not back down, her goods were confiscated, and she was sent into exile penniless.

Stuard says the record indicates the Small Council tried hard to avoid putting this harsh penalty on Nicoleta and they referred to this case as "the martyrization of Nicoleta de Mence." Stuard concludes:

"Nicoleta had no right to deprive [Jache] of her dowry or her person, and there the case rested. The law might be stretched or ignored to further the interests of family business and the larger interests of the mercantile class; it could not accommodate to a woman's demands for her individual freedom."[24]

It is easy to assume that women who were wealthy and had a modicum of power were exceptions to the constraints that pertained to less privileged women, but they were also dependent on men and obligated to them. A woman's power nearly always rested on the affections of a male, and she usually had nothing if he deserted her or, as they say in European history, "set her aside." Women have been made poor throughout history by virtue of their sex. The patriarchy has affected every one of them.

In the late nineteenth century, in Western Europe, North America, and Australia, radical revision of the laws regulating women's economic status was undertaken. The origin of that sea change goes back to the story of Christianity.

The Reformation cast a skeptical eye on the rules of the Roman Catholic Church regarding marriage. The Reformers did not hold marriage to be a sacrament and felt it should be dissoluble, but as the bloody changeover from Catholicism to Protestantism progressed, the Reformers argued among themselves about rules for the new religious institutions. A key figure in these discussions was the German Reformer Martin Bucer. He argued that marriage should be based on love and respect, so if a couple no longer felt affection for each other, they should be allowed to divorce. His opinion kicked off five long centuries in which the Western countries slowly converted to the idea that marriage should be based on love.[25]

Love in marriage would seem to suggest that the couple should not engage in violence, though we know that domestic violence continues to this day even among people who profess to love each other. But it is worth noting that it was during the Reformation that "wife beating" was at last criminalized. As an example, the first code of law in Puritan Massachusetts decreed that women did not have to tolerate being beaten by their husbands.

This new matrimonial ideal implied mutual trust and support, which seems to have led to a rethinking of economic arrangements; as the restrictions on divorce were lifted in the Protestant countries, economic restrictions often softened, too. Around the turn of the twentieth century, a series of laws was passed in Protestant Europe, North America, and Australia that began to tip the scales more toward fairness, though the changes happened in tiny increments.

In 1882, the principle of coverture was eliminated from British law by the Married Women's Property Act, legislation that inspired both Australia and Canada to do the same. In the United States, however, the process had to be done state by state. Between 1830 and 1880, most states granted women the right to control their own property if their spouse was incapacitated, the right to own (but not control) their own property, and the right to earn income and keep it for their own use. Gradually, coverture was wiped from American law, but it was not actually struck down until 1982, when the Supreme Court declared the Louisiana "head and master" law unconstitutional. It's both humbling and astonishing to learn that the formal end of coverture came in the United States less than forty years ago.[26] Some scholars writing today argue that the "companionate" marriage laid the essential groundwork for democracy, by seeding a preference for equality.[27]

As the twentieth century progressed and the nuclear family with its single male breadwinner came to the fore, another stock character was a wife who spent her daytime hours cleaning the house and taking care of the children. In the consumer culture that rose throughout the twentieth century, the nuclear family was idealized in advertisements for new goods and household appliances. The housewife became central to popular culture, but she was still dependent on a man. Women went from their fathers' homes to their husbands'. Divorce was easier, but shameful. Wives had few alternatives other than to stay in their marriages. Domestic violence continued to be a problem but was not taken seriously. To illustrate, a 1954 report from Scotland Yard remarked: "There are only about 20 murders a year in London and not all are serious—some are just men killing their wives."[28] Women were still economically subordinated under the threat of violence from the men on whom they depended.

The subordination of women in economics began with males using physical violence to force females into sex under the guise of trade— in essence, sex slavery. Under every unfair economic arrangement I have studied, fear of male aggression lies beneath women's choices, even if they apprehend only the potential attack suggested by a male colleague's rage at work. But now men are organizing to change the "born killer" profile forever, under several banners, including even professional sports players making public appeals to fans. And there have been some dramatic successes. For example, Michael Kaufman, who is an advocate for women's economic empowerment and the author of a book called *The Time Has Come: Why Men Must Join the Gender Equality Revolution*, founded White Ribbon, an organization of men working to eliminate violence against women. Since its beginning in 1991, White Ribbon has been joined by men in more than ninety countries.

I recently heard Michael recount an extraordinary story to a large meeting of women's economic empowerment people in South America.

A Pakistani man returned home to the Swat Valley after studying law in the capital. His attention was caught by the plight of rape victims whose credibility was to be tried in court. They needed to have four male witnesses testify that they had been raped, and barring that, they would be charged with adultery, for which the punishment was years in prison or death. He knew this was against Pakistani legal traditions and felt it was contrary to the teachings of his religion. So he defended these women and got them off the charges of adultery. But then the authorities put *him* in prison. There were swarms of men in the jail living in inhumane conditions. "You can imagine what happened to him," said Michael, and I could feel the whole crowd groan with the certainty that the lawyer hero was himself raped or beaten in jail.

But the story ended in surprise. When the other men in the prison found out why the lawyer was there, they all went on a hunger strike until he was set free.

Michael ended his talk by arguing how change would come. "Men are capable of seeing how others are harmed, of feeling another's pain. They may seem tough, but these guys have big hearts. An appeal to their compassion, changes in our ideals of what it means to be a man, and ending men's power over women will, together, finally stop violence against women." The human capacity to empathize, to see the distress of others even when it results from one's own cruelty, offers us an important reason for hope.

6 | ESCAPE FROM THE KITCHEN

adia and I rode into the village early. We were in no hurry, so I got out of the car and looked for a place to sit while we waited. Under a tree stood a tiled chair—a ceremonial seat, perhaps? I asked Radia and our driver if it was okay to sit in it. They both shrugged and said, "Sure." So I sat.

We were in Bangladesh to assess a rural distribution system that employed beggar women to deliver goods to household compounds, where the female residents are typically not allowed to leave home to shop. The program gave employment to women who desperately needed it, but had also been a surprising boon to the women at home. For the first time, they were able to buy for themselves instead of waiting for men to bring things in, and their isolation was broken by the saleswomen who brought information about the outside world. We were conducting interviews to see what impact this flow of information and goods had on the female residents' sense of independence. It was our second day in this village.

I had not been sitting for five minutes when the imam showed up. He politely explained, in English, that I was in his ceremonial seat and asked me to get up, which I did. He asked what country I was from. I said I lived in Britain but was American. He asked if I was Muslim, and I went with my upbringing. "Christian," I said. He asked whether I was married, and I explained that my husband was in the next village. I sensed every answer I gave was the wrong one.

I saw beyond the imam's shoulder that my driver had opened the car door and was gesturing to me to hurry up and get in. Nodding farewell to the imam, I crossed over and slid into the seat, but when I turned I was astonished to see that a crowd of twenty men had gathered behind me during that short conversation. They now began to close in around the jeep. The driver slammed my door and Radia stood against it. A man of about fifty, with a bright henna-orange beard and hair, began speaking for the group in Bangla. The others, listening intently, were visibly angry. The imam said nothing but stood in their center, facing me with an attitude of triumph.

Suddenly, a white jeep screeched into the square and our local male colleagues jumped out, their aviator sunglasses making them look like they were on a central casting call for Interpol agents. Quickly, the village men scattered. With the danger removed, I asked Radia what was going on. She explained that the orange-haired man accused us of fomenting discontent with our interview questions.

Once things settled down, our colleagues went on to the next village, leaving one man behind to stand guard with our driver. Radia and I walked warily toward the compounds to finish the survey. The women inside already knew what had happened. They said they realized we were there to help, but when one woman had alerted the men, none of the rest dared stand up for us. Violence against women is horrific in this country.

At dinner, our research assistants explained to us their own vulnerability to incidents like this one, as "city girls, uncovered." Though they were in fact covered from top to toe, they did not hide their hair or faces with a veil. In the countryside, their urban dress made them targets for conservative elements who resented the gains women were making in the cities. We crafted a plan to provide safety for our assistants. There were no more complaints, and the interviewees were surprisingly candid after the uproar, as if the men's behavior had given the women more reason to ensure we understood them. Most of them had husbands in the Middle East working in construction, they said. Men in the village, as well as some women, policed the wives in the absence of their husbands. The wives sat at home, captive, and waited for men, who often stayed abroad for years.

Bangladeshi culture is extremely patriarchal. Especially in rural areas, Bangladeshis practice purdah, a type of seclusion common in Muslim countries but also in neighboring India. The women we interviewed were afraid to step outside their compound because they knew it would invite rape, yet they are not really "protected" because the violence inside the home is just as bad. In societies like Bangladesh and many others around the world, men filter what women see, hear, and know, in order to keep them under control. Our questions had poked a hole in that screen.

Economic development experts would prefer the wives in Bangladesh go to work instead of staying at home, so as to stimulate economic growth. Increasing GDP allows countries like Bangladesh to build infrastructure—roads, schools, plumbing, electrification—as well as to develop social services to support the citizenry, especially the very poor. Growth, if handled with the population's well-being as the goal, increases household incomes, improving health, nutrition, and education. But men in low-income countries resist allowing women to work outside the home, especially if the women are married.

When the ready-made garment industry arrived in Bangladesh in the 1970s, young single women seeking their freedom ran to the cities to work. Today, textiles and garments account for 75 percent of Bangladesh's GDP, represent the only multibillion-dollar industry, and are the main source of growth. The garment-sector workforce is more than 80 percent female.

Factory work brings women autonomy and is often the first step out of poverty for them, for their children, and sometimes for their birth families.[1] Despite these workers' crucial contribution to the national economy, however, they are still reviled because they challenge traditional expectations of women. The workers use their wages to buy modern clothes and mobile phones, seeming to flaunt their independence and success. When they are attacked—as they often are—some authority will inevitably excuse the crime, charging that women are "out of their place" or immodestly dressed. Factory-girl behavior is a flashing red warning to village husbands: "Don't let your wife out."

The cultural shift underway in Bangladesh has occurred in many places over the past two hundred years. The garment and textile industry has usually been the first manufacturing to arrive in a poor nation; it moves from country to country, always seeking lower-cost labor. From the time textile factories first opened in the West during the early nineteenth century, these firms have hired young single women almost exclusively. Before the industry arrives, women work in agriculture and make homemade products to sell; when the production of textiles and other homemade goods moves to factories, the market for their wares dries up.

Single women see the factories as a means of escape. By leaving the village, they can have their own money, make decisions for themselves, and, especially, choose their own mates. The patriarchy never quite recovers.

The scenario is different for married women. For a long time, they stay home, which impedes growth because the vast majority of women in traditional cultures are married. But the historical pattern predicts that wives will eventually push through to the workplace. When that happens, there is a huge and sustained rise in GDP. Data sets for 163 countries have been analyzed, and the relationship between female labor force participation and GDP holds for all of them. There is no question: the best way to help a country grow is to get the wives out of the kitchen.[2] But no one knows quite how to do it.

Economists have long hypothesized why large numbers of married women suddenly rush into the workforce. They do multiple regressions trying to match some measurable influence, like an increase in education, to this dramatic shift. For decades, they assumed the decision was made by the husband, who chose to buy his wife "leisure" when he could afford it, instead of having her bring in wages. Analysts have also sifted through historical data from the rich nations, looking for clues about why husbands "let" their wives work, so they can apply them in the developing world today. But none of them have hit on what seems to me the obvious answer: married women stay home as long as there are gender-specific restrictions on them—like having no right to make their own economic choices outside of "obeying" their husband. As soon as these restrictions are lifted, women leave the hearth to work for pay because they yearn for autonomy.

Right now, economists in the West are wringing their hands because women in the rich countries have stopped coming to work. After decades of rising numbers, female labor participation has suddenly, unaccountably, slowed and flattened in North America and Western Europe. If women withdraw from work in these nations, GDP will drop and the world economy will take a huge hit. The trend is worst in the United States, where in 2000 women's engagement actually declined for the first time in more than one hundred years. For perspective, women's annual contribution to the U.S. economy is more than Japan's entire GDP—by about US$3 trillion.[3] Why, after two centuries of struggle, would American women sacrifice their gains?

American women arrived on the doorstep of the twentieth century with some newly won economic rights, but they were still carrying much of the burden of history. American men of the 1800s controlled all property and income, as well as the whereabouts and destinies of the females in the family. Even among the working class, most married women did not work outside the home. Working women were generally single and employed as domestics, sometimes working for cash, but usually for payment in kind, and the compensation often went to their fathers.

When a textile factory opened in Lowell, Massachusetts, in 1814, the daughters of farmers were recruited to work for cash wages. The girls despised the long hours, but loved being away from home and having their own money. By 1834, however, wages were declining, so the girls staged a strike, one of the first in America. They continued to organize, petitioning the state for labor rights, giving impassioned speeches, and publishing a radical paper. All this made them "public women," a term that referred to a woman made unrespectable simply because she appears, speaks, or writes on her own and outside the home. The factory workers also attracted censure by reproducing the clothes that the new fashion magazines featured in colored plates. Using their small wages and acquired sewing skills, they dressed "above their station."

Observers, seeing young women with no man to "protect" them while wearing such enviable costumes, assumed the girls must be prostitutes. How else would they get that much money?

You can imagine how all this played with a husband whose wife wanted to go outside to work. A wife who behaved the way factory girls did would lose her respectability. Her husband would be pitied, and she would be ostracized forever. To stop that from happening, he would resort to violence, if necessary.

Few American history books explain that the first U.S. economy was built, like the Chinese economy in the era of the Silk Road, on exporting textiles. As the economy boomed, factories proliferated, eventually moving into the cities from the country. New manufactures were added, such as notions, shoes, hats, and other accessories, as well as toilet soaps and face creams, and all these were marketed, sold, and bought by women. Seamstresses, designers, milliners, shop assistants, and writers for women's magazines found a new way to live and work, but they were viewed with suspicion by traditionalists. This incarnation of the Double X Economy grew into a system of exchange among women—even though the capital behind it was still controlled by men.

Meanwhile, signs of a women's movement appeared; many of the early leaders were professionals from the new economy.[4] These successful women founded a network of women's groups called the General Federation of Women's Clubs (GFWC). The network grew and flourished. Over time, it was populated by married middle-class women dedicated to winning a range of women's rights as well as other economic and social reforms. The GFWC allied with other women's groups that were focused on specific causes, including labor rights. By the end of the century, the GFWC was providing the foot soldiers of the First Wave.[5]

In the fight for working women's rights, the most prominent of the middle-class women's organizations were the Women's Trade Union League (WTUL) and the National Consumers League (NCL). The men's labor unions were unfriendly to female workers' rights because winning labor rights was to them a zero-sum game—one sex could win only if the other lost. These men also were emphatic about keeping wives at home. The loyalties of sex trumped those of class among American working men, so it was the women's movement, not labor unions, that came to the defense of female workers in America.

The NCL worked by uniting two ends of the Double X Economy, middle-class consumers and factory workers, in the fight for a common goal. The concept was that the "clubwomen" held economic power through their spending that could be used to pressure businesses to improve conditions for female employees. They began with retailers who employed women as salesgirls and who relied almost entirely on the shopping preferences of married middle-class women for their livelihood. The first action was to draw up a "Standard of a Fair House," a list of requirements that included equal pay for women, regular and reasonable hours, a paycheck every two weeks, paid vacations, holiday leave, and other employment rights. They then made a "White List" of stores that adhered to the standards and announced that their membership would only patronize stores on the list. Other stores, wanting to be on the White List, changed their labor practices accordingly.

The NCL manufacturing effort began with muslin underwear, again on the rationale that both buyers and employees would be women. If a manufacturer met their standards, the NCL allowed a "White Label" to be stitched into its garments (Figure 12). Once again, NCL members publicly vowed to buy only products with the White Label sewn inside and, again, it worked.

The NCL also successfully lobbied state legislatures to enact limitations on how long the workday for women could be, how much they

FIGURE 12. The "White Label" of the National Consumers League was sewn into garments made by factories whose working conditions the NCL had approved.

Source: By permission of the National Consumers League

could lift, and other protective rules. By midcentury, however, the women's movement had realized that these restrictions kept females out of the best jobs, and worked to repeal them. The NCL fought for equal pay, too. The justification for paying women less than men was that they all had a man somewhere who was the real source of their support, so there was no reason to pay females a living wage. In many charged debates, the NCL pressed the case for a wage substantial enough for a woman to live on her own. Labor unions, arguing that men should be paid a "family wage" since they were supporting families, believed that if women were awarded a living wage, it would jeopardize their case for men's family wage. Why would companies pay a man more to support a family if the females under his roof could earn just as much? In the end, the NCL won the living-wage fight, but only in principle. Women were still paid less than men, on the basis that their needs were fewer.[6]

The WTUL instead supported striking workers, offering important assistance during two long, violent strikes by the International Ladies' Garment Workers Union (ILGWU) in 1909 and 1910. The WTUL provided money, bought household necessities, intervened with authorities, and accompanied strikers to pickets. These prosperous wives locked arms with strikers, knowing police would hesitate to hit or arrest a well-dressed and probably well-connected woman. When they witnessed police brutality, they filed complaints and raised bail.

Though the strategy was effective, the strikers sometimes resented and mocked "the mink brigade." The class division was even more intensely felt after the 1911 Triangle Shirtwaist Factory fire, in which 146 workers, 83 percent women, died, some jumping from the top floors while helpless bystanders watched. Investigation revealed that fire escapes were blocked and doors locked; employers feared the workers would steal and leave work early.

In the wake of the tragedy, the women workers decided it would be more appropriate for them to break with the WTUL and instead make common cause with working-class men. The historic alliance across classes of women was thereby broken. By 1920, the ILGWU leadership had been taken over by men, and it remained a male-dominated union, focused mostly on men's labor issues, until it fizzled out in the 1990s.

To this day, unionized women in the United States are paid more than nonunion women, but substantially less than unionized men. Indeed, throughout the twentieth century, labor and socialist movements around the world were hostile to women's rights. Their political ideology typically drew a line between "socialist feminism," which capitulated to the "more important" claims of males and was acceptable, and "bourgeois feminism," which insisted that women had their own distinctive and equally important issues to be addressed—a premise that was not acceptable. Feminists in these movements set aside gender concerns, as they were shamed into feeling that "emphasis on the issues of their own sex would be selfish."[7]

Today, we see a similar conflict of interest between working men and women in Bangladesh. It begins with the familiar divide between men's work and women's work: hard, heavy, and dangerous versus easy, light, and safe, with men's work paying more. To enforce this division, there are protective restrictions on women's working hours and on jobs deemed too hazardous or "morally inappropriate," which effectively reserves the best-paying jobs for men. Ironically, it's clear that the underlying concern is not to protect the women, because none of the countries that have these kinds of restrictions have legal protections against sexual assault in the workplace, a significant problem. In high-income countries, there are few restrictions on women's work and more legislation to protect them from attack; consequently, more women work and GDP is higher (Figure 13).

In the factories of emerging economies, women are sparsely represented in supervisory or management ranks. The U.K. Department for International Development is investigating this apparent bottleneck with a five-year study in which the gender conditions in factories are analyzed. Its first inquiry was in the factories of Bangladesh. Both men and women were interviewed, as were both managers and workers.[8]

When researchers asked men working in Bangladeshi factories why women weren't being promoted at work, they answered:

RESTRICTIONS ON WOMEN'S LABOR ACTIVITY

Region	Percent of countries with jobs deemed hazardous, arduous, or morally inappropriate for women	Percent of countries with jobs that have industry-specific regulations against women	Percent of countries with jobs that have restrictions on women working during night hours
MIDDLE EAST AND NORTH AFRICA	65	55	55
SOUTH ASIA	50	63	63
SUB-SAHARAN AFRICA	43	51	9
EUROPE AND CENTRAL ASIA	36	56	20
LATIN AMERICA AND THE CARIBBEAN	19	16	6
OECD HIGH-INCOME COUNTRIES	6	9	0

FIGURE 13. The regions in the table with the most restrictions also have the lowest GDP as well as the lowest female labor force participation. Though the rationale for these restrictions would be "protecting" the women, these nations also have the fewest protections against sexual assault and harassment.

Source: World Bank Group, *Women, Business and the Law 2016*

- Women are unable to run the heavy machinery in the factory.
- Women can't shout.
- Women don't want the responsibility that comes with higher positions.
- Women don't stay employed in the sector long enough to be promoted.

The heavy machinery is operated by pushing buttons, so body strength is not needed. According to the men, shouting is required to assert the dominance necessary to lead in the factory. Women were no good at shouting, they said, so they can't lead anyone. And anyway, they added, men would never take orders from women.

When Bangladeshi women were interviewed, they were emphatic that they were *never* going back to the village. Women who had married since coming to the city admitted they were now expected to turn over their earnings to their husbands, but they hid some for themselves and felt this arrangement was still an improvement over village life. Women also said they were not given more responsibility at work because women were *unable* to operate the heavy machinery. They were echoing the men; they did not seem to know the equipment had push buttons. Men had also told them that supervisory jobs paid less—an outright lie. Since the women feared making mistakes, they were hesitant to take leadership roles. Women had to have more work skills than men in order to be promoted, according to these respondents, but they were always overlooked for training, even though they came into jobs with more education than the men had. They thought a female supervisor would be the target of violence from men insulted by her promotion.

Conflict at home was also a barrier. Women said they would not want to be a supervisor if their husband was not one, too, because they wouldn't want to usurp their spouse's position as the main breadwinner. A man would say his wife thought she was "bigger" than he, that she did not need him anymore. He would become suspicious that she was leaving him, and violence would result.

The women also mentioned that they had "duties" at home and did not want to be found wanting. Mind you, these women worked ten-hour days, six days a week, and still had to go home and do all the housework while their husbands relaxed. Women were dismissed from their jobs when they got pregnant; when they returned to the workplace, they were made to "start over," building seniority again from the bottom rung. Their status in the factory, therefore, was always viewed as temporary, regardless of how long they had actually worked. They were only temporary, in fact, because of the discriminatory policies against mothers.

Through these examples, we can see that the interests working men and women have in common are superseded by gender conflict. The men have an interest, both at home and at work, in confining women to the lower ranks. If these women were to join with male workers in forming a union, it is unlikely their problems would be solved.

Like the United States of the early twentieth century, Bangladesh has had major factory fires. The 2012 Tazreen Fashions factory fire killed 112, more than 80 percent of whom were women. The fire escapes were blocked and the doors locked; victims jumped from the top floors. International press coverage was intense, yet no journalist even mentioned that the vast majority of the people in that building were female. Five months later, the Rana Plaza factory collapsed, killing more than a thousand employees, again mostly women. In the West, various impromptu boycotts against clothing retailers began, in an attempt to spur reform in Bangladeshi factories, though few were sustained. But by 2013, propelled in part by consumer outcry, a coalition of global unions and more than two hundred international brands had formed to sign the Accord on Fire and Building Safety in Bangladesh. However, at no point were the disasters recognized as a woman's issue, despite the fact that both the boycotters and the garment workers were mostly women. Without this gender lens, the opportunity was missed to negotiate an end to the day-to-day discrimination the women endure. These women need a sisterhood, not male-dominated unions.

In early twentieth-century America, a new type of occupation appeared that was open to women but brought with it a fresh set of gender inequalities. White-collar companies—like insurance firms and law offices—were on the rise and needed clerical support. At first, clerical posts were filled by men, but by 1910, 30 percent of secretarial jobs were held by females. By 1950, this occupation was overwhelmingly "women's work," and it now employs a larger segment of American women than any other.

As with factory and domestic work, clerical posts were held by single women. American companies had policies called "marriage bars" that forbade employing married women. The "duty" a wife had to serve her husband at home was seen as incompatible with paid employment; most men, it was assumed, would not "let" their wives work. Any single woman a company employed had to be let go immediately if she married—regardless of her own or her husband's preference. These bars stayed in place through the 1930s, were temporarily suspended for war work in the 1940s, remained occasionally in place during the 1950s, and were at last outlawed at the federal level in 1964. As the marriage bars gradually eased up, the female labor force gradually grew.

Office work is not particularly hard, heavy, or dangerous, but it does require education. By the 1920s, most Americans had access to free upper secondary education—high school. Women were more likely to finish than men because there were well-paid skilled jobs for men that did not require a diploma. The typical high school curriculum was essentially the same for both sexes. Women and men with high school diplomas therefore brought identical qualifications to the job. There was no basis except gender stereotypes for putting men in one kind of job and women in another.

Gendered job distinctions were gradually implemented by personnel policies and recruitment procedures. The marriage bars themselves were a personnel policy—not a law—that created a gender division where women's work was "temporary," but men's was "permanent" or at least "long term." So, right from the start, career paths for men groomed them for senior posts, but for women, the "temporary" expectation meant whatever they did for the company needed to be of immediate value. Men were trained on the job in the specifics of the business, while women, if trained at all, learned additional secretarial skills that would apply in any office. So, though men might start in the mailroom and women in the secretarial pool, men were soon developing "specialized" skills, while women's skills remained merely "general."

Jobs that marked a potential career path for men—insurance salesman, loan officer—became "men's work," while dead-end jobs were "women's work." The conventional categories were formalized and disseminated into the economic culture by the newspapers, which, agreeably enough, advertised help-wanted ads for man-jobs and woman-jobs in separate columns. Readers learned to look for employment postings only in the column marked for their sex.

The temporary nature of women's work, as well as the lack of upward mobility, was supported by stereotyping: single women were said to be unmotivated to do more than the barest minimum of work because their futures lay elsewhere. Obviously, you would never give such a person complex tasks or serious responsibility. So, in addition to women's work being "temporary" and requiring only "general" skills, it was also "simple" and "not serious."

Women were, as a result, easier for a company to lose. When funds were tight, a secretary could be terminated without undue impact on the firm, but a man who had been groomed with "special" training and given "serious" responsibility was an investment that the company must try to keep. After all, a woman could find a job that "required no experience," but men, having "job experience," were harder to replace.

Office work therefore added a whole new set of descriptors to "men's work" and "women's work." In addition to "hard," "heavy," "important," "away," "dangerous," and "paid/paid more" versus "easy," "light," "unimportant," "at home," "safe," and "unpaid/paid less," there were now "permanent" versus "temporary," "serious" versus "not serious," "simple" versus "complex," "general" versus "specialized," and "requiring no experience" versus "requiring experience."

Women nevertheless considered secretarial work to have a higher status than factory jobs, retail sales, or domestic work, so they worked hard to get these positions. Women also thought the chances of meeting a well-to-do "Mr. Right" were higher in an office job. For a person who earned the barest subsistence wage because of her sex, the best economic outcome possible was to marry well. From the 1900s to the 1960s, secretaries were often depicted in popular culture as calculating and manipulative in their efforts to win, trap, or even steal a man. Popular magazines were full of comic scenarios in which a boss and his secretary have a go. Sometimes the secretary is seducing the boss. Sometimes the boss is running around the desk after the secretary. These images point to the tension between work and marriage, as well as to competition between different classes of women for economic survival. But they also point to a culture of sexual harassment in offices that may have been worse than in factories because the spaces were private and doors could be closed. And the sexual innuendo in popular culture further contributed to an ongoing prejudice that insisted single working women were immoral.[9]

"Good jobs"—those with security, opportunities for advancement, good paychecks, and benefits—belonged to men in the eyes of most Americans. A woman in a man's job was an affront to society because men were supposed to support families. When times were hard, a woman's holding any job implied there was a man somewhere without one. When the Great Depression of the 1930s hit, marriage bars were strongly enforced, even by public opinion, making it very hard for married women to get work, despite the fact that many husbands were unemployed and families struggled to get by.

This unwritten rule was quickly suspended with the outbreak of World War II, as was the prevailing gender division of labor. With American men away at war, even married women picked up jobs they would otherwise have been deemed *unable* to do, even ones using heavy equipment to make tanks, ships, and planes. These jobs, which were highly paid, but off-limits to women in peacetime, were suddenly essential for women to do.

Popular legend holds that women war workers were rushed back into the kitchen when the soldiers returned, expected once again to have babies and mop floors. But the employment facts tell a different story. During the decade immediately following the war, the curve for women's employment takes one of the steepest jumps of the century. Many women who had done wartime jobs remained in the workplace, and new women entered, both helping to fuel the postwar period of growth. You can see from the data in Figure 14 that the upswing in female labor force participation during the twenty years following World War II came entirely from married women.

There is, nevertheless, a notable shift in the popular imagery of the postwar period from war work to matrimony. As wartime technology was applied to civilian life, "miracle" household products made the work of the "little woman at home" look easy, modern, and even fun. That's when economists began thinking of wives as the recipients of "leisure time" their hardworking husbands bought for them. Housewives were "unproductive" because any work that wasn't paid didn't count. This attitude caused further diminution of women's economic contribution, even as female labor force participation skyrocketed. I have observed that many economists and some world leaders today fail to take women's economic subordination seriously because they still think of wives as a race of bejeweled poodles.[10]

Betty Friedan's 1963 *The Feminine Mystique*, a book often credited with kicking off the Second Wave of the women's movement in America,

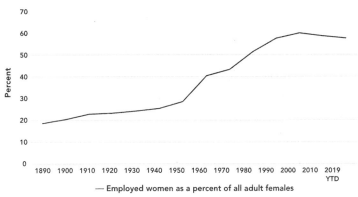

U.S. FEMALE LABOR FORCE PARTICIPATION, 1890–2019

— Employed women as a percent of all adult females

**U.S. FEMALE LABOR FORCE PARTICIPATION
BY MARITAL STATUS, 1890–2009**

— Married   — Single

arose from exactly this situation: women entranced by the postwar matrimonial imagery who became trapped in a life they found meaningless. In this feminist classic, Friedan focuses on the curse of educated housewives in the 1950s, specifically the graduates in her own class at Smith. Educated to the highest standard in their country's history, they were then expected to marry and stay at home forever. A malaise Friedan called "the problem that has no name"—a depressing sense that their gifts, and their lives, were being wasted—enveloped them. The only solution, Friedan advised, was for them to go to work. *The Feminine Mystique* went straight to the top of the bestseller list, and female labor force participation soared higher than ever.[11]

When this generation of women entered the workplace, however, they discovered that their opportunities were not much better than they had been in 1920. This realization sparked a new surge of women's activism, unseen since the end of the First Wave. Between 1963 and 1978, a combination of federal laws, court rulings, and executive orders removed every obstacle I have previously discussed:

- Employers were required to pay women equally for jobs that required the same skill, effort, and responsibility (1963).
- Marriage bars and sexual harassment at work became illegal (1964).
- Employers could not deny a woman a promotion on the basis of sex (1966).
- Employers could no longer pay a woman less for the same work just by changing the job title (1970).

FIGURE 14. (opposite) American women's labor force participation since 1890 is shown in the graph on the top. On the bottom, see that the curve represented by married women matches the overall trend almost perfectly—that's because married women drove the trend by going to work. Notice that the upsurge in married women's labor force participation begins its steep climb immediately after World War II. From 1930 to 1965, single women's participation ripples a bit, but does not rise overall. Because the number of married women was so much larger, it was their entry that drove the trend. After 1970, however, both segments rise, in tandem, for the rest of the century.

Sources: U.S. Bureau of Labor Statistics, "Employment Level: Married Women (LNS12000315)," Federal Reserve Economic Data, September 19, 2019, https://fred.stlouisfed.org/series/LNS12000315; U.S. Bureau of Labor Statistics, "Women in the Labor Force: A Databook," November 2017, https://www.bls.gov/opub/reports/womens-databook/2017/home.htm; Claudia Goldin, "Female Labor Force Participation: The Origin of Black and White Differences, 1870 and 1880," *Journal of Economic History* 37, no. 1 (1977): 87–108; Kristie M. Engemann and Michael T. Owyang, "Social Changes Lead Married Women into Labor Force," *The Regional Economist* (April 2006): 10–11, https://www.stlouisfed.org/~/media/files/pdfs/publications/pub_assets/pdf/re/2006/b/social_changes.pdf

- An employer could not refuse to hire a woman with preschool-age children if it was also hiring men with children of the same age (1971).
- Sex-segregated job classifications in newspapers were prohibited (1973).
- Barring women from night shifts or physically demanding work was ruled discriminatory, as were height and weight requirements (1978).

This more equitable environment fostered another rise in female employment, among both single and married women, that continued until the end of the century.

Conservatives are still making noise about sending women back to the kitchen, but the simple fact is that from an economic perspective, it is too late. If American women were suddenly raptured out of the workforce, the U.S. economy would lose 40 percent of its GDP just like that.[12] The system would collapse. All kinds of products would become unavailable and services would stop. The whole economic landscape would be scorched earth.

The Second Wave was not restricted to the United States, but was an international phenomenon that included other Western countries that had experienced a depression, a war, a baby boom, and a resurgent sisterhood (Figure 15). Though their experiences differed in the particulars, these countries arrived, rather uncannily, in the same place at the same time with regard to working women. All these countries enacted reforms along the lines of those in the United States. As a consequence, they all saw similar trends in female labor force participation, as well as the bonanza in higher GDP. Their conditions for women are now better than anywhere in the world, and their living standard the highest as well.

A very large segment of American women were, however, left behind by these events: stay-at-home wives and mothers who either had no working skills or did not find the feminine mystique stultifying. Many of us who joined the Second Wave as college students had mothers like that. As children, we had been bombarded with family sitcoms where the wife was an empty-headed but immaculate servant to the rest of

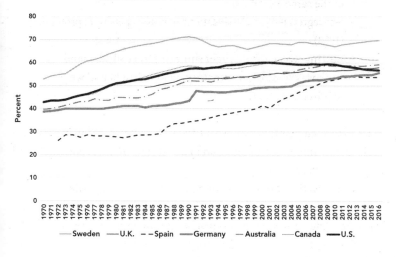

FIGURE 15. The female labor force participation trend lines for a sample of European and English-speaking nations illustrate the common trend among working women in the last quarter of the twentieth century. Most of these countries have experienced a plateau since about 2000, but the United States is the only one that has declined. Though the drop from 60 percent in 2000 to 56.7 percent in 2016 may not seem much, it is a reason for concern.

Sources: World Bank Database; Federal Reserve Economic Data; CIA, *World Factbook*, 2016

the household. Some of us felt sympathy for the women trapped inside the feminine mystique, whether they seemed happy or not, but most of us expressed disdain. To a great extent, the Second Wave, for its youngest members, was a rebellion against the image of the stay-at-home mom. One of the memorable slogans of the 1970s women's movement is "I Am My Mother's Revenge."

This attitude left an unfortunate aftereffect. As the movement focused on rights in the workplace and declared independence from the postwar ideals of matrimony, some housewives, feeling excluded, translated their alienation into a belief that the women's movement was undermining the family by attacking marriage. And so, tragically, the group that had been the First Wave's foot soldiers, housewives, marched in the opposite direction. They represented the biggest demographic segment of American women at that time. Not all housewives rejected the movement, of course, including my own mother and grandmother—exemplars of family values though they were—but this group of women, *as a group*, was effectively organized by Phyllis Schlafly into a movement to block what was to be the crowning accomplishment of the Second Wave, the Equal Rights Amendment (ERA) to the U.S. Constitution.

In 1978, I had an internship as a reporter for the *Dallas Times Herald*. One slow news day, the city desk editor, muttering under his breath that he "hated to give these people coverage," sent me to cover an anti-ERA rally where Phyllis Schlafly was speaking. Wanting to impress him, I decided to try to get an interview with Schlafly, by then a national celebrity. She was widely known for her ability to turn even the most reasonable question or argument into a weapon, but I felt confident I could take her on. I had been on the debate team in high school, after all.

When Schlafly left the stage, I ran to catch up. It wasn't hard to see her in the crowd: she wore pink ruffles and spike heels, her blond hair in an elaborate updo. I caught up to her in a corridor just inside the exit. She agreed to talk, and I began asking questions. But everything I said snapped back into my face, warped. I was floundering when I stupidly asked, "Well, don't you think women should have the right to work?" Steely-eyed and hissing like a snake, she said, "Don't *you* think women should have the right to their husbands' support? Don't you think *they deserve alimony*?" Then she turned on her stilettos and flounced out the door.

I saw in a flash that wives' dependency, the very core of women's economic exclusion, had been treated too casually by the movement. Schlafly's words were not spoken in the newspapers, on the radio, or on the TV talk shows, where all the spin was about how the ERA would bring abortion, lesbians, same-sex toilets, and the demise of Christianity. But she had let me in on the real issue: her supporters saw the ERA as a threat to their economic security.

I felt ashamed not to have made the connection before that meeting. My own mother and aunt had been housewives, but were divorced in the mid-1970s. Their economic vulnerability had made a life-changing impression on me. Seeing the threat of poverty hanging over my family was the real reason I decided to make a career for myself. But I had never until that moment in 1978 connected that particular aspect of Second Wave rhetoric and the housewives' political resistance.

Few people realize that the rise of the religious right in the 1980s sprang from the army Phyllis Schlafly led against the women's movement. There is even a YouTube video of Ronald Reagan thanking Schlafly for her support and offering a special tax accommodation to housewives.[13] The right recast feminism as an attack on "family values"—meaning women at work should be at home.

In the nearly forty years that followed, the right "owned" anything to do with family and, as a result, the women's movement mostly backed off issues like alimony, divorce law, and the care of home and children. Unfortunately, that reticence resulted in a lack of sufficient advocacy for supports to enable working mothers—paid maternity leave and, especially, affordable childcare. Approval for working wives has risen steadily since then, and the belief that working mothers are bad for children has declined. But the right has quietly played both sides: alimony rights for stay-at-home wives have been gradually "reformed" at the state level until they are only a shadow of support for these women who have sacrificed their own economic security for the sake of their families.

As a further consequence of the strangely distorted view of the Second Wave put forward by the radical right, as well as a popular tendency to demonize and ridicule feminism, few Americans realize just how impactful the Second Wave really was. Historians now agree that this surge of feminism was the most successful and transformative women's movement in history, not just in the United States but across the West.[14] And by the end of the twentieth century, the majority of the American public came to agree with the core principles first put forward in 1970—like equal pay, equal rights, equal opportunity, and reproductive freedom—as they had not before the movement began.

Since the movement had successfully recast the image of working women, however, employers next went after the millennials with all they had left: the care of children. Stigmatizing mothers in the workplace has become the norm of the day, and it is commonplace to pay them less than any other group, including other women. As we have seen, anti-feminists think this pay gap reflects their "bad choices"—having children but staying at work.

Economists have very recently identified one major cause of the decline in women's labor force participation in the United States: at least one-third of it springs from the failure of the U.S. government to institute federal policies, programs, and protections that support working mothers.[15] Another authoritative piece of analysis points to women's perception that the pay is not attractive enough, most likely a function of the trade-off between the "motherhood penalty" and the high cost of private childcare.[16] The right has successfully stopped progress by using gloomy predictions about child welfare to attack women who want autonomy.

Traditional ideas about the family, and women's role in it, continue to be used as weapons against women's economic participation all over the world, even at the highest levels.

Allow me to illustrate. One day in 2017, I was sitting at a round table in a high-end Chinese restaurant in Singapore. There were eight of us, mostly economists, who met twice a year, each from a different country. I had been appointed to add a gender perspective to their deliberations about making the world economy more inclusive, but I couldn't get a word in edgewise.

At each two-day meeting, we would take up one nation at a time for discussion, then sometimes one of the members would give a presentation on their work. For two years, I had been unable to get time on the program to present on gender. I tried to jump into the country-by-country discussions a few times. All countries have gender problems, as we have seen, but they all have, basically, the *same* problems, just to greater or lesser degrees. It seemed silly to keep saying it over and over, in two-minute installments. One of them would pick at me occasionally for criticizing *their* country—which never happened on any other topic—but usually they just stared at me. Since their traditional training in economics offered no way to conceptualize "inclusion," because it would not admit of "exclusion," we never talked about that, either.

At lunch on that particular day, however, I volunteered to give a quick update on the women's economic empowerment movement and was pleased when they all agreed. Since everyone was leaving for the airport after the meal, I would keep it short and light. A lot was happening at the global level, including the United Nations High-Level Panel on Women's Economic Empowerment and a push to get a women's interest group going at the G20 (already called "the W20"). I felt I had insights to share and thought the topic would at least be of interest in a public-radio kind of way.

I began with the W20, describing some difficulties we were experiencing as a result of the structure the G20 had imposed. Though I spoke cheerfully, I could feel the German economist sitting next to me bristling. "Why should the G20 care about women?" he blurted out. "They have *important* things to think about."

I was shocked, but no one else reacted, so I kept moving. I began explaining the connection between women's labor and growth, but he waved me off, announcing indignantly that attending to women "would be a waste of valuable time for the G20" finance ministers. "They have to think about their countries!"

I protested that women were half the citizenry of every one of those countries. He rolled his eyes.

The expert from China burst in to support his German colleague. "Women should not be in the workplace at all! It is bad for children when mothers work! Women should stay home and let their husbands support them!" I struggled for a response to that unbelievably retrograde remark when an eminent Harvard economist spoke up. He turned to our children's crusader and asked, "Doesn't something like 'Women's rights are human rights' apply here?" No response.

Gathering myself, I said that men are sometimes unable or unwilling to support children. I referred to the UNICEF research on how economically empowered mothers are the way to ensure children's well-being. The Chinese economist looked at me blankly, so I changed tactics. In many countries, I offered, the women are more educated than the men, so the country loses its investment if employers won't hire them at the level their education suggests. The economist from Singapore, who had turned his back to play with his cell phone, looked over his shoulder and said derisively, "College girls in Singapore are only there to find a good husband."

When the tea and cookies were brought in, I gave up. Without enough air to paint a comprehensive evidence-backed picture, I had defaulted to a set of disjointed facts they wouldn't believe anyway. My idea to slide this stuff in over lunch had been a bust.

I kept my cool to the end of the meal. Thank goodness, my car to the airport was already at the front door. I may have looked calm in the back seat, but inside I was roiling with emotion. What should I have said? How can I participate in these meetings if they can't even hear a sunny little report without losing it? I wondered whether I should leave the group in protest.

In the sky over the Bay of Bengal and the Arabian Sea, I imagined all the people, men and women, who were on the ground at that very moment, working hard to bring about women's economic empowerment. Some of them, I knew, were risking their own safety to solve a pressing world problem. My discomfort, I told myself, was nothing compared with the sacrifices others were making. I also did not want to disappoint the sponsor who had appointed me because I believed he sincerely thought an inclusive economy must encompass women. Somebody has to get to these economists, I thought. Maybe this is the mission I must choose to accept.

Although the women's economic empowerment movement includes important institutions and a few high-level players, the basic proposition remains a dubious concept to most policy advisors and government ministers. This was my first experience as the target of their resistance. I now felt I had been living for years in a warm bath of mutual support and was suddenly standing, cold and shaking, without a towel.

At that elegant restaurant in Singapore, I experienced the global equivalent of being surrounded in a Bangladeshi village. But the implications of seeing that kind of prejudice among people with this kind of power were much more disturbing.

I didn't quit. I should have. After I made two more excruciatingly polite attempts to bring gender into the conversation, they asked me to leave. They just did not want to know.

7 | PUNISHING MOTHERHOOD

Want to fight climate change? Have fewer children," read a *Guardian* headline one morning in July 2017.[1] The story was trending when I grabbed my phone to check the news, as I usually do to postpone getting out of bed. "This is insane," I thought, and burrowed back under the covers. All that day, this absurd notion from environmental scientists was blaring through news services. Yet not a single reporter questioned the underlying assumption that Western society can afford to have fewer children.

In the late 1960s when news of the "population explosion" first appeared as Armageddon, there was reason to worry. The generation then reaching adulthood in developed countries was the largest in history; if they had children at the same rate their parents did and the subsequent generation did the same, we were all going to be living in our own sewage. But that scenario never happened. The baby boomers did not replicate their parents' fertility; they barely replaced themselves. Their kids—the millennials—won't come close to that.

Nearly half the countries in the world are producing too few children to sustain their populations. Some countries' fertility rates are already below the "point of no return," the rate at which experts believe there won't be enough mothers to reverse the trend.[2] If the upcoming generation decides to have even fewer children in a crusade to "save the

GLOBAL FERTILITY RATES, 2017

Average number of children per woman

0   2   4   6   8

FIGURE 16. This is a 2017 world map of fertility rates. The low-fertility countries are dark; the high-fertility nations are lighter.

Source: CIA, *World Factbook*, 2017

planet," advanced economies would begin to shrink. But, you might reasonably wonder, isn't a declining population a good thing? Not from a socioeconomic standpoint, is my reply.

The map in Figure 16 shows the world's countries by fertility rate. Popular commentators often confuse fertility rate with birth rate, claiming that women having babies is a function of GDP and will vary periodically with nothing to worry about. What those people are actually talking about is birth rate, which is simply the number of babies born each year per one thousand women. The birth rate can vary with GDP, average rainfall, or who won the World Cup, but unless it turns into a long-term trend, the fluctuations don't really matter. The fertility rate is something else entirely: defined as the number of children the average woman in a society has during her lifetime, it is a measure of generational trends in childbearing. A change in a nation's fertility rate is a long time in the making and takes a long time to reverse.[3]

The fertility rate at which a population remains stable, called the replacement rate, is 2.1 children per woman—one to replace the mother, one to replace the father, and an extra bit for contingencies. A population is thought to reach a "point of no return" at a fertility rate of 1.5; after that, experts say, there are not enough mothers to reverse the falling numbers. At 1.6, the European Union is dancing on the edge of "no return," but all of eastern and southern Europe has already sunk below that number. France is roughly at replacement, held up largely by immigrant births. Australia and the United States have been falling gradually but steadily since 1960 and have now reached 1.8, where Britain has been since 1975. In East Asia, fertility rates are even lower: Hong Kong (1.19), Japan (1.41), Macau (0.95), Singapore (0.83), South Korea (1.26), Taiwan (1.13), Thailand (1.52), and Vietnam (1.81). The Scandinavian countries have all dropped below replacement. Canada has stabilized at about 1.6, after fifty years in free fall. Latin America is currently at the replacement rate, but it's falling like an anvil dropped from a helicopter.

What about the rest of the world? Approximately 55 percent of humanity lives in countries where the birth rates are still too high. The women have as many as six or seven children, and these populations stand to double in the next thirty-five years. If they continue unchecked, there will be 9 billion people living on Earth by 2050. High-fertility countries are heavily concentrated in Africa, with one or two in the Middle East and Central Asia, and are among the most politically unstable countries on the planet; they threaten the world not only with overcrowding but also with war.[4]

The proposed "have one less child" crusade is impracticable on both sides of the fertility divide, because mothers at each end of the spectrum have little latitude to affect childbearing outcomes. The root problem in both cases is gender inequality.[5]

When I interviewed Purity in Uganda, she was twenty years old and married to a teacher, with two children under the age of three. I was there to assess the number of polygamous households in the parish for a project on women's savings, so I asked whether she had a co-wife. Purity explained that she and her husband had fallen in love when she was still in high school, but it was only when she got pregnant that he had told her he was already married. He went to Purity's parents to say he would marry her, too. Her parents had little choice, so they agreed; her new husband set her up in a nearby village. He was still supporting her at the time of our conversation, four years later, coming to see her a few days a week and spending the rest of his time with his other wife.

The teacher did not pay Purity's parents the bride price, though he promised to do so when he could. That means she is not truly married in the eyes of her village, and since she was not married in a church, she has neither customary nor legal rights. She earned a little money selling vegetables from a small garden, but couldn't do much with two babies to watch. Her father-in-law was building her a house, but it was not clear to whom the dwelling would belong if push came to shove. I asked her whether her birth parents would take her back if things got tough. She said no—they wanted the bride price.

The seduction of secondary schoolgirls by teachers is a problem throughout Africa. Nearly all teachers in the rural areas are men, and most secondary-school teachers are not much older than their students. But they are the most educated people in these communities and the only ones with a steady paycheck, so the power differential is immense.

The chances this teacher will do to another girl what he did to Purity are high, and the risks for him are low. The community will tolerate his behavior; if his income can't stretch to support all his "wives," he will either give them less or choose one to abandon. If he abandoned her, Purity would be expected to find another man for support. More vulnerable children would follow. But a dozen children could follow that one teacher if he keeps spreading his joy around so indiscriminately.

Serena was a little older, twenty-three, and had only two children. She was in a customary marriage; her husband had paid a bride price. But now he had moved to the city for work, leaving her with his parents. Her in-laws had never liked her, and Serena was miserable.

When we spoke, Serena had recently learned that her husband had taken another wife. The next money transfer he sent was reduced, and she anticipated her in-laws would throw her out if she could not pay them enough to support her and the children. Serena was doing farmwork to save money, but had to take the children with her, which slowed her down. She was hiding cash in a small purse in the hopes of having enough to live on her own with her children when the ax fell, but if her in-laws found the money, they would take it as payment for her support. Serena was on the edge of disaster.

Most couples I met on this project were monogamous, and some had been together for decades. However, many young women were in the same straits as Purity and Serena. Some men "married" women at will and had children just as casually. Contraceptives for women aren't readily available, and men refuse to use condoms, so each time one of them decides to move on to another woman, more children are left behind. Most of these kids have no hope of an education; their mothers can't afford to pay for it. They do well to feed and shelter their kids.

Uganda has struggled with civil conflict since the horrible Idi Amin dictatorship ended fifty years ago. The government remains autocratic and unstable. Corruption is rampant; little is invested in education or health care—GDP buys military equipment or lines elites' pockets.[6] Fertility is six children per woman, life expectancy low, adolescent fertility high, and maternal mortality among the highest in the world. HIV has wiped out a generation, and young females are 2.5 times more likely to contract it than men because of male promiscuity and refusal to practice safe sex. An army of orphans is being left behind, cared for by sisters who must leave school to become surrogate mothers. One young woman I spoke to was supporting thirteen children left behind by her deceased siblings. She wept as she described her struggle to keep them fed and in school.

Women in such countries have low status and few rights; violence against them is the worst on earth. Of the thirty-five nations with the highest fertility rates, twenty-seven are in the bottom fifty of the Global Gender Gap ranking or—an even worse sign—haven't produced enough gender data to be ranked at all.[7] Uganda has the pyramid-shaped age structure typical of high-fertility countries: too many children at the base, compared to the number of adults (Figure 17). For four decades, countries with populations this shape have been eight times more likely to experience civil conflict than the global average, and 90 percent of them are autocratic states.[8] Of the thirty-five most fertile countries, more than two-thirds are among the most fragile states in the world.[9]

AGE STRUCTURE IN FOUR CONFLICT COUNTRIES, 2018

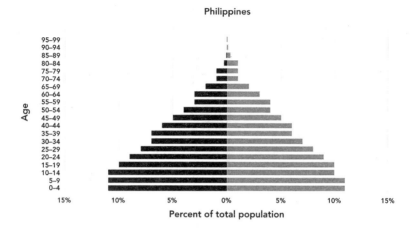

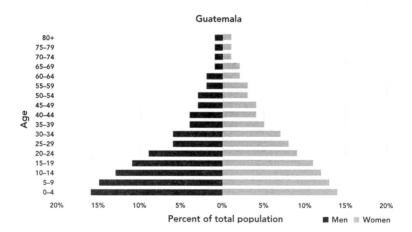

FIGURE 17. The bars on the left of each graph represent the men, and those on the right the women. Young people are represented at the bottom, with the age increasing as you go up the pyramid.

Source: United Nations Database

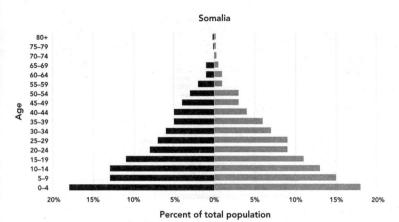

Somalia

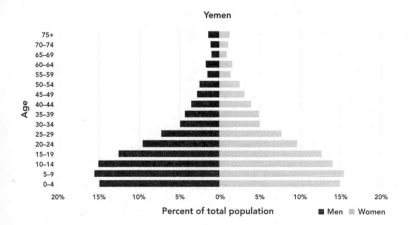

Yemen

A population that grows this quickly squeezes economic resources. Government services, already poor, are overloaded. Tensions and aggression rise. A disproportionate number of young men, compared to older ones, adds to the volatility. Older men usually keep a lid on younger ones, so their relative absence makes everything run to chaos. Citizens become desperate for order; dictators step into the void. Inevitably, conflict destroys resources, spills into neighboring countries, and spreads disease. And this all happens because women have no freedoms and men won't keep their trousers zipped.

In their authoritative book *Sex and World Peace*, Valerie Hudson and her colleagues in international studies explain, with detail and evidence, why there is a strong correlation between gender inequality and conflict. Beneath the ideologies, the shortages, and the poverty is a singular foundation of extreme male dominance. The rage typical of male-dominant settings means that the first response to any challenge will be a violent one. Conflict states typically have an "honor culture," in which men constantly fight over status and over control of women's sexuality. When an outsider violates a group's "honor" by sexually encroaching on "their" women, the ethic demands retaliation. Such men spend inordinate amounts of time in all-male settings, where they bond over their disrespect and violent intentions toward women. Females are often isolated from men and from each other. As tensions rise to conflict, war rape is common because it is the most direct way to offend the enemy's "honor."[10]

International agencies and NGOs emphasize contraception and reproductive health services as the first step toward controlling runaway fertility. By taking that step, they also reduce the risk of conflict. When conservatives in the United States cut off the reproductive health programs in these countries, they not only denied women basic medical services, they invested in producing more conflict and hunger. But when reproductive services focus only on "family planning" or abstinence, they fail to get at the root cause of high fertility: women don't choose. The reckless sexual behavior of the men, the brazen intrusion of sexual predators, and war rape, as well as the tolerance of forced sex, polygamy, and irresponsible fathers, keep fueling the fire. Solutions for high fertility always seem to focus on the women, turning away from a confrontation with men. But if you really wanted to solve this problem, you would focus on encouraging social sanctions against rape, bigamy, and desertion.

Women's economic empowerment cannot solve this whole cluster of problems, but it can help. Men sometimes show women with resources more respect. Females often have a voice when they have money. Either way, wives left by irresponsible husbands can at least provide for children. More widows can escape wife inheritance. Abused women can leave.

Giving women sovereignty over their own bodies, however, would be the place to start. Too often, women are forced to have sex with men who worry about neither children nor disease and are unwilling to use a condom at the expense of their own pleasure. To expect women to be able to *choose* to have "one less child" under these conditions is both unrealistic and cruel.

In contrast, women in low-fertility countries appear to have it all. They go to school and work for pay. They choose their partners and have sex for their own pleasure, using contraceptives that are easily available. But women in the West still struggle against men who want to push them back into the kitchen by punishing motherhood at work until they give up and go home—or skip having kids altogether. This male arrogance is poised to bring the rich countries down.

A crisis of epic proportions is now facing the low-fertility countries, one for which no one is prepared: aging populations. Most commentators assume the crisis is caused by longer life expectancies, and that is a factor, but the populations of advanced countries would not be aging so precipitously if their female citizens had not begun having fewer children.

The crisis of the coming decades will not affect citizens selectively. The impact will hit each and every individual, and it will be painful. A mushrooming number of old people will require more social services. Tax revenue will decline because fewer people will be economically active. There will not be enough labor supply to sustain growth. The bottom will fall out of the consumer markets. Savings will dwindle. The advanced economies will spiral toward ruin.

Inevitably, a care crisis will arrive, with elderly people competing with children for a larger share of care, attention, and spending. If "past is prologue," women will be expected to care for both the old and the young. Indeed, many women are already feeling that crunch—and it is a game-stopper. Each woman will potentially have to care for up to four old people—her parents and her partner's—as well as any children still at home. Chances are that fertility will drop further, given such overwhelming care pressures. The care burden will be so intense that many women will be forced to stop working, further depressing growth, taxes, livelihoods, and female spirits. The responsibility for maintaining income will fall on one partner, usually a male, who will have to support his immediate family and probably also supplement the resources of the older people. At the same time, his paycheck will be squeezed to accommodate higher government spending on social services, leaving him constantly on the edge of a panic attack.

What led to this march toward disaster? The answer is the same everywhere. Living costs in the rich nations, and especially in the cities where 80 percent of the population resides, are too high for new parents to live on one income. Mothers *must* work, and yet working mothers are penalized and stigmatized by employers. Governments have either ignored working mothers' needs or blocked them with outdated policies. Coworkers are hostile toward maternity leave and other concessions for parents. Unpredictable hours make every day an antacid commercial. If you know a working mother, would *you* change places with her?

Stay-at-home mothers don't have it much better. Most families with only one income have to endure years of financial stress and are unable to save for the future. Some mothers try to earn money and "stay in the game" by working part-time, but theirs is not a freely made choice—where data exists, it shows that about 75 percent of stay-at-home and part-time working mothers in rich nations say they would prefer to work full-time. These mothers live in isolation; they miss their friends and their freedom. A 2012 Gallup poll of sixty thousand American women showed that stay-at-home mothers are significantly more likely to feel depressed and worried than those who work.[11] If you know one of these mothers, chances are you wouldn't trade places with her, either.

Divorce rates are high in the developed economies; there is a strong probability that a young mother will be left to support her child at some point. In most cases, these mothers would experience a sharp reduction in daily resources; a significant number slide into poverty. I know from experience that being a single working mother is terrifying—like sitting in a runaway roller coaster racing along the edge of the world. Nobody believes it will happen to them, but a young woman is foolish if she doesn't think about that possible future before choosing to have a child.

Faced with the risk of twenty years of poverty, depression, stigma, and unrelenting stress, young women have increasingly decided against children. It's a sad state of affairs, but one that has been brewing for decades. We are now living with the impact of policy decisions made in the 1970s that were intended to keep mothers at home and then *never revised*. Let me show you two national examples of the negative impact.

Europeans already joke that Germany is "the nursing home of Europe" or "the country with no children." The nation's fertility rate has been under 1.5 since 1970, and in some years it has dropped below 1.25. Germany had a short-lived increase in births after World War II. When the women born during that time entered the workplace in the early 1970s, however, German culture pushed back with policies meant to encourage women to stay home instead. Fertility began to decline immediately, dropping back to wartime levels by 1978. Today, 78 percent of German households have no children in them.

Perhaps surprisingly, Germany's three-year paid maternity leave, one that women in other countries covet, was among the conservative policies introduced in the 1970s. But no day care facilities for children under three were authorized or built, by either the public or the private sector. That meant mothers had precious few childcare alternatives, whether they took leave or not. When children started school, mothers still did not receive a break, because all the way through the secondary level, German school is, even now, only a half day. Mothers whose children have finished school have a hard time getting good jobs, having been out of the full-time workplace for fifteen years. Given all these obstacles, only one in ten German mothers returns to work after giving birth.

As a consequence of this wrongheaded set of policies, the number of "permanently childless" women in Germany is the highest in Europe.[12] Childlessness is the new normal. These policies also affect the job prospects of all working women. When employers think about hiring a young female candidate, they can't help realizing that if she becomes pregnant while employed, she will be on leave for three years, and then there is only a small chance she will ever come back. This is a huge disadvantage for women coming into the workforce, and their representation shows it. Top German employers interviewed by the World Economic Forum in 2010, for example, said that only 33 percent of their entry-level employees were female, compared with 40 percent in the U.K. and 52 percent in the United States.[13]

Forcing qualified women to give up their careers and to sacrifice their education and experience, particularly when the labor supply is set to dwindle dangerously, is a poor strategy for staying afloat in an aging-population scenario. Furthermore, millions of women now entering old age will, as a result of past policies and practices, either have very small pensions or none at all. The gender pension gap—the difference between what men and women receive in pensions—is 60 percent in Germany. Many women will require government support.

In 2006, the German government finally woke up to the disaster it had created and began revising its policies. It's too late to save Germany from its aging crisis, but the changes might make it a little shorter.

A misogynist might ask why Germany did not simply force women to have more children by outlawing contraceptives and abortions. In response to that question, population experts point to Romania. In 1966, blaming abortion availability for population decline, the communist state outlawed both contraceptives and abortion, instituting a horrific system of enforcement:

Motherhood became a state duty. The system was ruthlessly enforced by the secret police, the *securitate*. Doctors who performed abortions were imprisoned, women were examined every three months in their workplaces for signs of pregnancy. If they were found to be pregnant and didn't subsequently give birth, they could face prosecution. Fertility had become an instrument of state control.[14]

Romanian fertility did increase, but the upsurge in births led to another frightening specter, the rise of government "orphanages" to house hundreds of thousands of offspring whom parents could not afford. Since the government did not allocate adequate funds to care for these children, Romania's next cohort grew up in horribly abusive conditions—underfed, underdeveloped, unloved, and unclean. That generation, now known as the *decreței* for the Decree 770 against birth control, spawned the revolutionaries that brought about the violent end of Romanian communism in 1989. The impact of this ill-advised policy continues to be felt in higher violence, substance abuse, crime, and suicide among the *decreței*. Demographers doing comparative studies in light of Europe's current population crisis argue strongly against such policies, recommending instead that governments invest heavily in the children they have.

Compared with Europe, the United States does even less to support working mothers. American women have no right to maternity leave,[15] and day care is privatized and expensive. Yet 70 percent of American women with children work—and 75 percent of those work full-time. Since American women don't stay out of the labor force for years and years after having children, they are more likely to build careers than women in Europe.[16]

Women now represent almost half the U.S. labor force, and working mothers are the norm. Both adults work in the majority of households with children and two parents.[17] American women, in addition to being essential to the national economy, are also essential to their households' economies: 42 percent of women contribute at least half of their family's income.[18]

Despite the record showing American mothers don't quit work, don't work part-time, and bear significant responsibilities for family support, however, American employers still use "They have children" as an excuse to pay them less and hold them back. A 2019 study shows that average pay for mothers takes a dip immediately after the first child

**PERCENTAGE CHANGE IN SALARY TEN YEARS
AFTER THE BIRTH OF A CHILD**

	Mothers	Fathers
DENMARK	–21	–1
SWEDEN	–27	1
U.S.	–40	–2
U.K.	–40	1
AUSTRIA	–51	0
GERMANY	–61	–1

FIGURE 18. Note that the policies and outcomes of the Scandinavian countries are better for parents than those in either the U.K. or the United States or in the Germanic countries, but that all countries show a significant, apparently permanent loss of income to the household when children are born.

Source: Henrik Kleven, Camille Landais, Johanna Posch, Andreas Steinhauer, and Josef Zweimüller, "Child Penalties Across Countries: Evidence and Explanations," National Bureau of Economic Research Working Paper no. 25524, February 2019, https://www.nber.org/papers/w25524

is born and then never recovers, even after a decade.[19] At the end, when you account for both salary history and reduced working hours, American mothers have absorbed a net 40 percent drop in pay.

Let's compare the American record on the motherhood penalty with different policies in other countries (Figure 18). The United Kingdom is similar to the United States in that government support for mothers has been negligible, though the British get a year of paid leave and a (wholly inadequate) childcare credit; the U.K. motherhood penalty after ten years nets out at about a 40 percent drop. The Scandinavian countries have the most liberal parental policies, including generous leave for fathers and sponsored childcare; in Denmark and Sweden, mothers' pay nevertheless ends, after a decade, down by about 21 percent and 27 percent, respectively. Germany and Austria, with long maternity leaves but no childcare at all, are the worst. Mothers' pay drops by 80 percent immediately after birth and is still down after ten years by 61 percent in Germany and by 51 percent in Austria.

The comparison with men's pay is unexpectedly alarming. The authors of this study remark that fathers' pay in all these countries is "unaffected." But what their data shows is that fathers' pay is flat from the time of their first child's birth, never rising again after ten years. Even if wages are stagnant for the male population as a whole, we should still see wages rising among men this age, as they acquire seniority and progress through their careers. But we don't: fathers are dead in the water from the time their first child arrives. You can imagine what a deterrent this is to having children. In total, households with children in all six Western countries are being penalized simply for having offspring. And employers are taking resources away from children to line their own pockets.

Put the American data together with the economic stress that the generation currently in their childbearing years suffers and the picture is more distressing. Like their cohorts in other countries, this generation came out of school to rising living costs and a declining job market. The crash of 2008 hurt them badly and delayed their careers, as well as their progress toward buying a home and starting a family. But unlike their cohorts in other rich nations, Americans, the majority of whom went to college, graduated with huge student debt. According to the American Association for University Women, two-thirds of student debt is held by young women, and they will come out of school making 18 percent less than their male classmates, regardless of their area of study, meaning their loans take longer to repay and therefore accumulate more interest.[20]

The comparatively liberal U.S. government of the 1960s and 1970s lifted some barriers in the workplace, but, as in Germany, there was also a lot of cultural pushback. Leaders of the private sector in the 1970s had gender attitudes much like those portrayed in the television series *Mad Men*. Most were deeply resentful of the coercion they felt from affirmative action policies, and made it clear to the young women entering their workplaces that their performance needed to be perfect if they wanted to stay—and that they must not call attention to their "duties" at home.

The big moment in history came when most baby boomer women, despite the inequitable terms and social disapproval, decided to go to work anyway. They dressed up in skirted suits, hid their families from sight, careened home at the end of every day to cook dinner, and let their bosses and partners preserve their masculinity in the unreformed way of that era's beliefs. The mean-spirited myth that these women selfishly wanted to "have it all" isn't accurate, but they were certainly *doing* it all.

Over the coming decades, this Second Wave generation of women was bludgeoned by conservatives about the presumed negative impact on their children as the price of their "selfishness." Numerous studies have tried to assess the effect on children of having mothers who work; for years, conclusions seemed to ricochet from one side to the other. In 2010, however, the definitive answer came. Rachel G. Lucas-Thompson, Wendy A. Goldberg, and JoAnn Prause did a meta-analysis of sixty-nine studies spanning five decades.[21] In a meta-analysis, the data from all the studies is combined, and the statistics run on the whole sample. The result overrides any individual study—the meta-analysis is the *last word*. This meta-analysis showed that children of 1970s working mothers displayed the same behavioral and academic outcomes as those whose mothers stayed at home. There was no difference. Boom.

Research conducted since the 1970s has suggested that men who live in households where both parents work, as well as share housework and childcare, are physically and mentally healthier—and happier. A 2019 study of six thousand American households in the *Personality and Social Psychology Bulletin* showed that men are actually happiest when their wives bring in 41 percent of household income—which is just about where American households are now. The cultural move away from the pressure of being the single male provider has done them good.[22]

What happened to the Second Wave children when they became adults? A Harvard Business School study of one hundred thousand men and women from twenty-nine countries found that the daughters of working mothers are more likely to work, make 24 percent more money on average, and are more often the boss than the daughters whose mothers stayed at home.[23] The sons, now men, do not have different career outcomes than those sons whose mothers stayed home, but they do have more gender-equal values and spend more time doing housework and caring for children, which creates a closeness between fathers and kids that was unknown in previous generations. The conclusion: The children of this historic wave of working mothers came

WHY EMPLOYERS THINK WOMEN ARE NOT ADVANCING

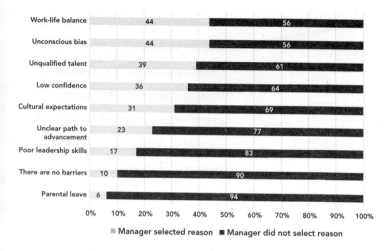

FIGURE 19. In this graph, employers attribute most of women's career-advancement problems to "unconscious bias," totally denying any responsibility. Other than that, the employers blame someone or something else, but most blame the women.

Source: Adapted from World Economic Forum, *The Industry Gender Gap*, executive summary, January 2016

out great. And they would be super parents if they got the chance. But they're not getting one.

American employers use motherhood as an excuse to hold women back, citing "work-life balance" as the euphemism for this systematic discrimination. Indeed, when you look past the show of "diversity planning" in big companies, you see that most employers are doing nothing at all to help women advance—and tend to blame the women instead of taking responsibility for the companies' own actions (Figures 19 and 20). They claim that if they are biased, it is only unconsciously. Notably, very few are taking the step most likely to result in pay equality—making compensation transparent.

The conventional "explanations" of women's slow career progress don't seem to capture what employers really think is the cause. In Fig-

WHAT EMPLOYERS ARE DOING ABOUT IT

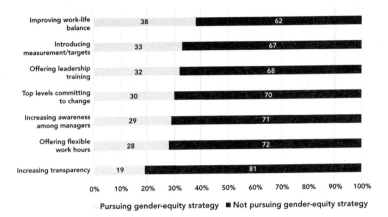

FIGURE 20. In this graph, we see how many employers are committing some kind of effort to help women advance. The dark bars show that 62 to 81 percent are not making even the efforts listed here.

Source: Adapted from the Future of Jobs Survey, as shown in World Economic Forum, *The Industry Gender Gap*, executive summary, January 2016

ure 19, we can see that *most* of them don't agree with *each* of the reasons given on the survey. Perhaps there is a more powerful reason, but it was not an option on the survey. What might this be? A 2010 study by the World Economic Forum, *The Corporate Gender Gap Report*, gives us a hint. This survey asked a large sample of employers from twenty countries to assess women's advancement, to see what was being done to help them, and to identify the barriers.[24] They found that, across *all* the countries except Norway (which had quotas for women on boards), women were a progressively smaller percentage at each level as you went up the ranks. Human resources managers for these companies were asked for their opinion of the main cause. Their answer was not "work-life balance" or "poor leadership skills" among women, but "patriarchal corporate culture" and negative attitudes toward working women in society.

A sense of the social rage behind negative attitudes toward working mothers can been seen in conservative blogs online. John Davis, an

American blogger, writing for the top website for misogynist hate groups, A Voice for Men, rants, "The birthrate [*sic*] in countries that pander to feminism and misandry (man-hating) are, without exception, showing huge declines in their birthrates [*sic*] and net population increases." He claims that Western countries are panicking because their "indigenous populations will be extinct within a century" and that "there are not enough young people to pay into socialist systems for the care of their elders." His antifeminist screed parallels racist talking points as he claims the European countries want to open their borders so North African men can come across and have sex with Western European women. Then, the victim statement surfaces:

> Feminism, in Western European countries, has been unchallenged for over 60 years, and, is now *de rigeur* [*sic*] in all institutions, especially Europe's public indoctrination (education) system. Hatred of men, and masculinity, in Western European nations, is open and oppressive to men. It is one of the factors driving the gender suicide gap world-wide (in which men are committing suicide at 4 times the rate of women). It is also the principal reason behind the decline in birth rates, and, the net population decreases.[25]

We can recognize this outburst as the precarious man's rage response; the rhetoric about socialism and immigration is also typical of the angry right-wing populism that brought about Brexit and the election of Donald Trump, while threatening the European Union with destruction from within. The single characteristic that best identifies the people behind this uprising, at least in Trumpism, is their score on a scale measuring "authoritarianism"—that is, their affinity with the patriarchy.[26] Indeed, among American hate groups, those that target women are growing fastest; the Southern Poverty Law Center, which monitors these organizations, says male supremacist groups are the most common point of entry for all other hate groups—and these groups' rise since the 1970s has been "fundamental to the foundation of the racist 'alt-right.'"[27]

A claim that the success of the women's movement in the United States—specifically women's alleged replacement of men in "good jobs"—has caused an uptick in the male suicide rate appears often in the discourse of American conservative politics, finding particular expression in the broadcasts of Tucker Carlson, an arch-conservative commentator on Fox News. However, the evidence proves this contention untrue.

Around the world, men *commit* suicide much more often than women; women, however, *attempt* suicide more often. Men are more successful primarily because they use more violent methods; in the United States, more than half of male suicides are effected by firearms. In fact, the most common cause of death from guns is suicide, not homicide or accidents. American men are 50 percent more likely than women to own guns.

The suicide rate among American males began to climb in 2000 and has not abated; during the same period, gun production has more than doubled and the geographic concentration of ownership has intensified. Both gun ownership and male suicide are now concentrated in the Upper Midwest and among older and white men. Gun ownership is also more likely among men who identify strongly with traditional masculinity.

Furthermore, the trend line for women's employment goes in the opposite direction from the male suicide rate (Figure 21). Thus, the rising white male suicide rate is attributable to increased availability of guns and the pressures of traditional masculinity—not women at work. The solution is taking guns away from men, not sending females back to the kitchen. Tucker Carlson's audience, however, is not likely to hear that truth.[28]

You can accuse the West of pandering to feminism by abandoning the traditional family structure, but in Southeast Asia, established family norms have remained strong. Nevertheless, the fertility rate in this region has dropped from six children per woman to just one, in the space of two generations. In 1950, Japan had a pyramid-shaped age structure. Fifty years later, the fertility rate has dropped to 1.44, and the age structure has inverted.

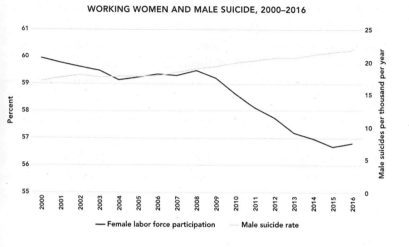

FIGURE 21. In this graph, we see that the male suicide rate in the United States increased significantly between 2000 and 2016. However, female labor force participation dropped even more steeply during the same period. This evidence shows that right-wing claims saying males are committing suicide more often because women are taking jobs away from them are false.

Sources: Federal Reserve Economic Data, https://fred.stlouisfed.org, accessed September 7, 2019, for women's labor force participation; U.S. Center for Disease Control, Table 30, 2017, https://www.cdc.gov/nchs/data/hus /2017/030.pdf, for male suicide rate

Southeast Asian women are not just skipping babies; they have stopped marrying. The graphs in Figure 22 show that over thirty-five years in Singapore, South Korea, and Taiwan, there has been a symmetrical change between women *going into* the labor force and women *staying out of* marriage—accompanied by a steep dive in the number of births. Even here, it seems, women are discontent with the constraints of traditional marriage and motherhood. *The Economist* observes that women in this region are well educated and have bright career prospects, but they are still expected to do everything necessary to care for their spouse, their children, and two sets of aging parents, without assistance. Why would anyone do that, *The Economist* implies.[29] Indeed, why *would* you?

The greedy institutions of the patriarchal economy also force fathers,

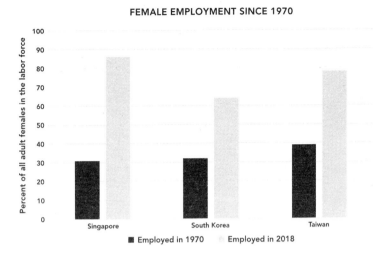

in Asia and elsewhere, to leave home for an absurd number of hours to endure an unsympathetic hierarchy of alpha males. In the West, an unexpected trend is emerging among millennial men in response to these overreaching institutional demands. This outspoken stance contests the validity of the traditional masculine model of fatherhood—and even of the image of masculinity itself. The term *toxic masculinity* is trending as one of the buzzwords of our times.

Fathers are the most important "alloparent"—meaning the caregiver "other than the mother"—and society is failing them, just as it is failing mothers. Josh Levs, now a member of the Power Shift Forum for Women in the World Economy community, stood up to Time Warner to demand paternity leave. He then wrote a book, *All In: How Our Work-First Culture Fails Dads, Families, and Businesses—and How We Can Fix It Together*, in which he interviews hundreds of young fathers. They express a passion to work more cooperatively in the care of their children, as well as an impatience with the mercenary power structure that keeps them from doing so.[30]

An investment in an "allomothering" infrastructure—that is, government-supported day care—would go a long way toward relieving this situation. Of all the policies and programs intended to support working mothers, sponsored childcare is the only thing proven to work. And, if thought and money were put into it, the system could be beneficial for child development.

Scientists have now alerted us to the capacity of even very small children to learn, as well as their need for stimulation. My own opinion, after recently becoming the main daytime caregiver for my infant grandchild, is that there is simply no way for *one* person, no matter how

FIGURE 22. (opposite) Since 1970, women in these four Southeast Asian countries have more than doubled their labor force participation, while also marrying at half the rate they did forty years earlier.

Sources: East-West Center, "The Changing Status of Women in Asian Societies," in *The Future of Population in Asia*, 2002, https://www.eastwestcenter.org/fileadmin/stored/misc/FuturePop05Women.pdf, for employment data in 1970s Singapore, South Korea, and Taiwan; World Bank Database for most recent employment data in Korea and Singapore; Wei-hsin Yu, "Women and Employment in Taiwan," op-ed, Brookings Institution, September 14, 2015, https://www.brookings.edu/opinions/women-and-employment-in-taiwan/, for Taiwan marriage rate data; Organisation for Economic Co-operation and Development Family Database, http://www.oecd.org/els/family/database.htm, for both years of South Korea marriage rate data; the 1970 Singapore marriage rate was conservatively estimated to be 9.5, based on the rate of change between 1995 and 2017 and comparison to Taiwan; Singapore Department of Statistics, https://www.statista.com/statistics/995762/singapore-crude-marriage-rate/, for the 2017 crude marriage rate for Singapore; National Bureau of Statistics of China: Taiwan National Statistics, https://www.statista.com/statistics/321428/taiwan-marriage-rate/, for the 2017 crude marriage rate for Taiwan; Vital Statistics of Korea, http://kosis.kr/statHtml/statHtml.do?orgId=101&tblId=DT_1B8000F&language=en, for the 2017 crude marriage rate for South Korea

loving that person is or how many learning toys he or she has, to provide enough stimulation. Further, the delivery of good childcare is so skewed by class that we contribute to future inequality by leaving early childhood development up to private wealth. I would like to see high-quality early childcare provided as an option for *all* children under five—similar to the public school system—so that we can make the most of this increasingly scarce resource and take joy in seeing children grow to their fullest potential. The cost of cultivating children to the standard that future societies will need—especially by investing in high-quality early childcare and excellent education—is too much to ask parents to supply privately, especially given their current economic situation.

The catch is always how to pay for it. As it is, the budget calculation frequently seems to rest on an underlying assumption that childcare is an unnecessary "gift" to women and therefore unworthy of diverting tax dollars from other, presumably more worthy expenditures. So, the calculation focuses on how the cost of childcare for a minimal number of families can be squeezed out of the pennies left over. The Brookings Institution recently proposed taking it out of the child tax credit![31] Under that scenario, only half of American children would get care. Not good enough. Some politicians propose taking the expenditure out of the pocketbooks of billionaires, and I'm happy with that. I also think the patriarchs could do without a few war toys in the name of a more life-affirming cause.

But if we apply an economic gender lens to the analysis, we can see that affordable, high-quality childcare would pay for itself. Brookings estimates that providing childcare to half the children in America would cost US$42 billion, so we are trying to cover a US$84 billion expenditure. Christine Lagarde, head of the International Monetary Fund, says that U.S. GDP would rise by 5 percent if women worked at the same level as men.[32] U.S. GDP is about US$20 trillion, so that's US$1 trillion. The tax revenue from that US$1 trillion would be US$271 billion—more than three times the cost of providing universal early childcare. A more conservative estimate would assume only one-third of the recent decline in female labor force participation, recovery of which would yield US$93 billion in tax revenue. So childcare would be covered, either way, by the incremental tax revenue *generated by working mothers.*

Women also now *pay* a significant portion of the taxes collected by the U.S. government. Treating something that, for women, would be an essential service as if it were an extravagance is unacceptable. Women have the right, as citizens and taxpayers, to expect benefits from their government.

The first priority for *any* economy is to provide for the material needs of its members and to support the reproduction of the species. An economy that can't do those things is a failure, no matter what the stock market is doing. The ethic of the Double X Economy is to prioritize this provisioning and to make careful use of resources—including both human and planetary capital—to ensure the future. These are the values women bring to the table. We should give them a seat.

8 | BRAIN BIGOTS

THE HARDWIRED DIFFERENCE BETWEEN MALE AND FEMALE BRAINS COULD EXPLAIN WHY MEN ARE "BETTER AT MAP READING," screamed a headline in the British newspaper *The Independent* in December 2013.[1] The story reported a University of Pennsylvania study that concluded the female "connectome"—the pattern of brain connections formed by learning and experience—is different from the male's. Women's brains, the research said, connected *from side to side*, and men's brains connected *from front to back* within hemispheres. A month later, eighty-seven articles had appeared on this topic in the mainstream press, and thousands of blogs and comments had been posted online. The actual findings of the study were quickly recast as "scientific proof" that males and females are biologically predestined to act out traditional gender roles, largely because women's brains are inferior.[2]

In September 2016, the London Science Museum had to change an exhibit where visitors could score "brain points" on a dial, called a "sex-o-meter," that went from pink to blue. An outcry exploded on Twitter and in the scientific community. "The stereotyped view of a 'hard-wired' link between sex and gender is wrong and potentially harmful as it implies that this is somehow the 'natural order of things,'" one neuroscientist objected. Curators removed the machine, claiming that it was a joke, and, anyway, it's hard to keep up with science.[3]

In August 2017, a Google employee called James Damore circulated a memo to coworkers claiming that women should not be hired by tech companies because "science says" their minds are biologically unsuitable for doing the work. He was fired only after news of this outrage had exploded on social media, but he sued for wrongful dismissal, claiming that Google had discriminated against him for his "heterodox political views."[4] Overnight, Damore was endorsed by *Breitbart*; he quickly became a poster child for the alt-right.[5]

Fifty years ago, some scientists were still trying to prove that the brains of black and white people were different, but the overwhelming weight of better science, along with rising awareness of racism, caught up with them. They were shut down, shunned, and relegated to a dark corner of scientific history. Academic journals stopped accepting that kind of paper, and even the popular media eventually stopped promoting these poisonous views. But we have the same attack still being leveled at women—and it just keeps spreading.

Picture this: A Google employee circulates a memo claiming that ethnic minorities, especially blacks, should not be hired by tech firms because they are biologically unsuitable. Or the London Science Museum opens an exhibition suggesting Muslim brains are different—and then apologizes for its "mistake," calling it a joke. Or a leading newspaper prints a puff piece about brain research showing gay men are "more intuitive" than straight men.

Horrified? You should be. But somehow hate speech about women's brains is not regarded as offensive. For centuries, male scientists have tried to find physical properties that prove a difference between men's and women's brains, but none of these attempts went anywhere. When all is said and done, brains are more like livers or eyeballs than testes and ovaries—they just don't reflect sex the way some would like to think they do.[6]

There is nevertheless a seemingly insatiable hunger among the public for proof that women and men are cognitively different—and that women are inferior. Any study that seems to prove that female brains are dissimilar spreads through social media like wildfire. Studies that demonstrate human brains and cognitive abilities are basically the same, regardless of gender, are far more numerous and of better quality, yet they seldom scratch the surface of public awareness. That's because the media chooses to publicize more marketable research, writing up misogynistic findings under the guise of light entertainment.

Neuroscience is in a crisis over this phenomenon. Scientists see their findings used by vicious people to vicious ends, such as when people say public schools should be segregated by sex, or that they should exclude girls from the science and math classes because they won't "get it," anyway.[7] But it's not up to science to put a stop to this problem; it's up to the rest of us. What we can do is curtail the misuse of scientific information by calling out shameless bigotry when we see it.

A softer term, "unconscious bias," is now widely used as a euphemism for attitudes that shouldn't be excused. Our brains do produce rapid-fire judgments that result in biased decisions about other people; we learn to make them by immersion in a culture with pervasive prejudices. Bigotry is something entirely different: it's intentional, conscious, and often manifested in speech and behavior. Bigots reject, refuse, or reinterpret new information that contradicts their beliefs in order to maintain their hatreds. This is what James Damore did: weaponize science to contribute one more bigoted meme to the culture that produces unconscious bias.

Damore also gave permission for other bigots to come forward, normalizing the worst impulses of Silicon Valley. When the Google incident was reported in the press, quick-and-dirty surveys were conducted among other Google employees and those of other tech companies like Uber and Apple, and over half those surveyed supported Damore. The incident reinforced their biases. So, can the attitudes of this band of bros be called *unconscious bias*? No, because when they have articulated their beliefs, there is no way to call it *unconscious*. What those surveys were documenting was bigotry, plain and simple.[8]

Can you imagine being a woman in tech when this was happening? How would the unbridled disdain your male coworkers were expressing make you feel about being there? And would it affect your career?

Neuroscience answers that question. No matter how capable a woman was when hired, her performance will suffer from hearing this bigotry expressed. When confronted with the stereotype, she has to marshal a cognitive effort into resisting the denigration, which takes "brain space" away from the task at hand. If she is in that disabling environment day-to-day, she will perform consistently less well than she is capable of performing. This phenomenon, known as "stereotype threat," is one of the most robust findings in social science. Importantly, the most capable woman is the most vulnerable because she has the most identity invested in the activity. But she doesn't crumble into self-hatred or "thicken her skin." Instead, she packs her bags and goes off to do something entirely different, another star gone from a field with too few women.[9]

The pink-and-blue exhibit in London also has abiding noxious effects. People who are exposed to gender stereotypes in the public domain become "primed" to express bias and are more likely to make discriminatory decisions at work.[10] The mandate of a science museum is to *keep up with science*, accurately translating that knowledge to the public, rather than to bolster ignorant prejudices that disadvantage people in work or school. We must demand that such institutions show the same consideration for women that they do for minority groups— and exert the same meticulous effort to translate science as accurately on this topic as any other.

The media can take these harmful messages to an even broader audience. The public relations team at the University of Pennsylvania inserted the bit about map reading in their press release, though the study did not show evidence for the claim. This bit of spin, undoubtedly intended to make the research more interesting to the media, then ended up in the *Independent*'s all-caps headline. In an interview, one of the study's authors was quoted as saying her research explained why men or women were better at different occupations, a comment that wasn't *at all* justified by her findings. The researchers must take extra care, because once the popular media has the story, a study about brain differences will have more stereotypes added. In this case, the press added the following points, none of which had been in the study, the press release, or any interview of the authors: (1) women are better at multi-tasking; (2) men are rational, and women are emotional; (3) women are "wired" for housework, and men are not; and (4) the underlying causes of gender differences are biological.

In the online comments responding to these media stories, some readers spun the discussion in a particularly negative way, for instance claiming that women's multitasking was really just scattered attention that resulted in unacceptable performance. "You could argue that women are incapable of focusing on the job at hand—multitasking often being a euphemism for never being able to complete anything," said one writer.[11] An angry defensiveness was apparent among those who had endorsed male superiority, and several made snide remarks about women never winning Nobel Prizes or chess tournaments. Online remarks from around the world showed the impact of this barrage: "Men are performing better than women in each and every field in reality especially in India, in spite of the fact that women get all sorts of facilities and reservations . . . So men are much superior to women whether it is single-tasking or multi-tasking."[12]

A University College London research team tracked the response to the University of Pennsylvania study and concluded that the public was not concerned with the actual content of the study, but had seized the opportunity to declare "proof" that the sexes were unequal.[13] The UCL team ended with a warning that neuroscientists would recognize all too well: "The neuroscience of sex difference does not merely reflect, but can actively shape the gender norms of contemporary society."[14]

We must also become more mindful that, in the process of discovery, theories are proved and disproved. Methods come and go. For example, thirty years ago, a theory in neuroscience claimed that females and males function differently because boys in utero are washed with testosterone from their own developing testes—and it changes their brain. After that, the brain differences between the sexes were set in stone; now filled with all kinds of stereotypical preferences and propensities, these infants were then trapped in ruts they would follow for the rest of their lives. This theory, when new, had a long way to go in connecting the dots between the presence of a hormone to a changed brain and from there to a difference in a thought or behavior. Of course, they never got there; not every juicy scientific tidbit you read in the news proves out under subsequent testing.[15] This theory never proved out, but you can still see it floating around popular culture, put there by people like James Damore.

The gender differences researchers find are also often trivial, but touted as "statistically significant" because that is what it takes to get published. There is a difference between a finding that is statistically significant and one that is important to daily life. For instance, Robert Plomin, a professor of behavioral genetics at King's College London, remarks, "If you map the distribution of scores for verbal skills of boys and of girls, you get two graphs that overlap so much you would need a very fine pencil indeed to show the difference between them. Yet people ignore this huge similarity between boys and girls and instead exaggerate wildly the tiny difference between them."[16]

Sometimes the sample isn't big enough to support a claim. The original study that claimed biology caused boys to be better than girls at math appeared in the United States in the 1980s. C. P. Benbow and J. C. Stanley published two studies that analyzed the performance of fifty thousand thirteen-year-olds on the math section of the Scholastic Aptitude Test. Ten years of data regarding one test, in just one country, was used to generalize to the whole species. The sample was large, but not large enough to declare a biological difference.[17]

In 1990, Janet Hyde, Elizabeth Fennema, and Susan J. Lamon ran a meta-analysis on one hundred studies of girls' and boys' math performance and found—only ten years later—that there was no gender difference in performance; indeed, overall girls outperformed boys, but by a negligible amount. However, in high school, girls dropped behind boys in complex problem-solving. By 1995, girls' absence from advanced math classes, chemistry, and physics had been identified as the cause. During the next decade, the number of girls taking advanced math rose to match that of boys, and by 2000, analysis of more than seven million math performance tests showed that the gap that Benbow and Stanley had identified had disappeared. These changes over time could not have occurred if the underlying cause were an inborn biological difference.[18]

One of the most interesting studies to falsify the "girls can't do math" meme appeared in *Science* in 2008: it showed that female performance in math tests varies directly with the World Economic Forum's Global Gender Gap Index.[19] Where gender equality is high, female math performance is also high, but where it is low, female math performance is also low.[20] This suggests that the effect of gender practices is strong enough to influence test results, and if these kinds of systematic variations occur, biological difference can't be the cause.

The last gender math gap left standing was in spatial reasoning. But in 2007, a study by Jing Feng demonstrated that the gender gap in spatial cognition closed after girls had just ten hours of video game instruction. Today, primary school children do not demonstrate this gap at all, likely because of early exposure to games, phones, and tablets.[21] The difference in their experience overrides what was once regarded as a biological sex difference.

Also in the 1990s, mathematicians demonstrated that the gender gap in the highest percentiles of math achievement (and other achievements, such as chess) was a function of the pool of boys being larger, and not a real performance difference.[22] Given these findings, it was no longer possible to claim biological superiority as the reason there were more males among leading scientists, chess players, or Nobel laureates.

As all these studies debunking a biological math gap grew, however, the popular media continued to advance the theory that men's and women's psychologies were vastly different. So, in 2005, Janet Hyde proposed the "Gender Similarities Hypothesis," which says that women and men are the same on most psychological variables, including cognitive abilities.[23] She backed up her theory with a massive meta-analysis of research into gender differences in temperament, preferences, habits, and many other aspects of personality and ability. Hyde found that women and men are generally more similar than different; however, there were a few differences at the population level that were pretty true to stereotype. At the individual level or in small groups, she warned, these differences could not be predicted because there is simply too much variation to walk around expecting that all women sew and all men watch football. There are men who sew and women who like football.

An elegant new theory of the brain has now risen to explain all these similarities and variations. We now know that humans learn to think by creating synapses that connect parts of the brain. A newborn must generate a hundred billion synapses in order to function as an adult. But only six thousand genes are available to do that at birth, a number sufficient to produce only 10 percent of those connections. The remaining work is done through experience and learning. We are absorbing information and building synapses each second of our individual lives. The connectome grows, reconfigures, and recedes as you learn and forget; studies have shown the connectome acquiring and then losing map information, juggling skills, and piano-playing prowess. Many of us have lost the ability to speak a language we once felt we knew. As these lessons and losses collect, the pattern of connections in each person's connectome becomes as unique as a fingerprint or a snowflake.[24]

Cultures normally teach boys and girls different things. So we might expect to see systematic differences in their knowledge at the population level, such as those Hyde observed. Therefore, their connectomes *may be* differently patterned. But we don't know yet. There is currently an international effort to "map" the variations in the human connectome, much like the project on the human genome thirty years ago. In the United States, the National Institutes of Health has funded a five-year, US$30 million Human Connectome Project, and a similar international project called the Developing Human Connectome Project is underway, collecting brain scans on hundreds of people as well as animals.[25] We must wait until that work is done before we can say for sure whether men and women have different connectomes—and find out what that means. In the greater scheme of things, then, that University of Pennsylvania study was just a trial balloon.

Throughout history females have been excluded from educational institutions. Male elites withheld knowledge of writing from "lesser" groups, including women, as the technology spread around the ancient world. Literacy remained uncommon among women for thousands of years. As late as the nineteenth century, women in the developed nations lobbied to be allowed the same education as men. The girls in Africa today are fighting a very old battle. Elsewhere in the world, girls are now pushing their way into postsecondary education, and it is having a dramatic effect on their national economies. However, the trend toward education does not cause women to take jobs; the opposite is true: job availability for women spurs them toward education.

The shining example of this phenomenon is Latin America and the Caribbean. Figure 23 illustrates trends in female higher education enrollment in that region since 1970, alongside female labor force participation and GDP. You can see the relationship between growing numbers of working women and the increase in higher education; because there are now more and better jobs open to Latin American females, girls and their families invest in education and expect a different kind of future.

Across the Western nations, women outnumber men in higher education, achieve better grades, graduate at higher rates, and more

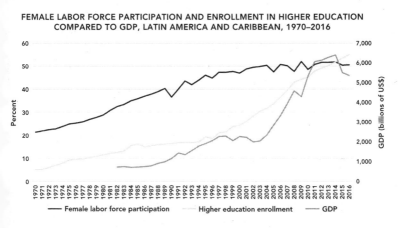

FEMALE LABOR FORCE PARTICIPATION AND ENROLLMENT IN HIGHER EDUCATION COMPARED TO GDP, LATIN AMERICA AND CARIBBEAN, 1970–2016

— Female labor force participation   Higher education enrollment   — GDP

FIGURE 23. In the graph above, the light gray line represents the percentage of all females enrolled in higher education in Latin America and the Caribbean from 1970 to 2016. The black line shows the percentage of females participating in the labor force, with a trend line that closely follows educational enrollment. Similarly, GDP grew alongside both female education and labor force participation, as is the global pattern. The drop-off in GDP in the last few years was caused by political instability, especially in Venezuela.

Source: World Bank Database, accessed July 17, 2018

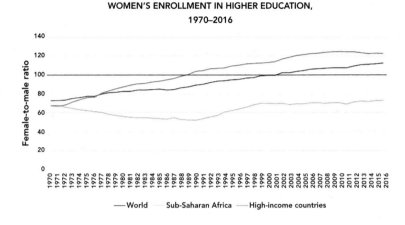

WOMEN'S ENROLLMENT IN HIGHER EDUCATION, 1970–2016

FIGURE 24. In the graph above, the bold black line indicates where equality with men would be. Females in high-income countries passed the equality mark around 1990. The world total shows females passing equality in about 2000. The bottom line represents sub-Saharan Africa, the only region where women do not now enroll in higher education at a rate equal to or higher than men.

Source: World Bank Database, accessed July 17, 2018

frequently go on to postgraduate work (Figure 24).[26] But when brain bigots are presented with data about women's dominance in higher education, they dismiss the evidence by saying that women don't study the "right" subjects and so the rise in their educational achievements is unimportant. The "right" subjects are digital technology, engineering, math, science, and business, which they regard as the most challenging, the most important to the future economy, the most thoroughly dominated by men, and the ones that scare women the most.

Let's take a look at where women really do focus their education (Figure 25). Females are indeed only half as likely as males to study information and communications technology (ICT), but the proportion of *all* students studying ICT is less than 5 percent. The difference between 6.5 percent (male) and 3.2 percent (female) is not sufficiently important to make a big deal about. Males do dominate the field, but the big picture is that almost *nobody* is getting those degrees.

RECENT GRADUATES' AREAS OF STUDY, 2017

	Estimated total % of students	Males (%)	Females (%)	Female-to-male ratio
BUSINESS	27.1	26.3	27.8	106
ENGINEERING, MANUFACTURING, AND CONSTRUCTION	12.2	19.4	6.1	31
EDUCATION	14.2	10.4	17.3	166
SOCIAL SCIENCE, JOURNALISM, AND INFORMATION	9.1	7.9	10.1	128
HUMANITIES AND THE ARTS	9.2	7.7	10.4	135
INFORMATION AND COMMUNICATIONS TECHNOLOGY	4.7	6.5	3.2	49
HEALTH AND WELFARE	9.8	6.4	12.6	197
NATURAL SCIENCES, MATH, AND STATISTICS	5.0	5.3	4.8	91
SERVICES	2.9	3.7	2.3	62
AGRICULTURAL SERVICES AND FORESTRY	2.3	2.8	1.8	64

FIGURE 25. These figures reflect the total for all nations for which there is information, unweighted by population. The "Estimated total" column is weighted for the greater pool of females. I have highlighted information and communications technology. You can see that this field is very small, so the difference between male and female enrollment is not large in terms of absolute numbers.

Source: World Economic Forum, *The Global Gender Gap Report*, 2017

The stereotype is that females study the "easy subjects," like the liberal arts.[27] It's true that women do study the humanities, education, and social sciences more often than men, but they also major in business more often. In fact, three times more women study business than study the humanities. Forty years ago, business education was very male dominated, and it is still heavily quantitative and competitive. Women don't seem daunted. Those trying to sell this stereotype haven't done their homework; they merely assume women don't do business because they're too busy doing art.

Let's get a better sense of how this pattern came about by focusing on the data from the United States, which is more detailed and goes back further than other countries' while showing the same trends (Figure 26).

Women enrolled in higher education in equal numbers as men beginning in the early 1970s, probably encouraged by the workplace reforms of the Second Wave. The trend continued upward for twenty-five years, until the daughters of the 1970s movement were finishing high school and the rate of increase ratcheted up again, the result of an increased emphasis on careers for women in the 1990s as well as the influence of working mothers.

The increasing number of women enrolling in higher education put pressure on the capacity of American universities. Universities use admissions criteria to recruit the best students for a limited number of places, so the greater presence of females in the student population testifies to their better ability to meet the requirements. In the late 1990s, private schools in America began accepting lower admissions standards for boys, in order to maintain a gender balance.[28] Over time, these practices have resulted in an admissions system that makes it harder for girls to get in, even if they have better academic records. In spite of this intentional disadvantaging from school admissions officers, 57 percent of all students today are female. Overall, slightly more American women than men hold degrees across the entire population, not just the young, which is also true for the G7 countries as a whole.

When female students began to attend college in higher numbers than males, there was a huge outcry. In her book *The War Against Boys: How Misguided Feminism Is Harming Our Young Men*, Christina Hoff Sommers argued that boys should not be expected to sit still and pay attention in school, so the way school was taught was discriminatory.[29] This argument was rather odd because educators had insisted for decades that

FIGURE 26. (opposite) On the top, you see the number of U.S. bachelor's degrees awarded to men (dotted line) since World War II. The trend is flat from 1970 until about 2001. Degrees awarded to women (solid line), however, have consistently climbed since females hit equality with males about 1983. A trend like this takes a long time to work through an entire population, but as you can see on the bottom, in the past couple of years, adult women in the United States have become more likely to have a college education than adult men.

Source: National Center for Education Statistics, https://www.statista.com/statistics/185157/number-of-bachelor-degrees-by-gender-since-1950/

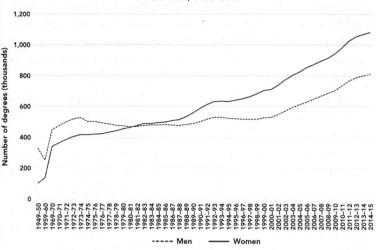

**BACHELOR'S DEGREES AWARDED IN THE UNITED STATES
BY GENDER, 1950–2015**

Number of degrees (thousands)

----- Men ——— Women

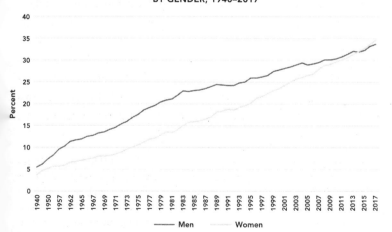

**TOTAL U.S. POPULATION WITH AT LEAST FOUR YEARS OF COLLEGE
BY GENDER, 1940–2017**

Percent

——— Men ——— Women

the reason boys got into college more often than girls was that they were simply smarter, better students.

The actual explanation for lower numbers of males in college is that young men don't *need* as many credentials as women do for the same jobs. A North American study that used 122 million professional profiles found that female software engineers needed a master's degree to get the same job that a male with a bachelor's can get.[30] North American men also continue to advance more rapidly, earn more money, and monopolize leadership, even when they have less education.[31]

These trends tell us that women's lower status in the world of work is not a result of their being less intelligent, motivated, or disciplined. But what did they study? Since 1970, women's areas of preference have changed dramatically, showing much more intentional orientation toward careers, according to the Harvard economist Claudia Goldin.[32] The overall trends for topics of study are shown in Figure 27. Though this data reflects the interests of students as a whole, the driving force is the increase in women's enrollment. The majors that grew were the ones chosen by females, while the topics with flat lines did not attract them. Business won the most students, followed by health sciences. ICT and engineering have been comparatively unattractive to all students for most of the last fifty years.

In the latest available data from the U.S. Department of Education, we can see the current gender breakdown (Figure 28). The students studying something other than science, technology, engineering, and math (STEM) topics—a category that includes majors as various as geography, economics, forestry, and art—are 51 percent of the total. Today, males are hardly present in studying the health professions (which includes doctors and veterinarians, as well as nurses and speech pathologists). The sexes are roughly even in business, and pretty close in mathematics and statistics. The biggest gender difference is in engineering and ICT.

Far from being cowards who "fear science," as brain bigots claim, women have shown courage as they've entered male-dominated disciplines. Today, women are 50 percent of all American medical students—in 1965, they made up less than 10 percent. They are a solid majority in

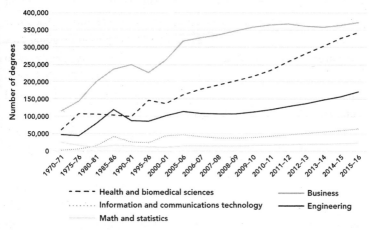

**BACHELOR'S DEGREES AWARDED IN SELECT FIELDS
IN THE UNITED STATES, 1970–2016**

- - - - Health and biomedical sciences   ——— Business
· · · · · · · · Information and communications technology   ——— Engineering
Math and statistics

FIGURE 27. Note that the trends here reflect changes in the interests of undergraduates, but the influx of female students affects them even more. The two fields increasing the most are the ones that attracted women. The others are flat because they did not.

Source: National Center for Education Statistics

the biological sciences. If you take all science into account, women get more than 50 percent of doctorates.[33] But interestingly, the life sciences suddenly don't count as STEM.

The right to enter medicine was hard won. As women pushed against the barriers placed in their way, they were forced into segregated schools and often met fierce opposition. In 1869, the dean of the Women's College of Medicine of Pennsylvania convinced the teaching hospital to allow her students to attend clinical observations. When word got out, hundreds of male medical students gathered to express their disapproval: "Ranging themselves in line, these gallant gentlemen assailed the young ladies, as they passed out [the door], with insolent and offensive language, and then followed them into the street, where the whole gang, with the fluency of long practice, joined in insulting them . . . During the last hour, missiles of paper, tinfoil, tobacco-quids,

**BACHELOR'S DEGREES AWARDED BY SUBJECT
IN THE UNITED STATES IN 2015**

	Percent of all students awarded degrees	Number of females	Number of males	Percent female
HEALTH PROFESSIONS AND RELATED PROGRAMS	11.4	182,570	33,658	84
BIOLOGICAL AND BIOMEDICAL SCIENCES	5.8	64,794	45,102	59
BUSINESS	19.2	172,489	191,310	47
MATH AND STATISTICS	1.2	9,391	12,462	43
PHYSICAL SCIENCE AND SCIENCE TECHNOLOGIES	1.6	11,560	18,478	38
INFORMATION AND COMMUNICA-TIONS TECHNOLOGY	3.4	12,509	52,207	19
ENGINEERING AND RELATED PROGRAMS	6.0	21,521	92,948	19
OTHER	51.4	607,431	366,504	62
TOTAL DEGREES AWARDED	100	1,082,265	812,669	57

FIGURE 28. This table shows the breakdown by gender for science, technology, engineering, and math (STEM) majors in the United States in 2015. You can see that the main difference is in the fields of health/biology versus ICT/engineering. Notice that about 60 percent of "other" majors are females, while about 40 percent are males. "Other" includes a very wide range of topics, including economics.

Source: National Center for Education Statistics

etc., were thrown upon the ladies, while some of these men defiled the dresses of the ladies near them with tobacco juice."[34]

Today, evidence of this kind of behavior in ICT and engineering is accumulating. "The Elephant in the Valley," a study of senior women in tech, reported that 87 percent had experienced demeaning comments from male colleagues; 84 percent had colleagues or clients who wouldn't look them in the eye; 84 percent had been told they were too aggressive (42 percent more than once); and 90 percent had seen sexist behavior at off-site industry events. In addition, 59 percent felt they had not been given the same opportunities as men, and 47 percent had been asked to do low-level tasks that males were not asked to do. The most shocking statistic is that 60 percent had received unwanted sexual advances, of which 65 percent had been from their own supervisor (50 percent more than once).[35]

A recent Pew study further reported that women who work in STEM jobs where the majority of workers are men are significantly more likely to experience sexual harassment, demeaning social behavior, and sex discrimination.[36] The World Economic Forum says half of young women entering the ICT industry have left by their twelfth year, twice the frequency in other industries. Their average tenure is only seven years.

When assessing probable outcomes, it's unlikely that a young woman and her parents considering the "right subjects to study" see an attractive proposition in studying tech or engineering. The up-front investment is large and entails lifelong opportunity costs, the period for payback is unacceptably short, and the risk that the decision wouldn't be worth it is high. To choose one of these disciplines, given the working conditions a woman could expect, is economically irrational, even if the pay is higher in the short run.

So young women have been making what, for them, is a better choice. In the United States, health has become the largest employer (accounting for many more jobs than the tech sector as of 2018), and it is projected to create more new jobs than any other industry in the next decade. Jobs in health care are much more secure than jobs in tech. Manufacturing is in decline.[37] Furthermore, some of the most important and profitable technological breakthroughs are coming not from ICT or engineering, but from the biological and biomedical sciences. Since women are the majority in these sciences, it does not appear that they are poor at math, afraid of science, unable to innovate, or lacking confidence. They are ready to help their countries grow *and* provide care for their fellow citizens. There is *nothing* wrong with their brains.

9 | THE FAILURE OF EQUAL PAY

The British government did something extraordinary in spring 2018: it stipulated that all businesses with more than 250 employees should reveal their gender pay gap online. When the data appeared, the controversy was immediate and intense. There, for all to behold, was a consistent pattern of inequality among some 15 million employees. Across companies and industries, there were gender gaps in pay, some of them huge. And women were almost completely excluded from the top quartile—the best-paid jobs.

"The concept of extreme pay disparities in City finance is not particularly new, but what is arresting about the site is the way it offers an x-ray of the inner workings of diverse organizations from universities to meat-packing businesses, government departments to high-street fashion retailers, sewage companies to the Ritz," Amelia Gentleman wrote in *The Guardian*. "Companies are stripped naked . . . and attitudes towards women are revealed with uncomfortable clarity."[1]

Of all the companies, airlines and banks were the worst offenders. The airlines had men flying planes and women serving drinks, with the former paid very well and the latter paid rather poorly. As an example, 94 percent of the pilots at easyJet were male, compensated at £92,400 (about US$121,000) on average. Flight attendants were 69 percent female, compensated at an average of £24,800 (about US$32,000). The airlines seemed to think this split was perfectly normal, even though the 1950s sex-role stereotyping had the irony of a refrigerator magnet. They set a goal of having 20 percent female pilots by 2020—and expected everyone to be impressed by that neck-stretching. Had they been asleep in the cockpit since the Equal Pay Act of 1970?[2]

Across the board, corporate spokespeople seemed unaware that British women had outstripped men across a wide range of qualifications. For instance, the managing partner for talent at Deloitte (which posted a 43 percent gender pay gap) complained that progress at a firm like theirs would not happen in a flash. "For us, you can't just magic up a load of senior women and plonk them into our organization. We need to make sure that we enable our women to progress," she said. "I frequently say this is for us a 10-year journey."[3] Deloitte has already had fifty years to create a level playing field—now they need a ten-year extension? Maybe they should "magic up" someone else to manage the talent.

In the U.K., women have been educated equally to men for decades. There are currently 31 percent more women than men in higher education—and that is not breaking news. As with their counterparts in the United States, British women take more places at university, make better grades, graduate at higher rates, and go on to postgraduate work more often than men. Despite these wide advantages in their credentials, the government, the press, and businesses persistently suggest that women should have more training so they can get the big jobs.

If, in the aggregate, women are more qualified but not getting promoted, then widespread sex discrimination *must* be happening, and happening consistently. That is the only way to reconcile those facts. So where are the lawsuits? The BBC looked at court statistics, expecting to find masses of equal pay lawsuits clogging the employment tribunals, but was surprised to learn that not a single equal pay case had been decided since 2010.[4] Zero.

The Western countries have had equal pay laws since the 1970s. Employers have had plenty of time to comply, but equal pay has not been achieved anywhere. Today, analysts point to three main causes of the gap: the motherhood penalty, clustering in female-dominant industries, and the lack of advancement. Reading only the "big data" and using their prejudices to project a reason behind the numbers, most pundits, HR managers, and government servants blame the women for having children, working in all the wrong places, and, in one way or another, not trying hard enough. In this chapter I will offer a different explanation via two illustrations: Britain, where the equal pay laws were made toothless when drafted; and the United States, where the enforcement system was perhaps too effective and so was subsequently rendered impotent by reactionaries who took over the courts. Across the Western countries, it has been an absence of will on the part of governments that has kept the gender pay gap in place.

The origin of Britain's first equality legislation sets the stage. The European Union asserted the principle of equal pay for women at the formative Treaty of Rome in 1957. At that point, Britain's leaders had no taste for gender equality; anyway, they weren't part of the EU. A few resolutions were passed by the British trade unions in the early 1960s, but neither the union leadership nor the government took concrete steps toward making equal pay a reality. In the film version of the story, the roadblock in the government was broken by a sewing machinists' strike at a Ford plant in Dagenham in 1968. Polling that year did show that three-quarters of U.K. citizens were in support of equal pay for equal work, but it seems more likely that Britain adopted equal pay legislation because by then the government wanted to join the EU, which required that all members have provisions for equal pay for women in place. So Britain's Equal Pay Act of 1970 supported application for admission to the EU in 1973. This would not be the last time that the EU would compel a reluctant Britain to liberalize its gender practices.

The U.K.'s Equal Pay Act of 1970 is just ten pages long, but it contains a provision that held equality by the throat for the next fifty years: there could be no different treatment of one sex versus the other.[5] Those drafting the law protected themselves from male citizens' rage and ensured their own interests with this provision. Though the rule sounds right and reasonable on its face, it does not recognize the inequalities that already existed between men and women, nor that past discrimination had created a massive heap of male advantage, nor that women suffered as a result of attitudes that were tightly integrated into the social structure. Such a rule also fails to acknowledge that sex discrimination is an ongoing process by which one sex uses its advantages to disadvantage the other.[6]

So, from the beginning, any kind of concession or support for a British woman over a man was called "positive discrimination"—what is called "reverse discrimination" in the United States—and it was illegal. The positive discrimination doctrine led to employment dilemmas that were counterproductive to the aims of gender equality. If two people were working in the same role, it was clear that they had to be paid equally, but if an employer was choosing whether to hire or promote an equally qualified man and woman, either choice could theoretically invite a lawsuit for sex discrimination. As personnel practices evolved, however, men could get jobs and promotions if they were only *equally* qualified to the women applying, but a woman had to be clearly *superior* to all the male applicants to win.

This structural flaw in British law was compounded by issues of enforcement. A woman who felt she was being treated unfairly had to prove it by showing what additional pay, promotions, or other advantages had been given a male *and* that she was performing just as well in the same job. However, an employer could legally sack any employee who spoke to another about pay. That made it unlikely a woman would know that a man was being paid more and dangerous for her to ask.

Even today, the court process can take years, and the most a woman can win is her back pay, plus other damages that are capped at inconsequential levels. Unless her salary is very high, it is unlikely that the back pay will even cover her legal costs—and British courts don't ever make the guilty employer pay the plaintiff's legal fees for getting what the plaintiff should have had in the first place. By contrast, the law does provide that if the court and the employer think the complaint unworthy, the judge can order the employee to pay the employer's legal costs as well as her own. Since the British system does not have class action suits, there is no cost-sharing for plaintiffs. Furthermore, strict libel laws keep any whiff of a case being tried from getting to the public or press. The entire process is secret as a star chamber.

The risks of pursuing an equality claim vastly outweigh the possible benefits. The employer's risk is so minimal that it makes economic sense to pay women lower salaries and bet that nothing will ever come of it. Predictably, the features of the U.K. equality system have resulted in just what the spring 2018 explosion revealed: few women at the top, large pay gaps, dark courtrooms, complacent employers, and a shocked public.

In the late 1990s, the European Union began to recognize that efforts to achieve equal pay were failing across all the member nations. They proposed adopting a policy of "positive action" (what Americans call "affirmative action"), and conservatives in Britain went nuts, starting a heated negotiation for a new equality act that would reconcile the EU directives with Britain's positive discrimination doctrine. Opponents to the EU policy began talking about the legal "tradition" of positive discrimination as if it were the Magna Carta and not a 1970s expediency.

When the Equality Act of 2010 was finally announced, the big story was that the new legislation now made it legal to hire an *equally* qualified woman, a claim that was highly misleading. Since the act still made positive discrimination illegal, it was a new feature, the "tiebreaker," that was offered in order that the government could argue something real had changed. The conditions under which the tiebreaker can be used are unbelievably complex, and make it clear that the risk of hiring or promoting a woman who is not head and shoulders above the nearest male candidate is still high.

Under the tiebreaker, an employer could hire an equally qualified woman *if* it can prove she is absolutely equal in every way, but it must also be able to prove the following:

- There is a documentable diversity problem in the company or in the sector.
- The action is "proportionate to the need" (whatever that means).

- The company has thoroughly evaluated every possible relevant aspect of every candidate's background.
- The qualifications of the woman are directly necessary for the job.

If there is any doubt, the male candidate must have an opportunity to provide more information that might tip the scale in his favor. Human resources experts recommended that any employer hiring a woman keep extensive records about how and why the decision was made, just in case it was challenged by the male.

And then the government was actually surprised when, five years later, no employers had used the tiebreaker.

The British approach relies heavily on the expectation that employers make objective judgments, which presumes bosses are aware of their own potential for bias, as well as the certainty that any judge would make the same call. If you lined them all up, studies that prove gender bias systematically affects employment evaluations probably would circle the globe. They are usually some version of this:

1. You have a false set of CVs, some identified as belonging to females and some to males.
2. You give them to a group of employers and ask them to evaluate and choose the top candidate.
3. Then you swap the male and female CVs, such that each "candidate" has a CV that belonged to the opposite sex before.
4. You get another evaluation.

You might be able to guess how it comes out: people rate the men higher than the women even when they have an identical CV. If you ask respondents to explain their choices, they express doubts about the woman's credentials and devalue her accomplishments, while finding the same credentials and accomplishments superior when the name at the top of the CV belongs to a man. Researchers have studied this effect using many tasks and measures, and I do not know of a single study that has concluded that men and women are rated equally. So, for a woman to be judged as equal to a man in any circumstance, she would actually have to be better than him.

Company spokespeople trying to defend the gender pay gap in 2018 spent a lot of time "mansplaining" the limits of the government's reporting requirements to outraged women. They complained that the government's method of calculating the pay gap was too simplistic to reflect the complexity of their payrolls. The truth was that the "simplistic" formula, while making all businesses' numbers comparable and keeping the reporting burden to a minimum, did not allow employers to massage the pay gap out of their numbers. As *Bloomberg Businessweek* explained in a story headlined "New Numbers Show the Gender Pay Gap Is Real," "The rigid [U.K. government] approach leaves companies nowhere to hide, no statistical mechanism to cover up their failure to mentor women, no rhetorical way around the fact that their higher-paid divisions are largely male."[7]

The EU had been criticizing Britain's government for years because its cost of childcare was the highest in Europe (maybe in the world), the U.K. was not offering help to working women to defray it, and unequal pay was the visible result. Nearly 40 percent of British women in the labor force work part-time, one of the highest rates among developed nations, which adds substantially to the pay gap because part-timers are paid less, even by the hour, for the same work. Most of them are young mothers, though increasingly they are also women caring for the elderly. Surveys show that young couples in the U.K. do not want to live in single-breadwinner families; mothers would prefer to work full-time. But because childcare is so expensive, young families are forced to have one adult remain at home—and it's nearly always the woman. These women end up staying out of the workforce for a long time, and when they return, their careers resume in a lesser role at lower pay. Their education and career have been sacrificed. Conservatives (and many businesses) argue this is not a gender phenomenon, but just the "natural" outcome of mammalian reproduction—or a private choice made freely in a free-market system.

The pattern of industry segregation is the same in Britain as it was fifty years ago; in fact, it's the same as it was in the Paleolithic Age—women are clustered in care, clothing, and food. Better-paid industries are unwelcoming to women, especially to mothers, which leads them back to the friendlier sectors to avoid mistreatment and find greater flexibility. Pay equality by occupation is no better: women are paid less in every job.

Another "manscuse" voiced during the 2018 scandal was that women were paid less because they are poorer negotiators. Back in 2007, a book called *Women Don't Ask* said women get paid less because, unlike men, they don't negotiate for more money.[8] The authors' solution was simple: women should "man up" and ask for pay increases. Subsequent studies showed, however, that there is a good reason women do not try to negotiate higher salaries: those who do tend to get punished. Asking for money is seen as inappropriate behavior for women, as is the assertion of one's own value that must underlie the request. The less transparency surrounding pay parameters, the worse the women do when they ask for more money, and having another offer in hand doesn't help. One much-hyped study argued that women could win salary negotiations if they asked nicely enough, but that was disproved by still more studies. Turns out, if you are a woman, you can't ask nicely enough. Most women already know that. Which is why they don't ask.[9]

In both the United States and the U.K., controversy over the right way to calculate the gender pay gap has been haunting the effort to advance gender equality. Extreme-market economists want to prove there is no gender gap because it fits their self-interested version of the way the economy works; their idea is that if there really were a gender pay gap, companies would hire only women in order to save costs. (This argument ignores the practical reality that doing such a thing would be illegal in pretty much every country on earth.) These economists pursue their ideological agenda by "controlling variables" in national data sets until the gap in pay between men and women disappears. They conclude that if women made the same choices as men, there would be equal pay. They then put the studies out to the media, who jump on them the same way they do studies about brain differences, until everyone has heard something about the gender gap being a fiction.

Sometimes it is appropriate to control variables, but it is also true that you can make nearly any effect disappear if you control for enough of them. These analysts control for items like "works part-time," "works from home," and "works in health care, education, or fashion," which describe women so much more often than men that they're really just another way of saying *female*. When analysts control for these factors, they have not discovered that the pay gap is a fiction. What their manipulated data really says is, "Women were paid the same as men once we removed all the factors that enforce and reflect gender bias in the workplace."

An analogy often makes the problem clearer. African American men are paid less, on average, than white males are. Imagine someone takes the data set on male pay and controls for variables like living in a disadvantaged urban zip code or having been unemployed recently or having been arrested. After all those factors have been thrown out, the white men and black men are paid the same. The analyst announces, "There is no racial discrimination in America! Black men would be paid the same if they acted more like whites!" But the conclusion is not valid because the variables eliminated are each either a reflection of racial discrimination or a means by which racial discrimination is accomplished. We would also be very suspicious of the motives behind an analysis like that. We should be equally suspicious when the data set is women.

The World Economic Forum, the Organisation for Economic Co-operation and Development, and the EU have published estimates of the gender pay gap in the U.K. that range from 18 to 45 percent. It depends on what source they use and how they calculate the gap, but the unavoidable fact is that they all show a big difference. Even within the same industry or the same occupation, even when working hours are matched, women are paid less than men.

The damage the pay gap does to Britain's economy is considerable. British women lose £140 billion a year in pay due to the gender gap, an average of £9,112 (about US$12,000) a year per person. And Britain sacrifices about £123 billion a year because of lost productivity associated with unequal compensation. Nevertheless, the government resists real reform. As one furious woman told *The Guardian*, "We try to get change, but men are holding the levers of power. We're expecting our oppressors to change the system—it's like asking the turkeys to vote for Christmas."[10]

The United States started this journey from a different place and, for a while, it was making better progress. The legal guarantee of women's equal pay arose in America on the heels of the civil rights movement, because sex was added to the protections given to race. So, the impetus behind all the equality legislation was the desire to correct the mistreatment of the past and its effects in the present. Unlike the U.K. legislation, therefore, U.S. law recognized a disparity of rights and opportunities, which meant barriers had to be lifted, counterbalanced, and outlawed. Implicit in this approach was an acknowledgment that white males, the most dominant group in America, had been responsible for discrimination and continued to benefit from it. Also implicit was the recognition of significant prejudice currently in the society that emerged in unfair attempts to keep the disadvantaged groups down. No one fooled themselves into thinking blacks and whites, or men and women, were starting fresh from the same place when the equal pay law was enacted in 1963.

The American program of gender equality came from two directions. From Congress and three presidents came laws and executive orders, while from the grassroots came lawsuits. Here, too, the burden of enforcement was on individual women, but provisions of the system evened out the chances of success: affirmative action, class action lawsuits, punitive damages, and contingency arrangements. Add to all that the American taste for watching important court cases like it was a blood sport, and you've got an enforcement system that might work.

Affirmative action was established and implemented via presidential orders that banned sex discrimination in the federal government and among federal contractors. So, all government suppliers had to demonstrate a serious and impactful effort to equalize advancement of women and minorities or risk losing their contracts. The U.S. government is not only the country's largest employer but also the biggest purchaser of everything from mayonnaise to missiles. Threatening to pull an employer's federal contract is tantamount to cutting off somebody's life support. It's a testament to the power of this threat that the government has never had to do so.

Employers who ignored the new laws also became vulnerable to civil lawsuits. The U.S. legal system allows civil suits to redress grievances brought by individuals, but it also provides a venue from which to publicly test government mandates, to expose offensive practices within institutions, and to raise issues in the public consciousness. For a socially charged matter like equal pay, these civil proceedings can be more like a soapbox than a star chamber.

Sex discrimination cases presented a very high risk for defendant institutions. The United States has class action suits, which are lawsuits where a group of harmed individuals sues the same party, and the requirements make it fairly easy to raise a very large class of plaintiffs. The biggest sex discrimination suit ever, launched against Walmart in 2001, had 1.6 million plaintiffs. On top of that, the courts can and do award punitive damages in the most egregious cases—the law makes that provision so that court decisions will act as a strong deterrent against bad behavior. So, in addition to the recovery of financial harm directly to the plaintiff in a sex discrimination case, the court can add an award in an amount calculated to hurt the employer. If a large class of plaintiffs wins a sex discrimination suit, the employer has to pay for any harm (such as back pay) to *all* members of the class, *plus* the punitive damages.

We're talking about big money. Because the award can be so great, lawyers who defend claimants in class action cases often take the work "on contingency," which means they are paid only if they win, taking a percentage off the top, rather than getting a fee for the hours spent. The potential notoriety may also increase their eagerness to work on contingency, as national media exposure might attract more clients.

From the 1970s to the 1990s, the provisions of the American legal system made it affordable to create huge pools of plaintiffs easily, raise the stakes very high for the employer while reducing plaintiff risk, and, consequently, pump up the entertainment value of the fight. Sex discrimination became a public interest matter rather than merely a private dispute between a woman and her employer, as it is in Britain.

Two frequent misunderstandings about U.S. sex discrimination law—on both sides of the Atlantic—have to do with quotas and reverse discrimination. In the 1978 *Regents of the University of California v. Bakke*, Allan Bakke, a white male, claimed he had been rejected for admission to the university's medical school, which was using quotas to favor black candidates, and thus had been a victim of "reverse discrimination." The court's opinion essentially argued that if white males could claim discrimination, the Bakke argument, if allowed, would undercut the intention of the law—to make up for the suffering of those groups who had experienced discrimination in the past. Reverse discrimination was rejected—in effect, putting the concept to bed forever. Since white males were entitled to equal treatment under the law, however, the court ruled that when the University of California used quotas to effect equality, it was acting unconstitutionally. So, contrary to popular belief, American affirmative action has *never* required quotas.

In the United States, women's pay as a percentage of men's rose steeply from 1973 to 1990, a gain of about 30 percent overall. But beginning about 1990, the rise plateaued; over the next three decades, American women saw a gain of only 12 percent, in total, against the gender pay gap. Had the Americans kept up the same pace that was experienced between 1973 and 1990 to the end of the twentieth century, they would now be at equal pay.

The slowing in American progress is attributable to the rise of the right wing and its success appointing conservative judges, especially to the Supreme Court. The swing toward a right-wing judiciary has already essentially destroyed the 1970s women's employment rights using three drastic measures: (1) allowing employers to use employment contracts to override equal rights, (2) pushing courts to limit the use of punitive damages, and (3) declaring that women do not constitute a class.

Beginning in the early 1990s, employers began making new hires sign employment contracts stipulating that any employment complaint had to be resolved through arbitration, a practice that consistently works against the employees. Employees also must sign away the right to enter a class action suit. A series of lower court rulings initially said these contracts were illegal. But, in 2018, the Supreme Court declared "forced arbitration" requirements constitutional. By that time, 60 million women *and* men, representing nearly 50 percent of the American workforce, worked under such arrangements. For the women bound by forced arbitration, the Supreme Court had negated the system of provisions that had been propelling the U.S. toward equal pay.[11]

During the same period, courts deciding discrimination cases began limiting awards to restoration of back pay and eliminating punitive damages altogether. Again, this change can be chalked up to conservative strategies to gain control of the judicial system.

The Walmart case, *Wal-Mart Stores, Inc. v. Dukes, et al.*, was another situation in which all the lower courts had held for the plaintiffs, but the Supreme Court reversed them. In 2004, that case had been certified by a U.S. federal court as a class action suit on behalf of all past and present female Walmart employees; however, the 2011 Supreme Court decision held that women could not be a class. The ruling was split along both gender and ideological lines, five conservative male judges against four liberals, three women and one man.

The story has gone down in popular culture as Walmart winning the biggest sex discrimination suit in American history, but the question that decided this case was not whether there had been sex discrimination at Walmart, but whether women as a group have enough "commonality" to call themselves a class. The conservatives claimed the complaint was just an aggregation of singular experiences, so the women had to pursue their case on an individual basis.

The SCOTUS objection to thinking of women as a class had lurked under the law for a long time, because of the implicit comparison with race, on which U.S. equality legislation is based. In the 1978 *Bakke* case, for instance, the opinion of the court emphasized the historical mistreatment of African Americans as the basis for class status, but explicitly rejected women's similarity because "the perception of racial classifications as inherently odious stems from a lengthy and tragic history that gender-based classifications do not share."[12] This attitude is similarly visible in the 2011 Walmart decision, and it is clearly attributable to the fact that *women did not have a written history* until recently and the public has not been made aware of it now that it exists.

Since the Walmart case was decided, multiple cases going through the courts have been decided on the basis of the precedent saying women do not experience enough commonality in employment discrimination to constitute a class. The plaintiffs were denied class action status in a lawsuit against Microsoft, despite two massive, authoritative, and independent reports concluding there were statistically significant patterns of women being paid unequally and promoted less often—and multiple lawsuits pending from other women.

Though the Obama administration made a significant contribution to women's employment rights by passing the Lilly Ledbetter Fair Pay Act of 2009 (which broke the power of salary secrecy to minimize recovery of damages), the right wing has continued to push equal pay backward. Trump abruptly canceled an order, made under Obama, to require companies to report detailed pay information by gender; fortunately, a federal judge ordered the administration to continue collecting the data required under the law. But several bills addressing the equal pay problem are languishing in the U.S. Congress, blocked by conservatives.

At this point, the U.K., the United States, and all the Western nations have failed to protect the equal rights of half their citizens. That was the conclusion reached by the European Commission in 2009 when it studied the results achieved by the EU member countries, Canada, South Africa, and the United States.[13] The fatal flaw in all the equality procedures was that the burden of enforcement had been placed on individual women, who bore the cost and risk of lawsuits unlikely to be decided in their favor. Women had lost confidence in the judiciary entirely, and neither unions nor governments had the will to do anything about the situation. Employers had skulked through the end of the twentieth century discriminating with impunity.

In 2010, the European Commission published another report that analyzed the available mechanisms for reform.[14] The conclusion was that the main solution would be to move the responsibility for enforcing gender equality laws from the shoulders of individual women—and take the entire matter out of the hands of the judiciary—by returning oversight and enforcement to the governments, in much the same way that tax avoidance, bank fraud, and safety violations are monitored and prosecuted.[15] There would be regulations, a reporting requirement, an office that monitored compliance, a force of people tasked with periodic assessments of individual businesses, and a set of penalties. Specialist tribunals would adjudicate complaints, should they arise, and labor unions would be required to submit collective agreements for approval.

This suggestion, or some other drastic reform of the way women's employment rights are enforced, is essential if we are to make progress. All the headlines saying it will take fifty, one hundred, two hundred years to achieve equal pay are wrong: this is not a slow but automatic process; it's a long push against entrenched resistance.

Women are not paid less because they are less educated, less motivated, less ambitious, less willing to ask for more money, weaker, more cowardly, lazier, meant to be stay-at-home mothers, or any of the hundreds of "blame the women" excuses that popular culture spits out. They are paid less because hostile men, and the institutions they create, keep finding ways to frustrate gender equality.

It's time to stop pretending this isn't a fight. Women can use marches, strikes, and votes in protest—or they can turn to the one place in the world economy where *they* are in control and use that power.

10 | THE 80 PERCENT CHRISTMAS

Picture this: Women in all nations where Christmas is celebrated pledge they will spend only 80 percent of what they spent last year. They swear to continue reducing spending by the same amount every year until the gender pay gap is closed. There's a hashtag, T-shirts, buttons, bumper stickers. News coverage. Retailers, manufacturers, and economists quake in their boots.

Even a 20 percent reduction in Christmas spending sounds a big alarm. For the national economies of the West, the holiday season is extremely important. Consumer spending keeps the juices of an economy going; where Christmas is the main annual celebration, a large percentage of any year's spending occurs in the last quarter of the year. In the United States, for example, consumer spending accounts for 70 percent of GDP, of which more than a third occurs in November and December; this burst of shopping generates about US$23 billion in retail sales in department stores alone and US$60 billion in online shopping. The single category of toy sales generates about six hundred thousand jobs. Christmas shopping affects almost every sector: food, housewares, toys, jewelry, perfume, clothing, consumer services, travel, beverages, electronics, books—you know the rest.

As they say, Christmas happens only once a year. You get the money or you don't—there's no making up for the loss in the next quarter. A

20 percent slowdown in consumer spending during the holiday season is enough to throw the Western economies completely off track. To illustrate: from year to year, growth in holiday shopping of 2 to 4 percent is considered the sign of a healthy U.S. economy; anything less keeps businesses awake at night.[1]

Now imagine: Just as the West has caught its breath from the Christmas shock, the world's women are gearing up for the 80 percent Chinese New Year. The Lunar New Year is the biggest holiday in the world. In 2018, roughly US$142 billion was spent in China alone. The Chinese economy depends increasingly on consumer spending for growth; a decline of 8.5 percent in 2018 spending for the Lunar New Year had economists wringing their hands.[2] Think what a 20 percent drop would do.

Ramadan, another holiday with big economic impact, comes in the spring. Then, in the fall, there's Diwali—the mother of all festivals in India's festival-based economy. At the end of the year, the women's action trajectory would come full circle back to Christmas, where the spending will now be 80 percent of 80 percent. The whole action is orchestrated by social media, something the women of the world proved they could do with the Women's March in 2017.

None of these holidays would happen if women did not make and buy all the things needed to pull them off. The spending is totally under their control.[3] It's a slam dunk.

Consumption is an area of the economy that is often overlooked or undersold by both economists and feminists. But the purchase decisions that affect consumption drive the economy with a similar impact to investment decisions, and no one has more control over those choices than women. In Western Europe and North America, women control upwards of 75 percent of consumer spending. Boston Consulting Group calculates that the market represented by women's spending worldwide is three times China's GDP and six times India's—the two most populous countries on the planet.[4] This is the one part of economic life where the Double X Economy rules. Why is this power being wasted?

I think it's because the women's movement long ago bought into a production-centric view of economics. This is a male-oriented approach that says making stuff is important but buying stuff—because it's a girl thing—is not. We have lost sight of the power that buying has over the economy—and women have only recently come to control it.

In the early twentieth century, Western women were already depicted as consumers in magazines, but in reality, men still controlled household budgets. By the 1960s, women had more autonomy to decide purchases and so began to wield greater influence in selecting purchases from household product categories, such as laundry detergents, household cleaners, food, and clothing for the whole family. The husband would give his wife an allowance to buy goods for the home at her own discretion, but he still had the final say about luxuries and major purchases. As women began to work for pay, however, female consumers gained authority over a growing purse and a widening array of goods. Today, women in the West still buy household necessities, but they also influence or control purchases of big-ticket items and luxury goods—much of the time buying them outright.

Gaining the ability to make decisions about household buying was a major milestone for women. We can see why by looking closely at the women who still lack that power. The impact of many women's economic empowerment interventions in developing countries is measured by the change in women's ability to influence household decision-making, especially for big-ticket purchases. My own preference is to measure whether the woman can buy small luxuries for herself. Here is the story of how I came to think of that as a better question.

Laurel Steinfield, my doctoral student, and I had been struggling to find a way to assess where items such as sanitary pads stood in the pecking order of Ugandan family purchases. One morning, in the truck on the way to the field to do focus groups, we had an inspiration. With our colleagues from the NGO Plan International to advise us, we stopped at the market to purchase a basket of goods we thought would represent a spectrum of uses and users: daily necessities, treats, infrequent purchases, frequent purchases, objects for men and for women, objects given to or used for children, sugar, spices, and perishable or nonperishable food. We took all that loot to our first focus group of the day.

A mix of men and women were sitting at a long table in an abandoned school. We put everything we had brought in front of the group, and then we asked them to arrange everything on a spectrum of "necessity" to "luxury." Bemused, they began to rearrange the products, and before long a lineup began to appear. When they got to the luxury end of the spectrum, the group began to argue softly. The contested items? Beer, batteries, a SIM card, toilet soap, a hair extension, facial cream, and, interestingly, sanitary pads.

The next task was to order frequent and infrequent purchases. At the "frequent" end were paraffin, salt, sugar, and cooking oil, along with beer, batteries, and phone cards. On the "infrequent" end were rice (a special-occasion food in Uganda), toilet soap, spices, candy, facial cream, and a hair extension. Roughly in the middle, next to the vegetables, were the sanitary pads.

Laurel and I exchanged an "aha!" glance, and I spontaneously asked the group to pull out items that men thought were necessary but women did not. At this point, they really began having a lot of fun, frequently bursting into laughter. The objects chosen were beer, batteries, a phone card, and a soft drink. Okay, I said, let's do items women think are necessary but men don't.

The men and the women looked at each other and smiled knowingly, as if to say, "Now comes the real fight." The women went straight to the objects of dispute, dropping them in the middle of the table with a thump of defiance. The whole table laughed out loud. Four objects stood for review: toilet soap, facial cream, sanitary pads, and the hair extension.

We used our new "grocery method" with more focus groups all that week, doing some with mixed groups and some with same-sex groups. Along the way, we took some objects out, and we added red lipstick. We learned a lot.

The determining factor for all the choices was that the man of the house controlled spending. In this community, most of the women did not work away from home, while the men commuted to a small town nearby. The men were paid in cash, while the women bartered goods among themselves. The men, therefore, always had coins and bills, while the women had only the cash that their husbands gave them to buy "necessities"—or what passed as "necessary" by male estimation.

None of the women knew how much her husband earned or how much money he might have squirreled away somewhere. Nor did they know what we discovered: that at midday he bought a meal of rice and meat, foods she and the children very seldom ate, and he washed it down with a soft drink. Occasionally, he would use whatever money he had left in the evenings to treat the kids, and sometimes his wife, to a soda and candy. Of course, being the only one who can give a gift is an expression of power, and wives could never treat the children at all. As for phone cards, they were considered necessary items for men who went to town for work. Batteries were for "his" radio. He also needed shiny new shoes and good-looking clothes for working in town, while clothes for the women were not considered a necessity.

To a person, every woman we interviewed insisted that her husband did not drink beer except when another man treated him. Yet the men, when they were in a same-sex group, admitted to drinking every evening. They also said they paid in rounds with a different man paying each night, so that all but one of them could go home and honestly say he had been treated by another man to beer. Over time, each man's bill averaged out to be several dollars a week; the households in this community made about two dollars a day. But the men explained that the beer-drinking ritual was part of being a man, and that you really could not refuse to participate.

I understood this completely—such rituals are common among humans—but it irked me because of the ongoing controversy about sanitary pads. NGO workers could be pretty high and mighty in those days about how frivolous sanitary pads were, always insisting that they were too expensive for these poor households. But once we learned about the money being spent on beer, I began asking the NGO people if they knew about it. They all did, of course. Though they did not know exactly how much was being spent, they knew it was probably significant, in proportion to the income levels. No one had ever spoken to the men about whether these expenditures were appropriate. We had learned by this time that most girls could get by on a packet of pads that cost a dollar a month—versus *at least* ten dollars a month for beer. The men, when speaking in their own groups, admitted they knew the schoolgirls needed the pads, but no one ever talked to them about it because the topic was taboo. This silence enabled them to "play dumb" and ignore the issue altogether.

In fact, all the toiletries were problematic for the women. In rural parts of the developing world, people use the same soap for everything. In Africa, it's a narrow blue bar of about twelve inches long. You slice it like a sausage and use it to wash the floor, the dishes, your baby, or your face. It's harsh, which is why the women value toilet soap so much—both the soap and the face cream make their skin feel and look better. Their explanations were poignant. Using such products made them feel like a human being, not a work animal. When someone gave them soap or cream, they felt recognized as a person of dignity. The women said that if they could have hair extensions all the time, they would choose to do so, but they usually only had them for special occasions like weddings, funerals, and Easter, and then only if their husbands gave them the hairdressing session as a gift.

The red lipstick was a lightning rod. We used it for an exercise where we would assemble five or six items and then ask the group to tell us what kind of person would own the things they saw. The men always identified the red lipstick, especially as paired with face cream, toilet soap, and a phone card, as belonging to an urban prostitute. In one particularly vocal mixed-sex group, one of the women pushed back and charged, laughing, that men said only prostitutes wore makeup so that they didn't have to buy it for their wives. The other women laughed and nodded—and so did the men.

One group of women, high up in the mountains where the people are very poor and there isn't much of anything to buy, said they admired the woman with the red lipstick, face cream, phone cards, and toilet soap. When I asked why, they answered that she had bought those things herself, with her own money, and she respects herself enough to buy the things that make her look nice. How does she make her money? I prodded. She's empowered, they said emphatically; she has her own business. But is she a good mother? I asked. Does she take good care of her children? Yes, they answered, she buys things for herself only after the children have what they need. It was clear from their expressions that this line of questioning had touched a nerve—these respondents neither had lipstick nor felt empowered.

Ever since that fieldwork, I have put questions about women's freedom to buy their own face cream and toilet soap into my economic empowerment research. The answers cut right to the heart of the inequality between men and women.

These focus groups in Uganda further illustrated that the person with the power to decide what the household buys will, in the process of choosing, enable some habits and discourage others, give some family members what they need to develop and frustrate the dreams of others. This is the person who sets aside funds for education or pisses them away on beer. Purchase decisions determine, in a fundamental way, what a community will become. Whoever is the one doing the provisioning affects a community's future, directly and forcefully. In these focus groups, the man decided, and he would often put more value on his own pleasures than he did on expenditures that would benefit his developing children.

We observed similar issues in our work on the rural distribution system designed by CARE Bangladesh. In this situation, the power to purchase is mediated by access to cash, as well as mobility, as the would-be shoppers are not allowed to leave their home. CARE drew the saleswomen from the extreme poor and gave them the name *aparajita*, which means "woman who will not accept defeat." The system itself is called Jita.

The economic development team who devised the system negotiated with local and international businesses to let women sell small packages of things, including shampoo, laundry detergent, soap, and toothpaste. They also carried phone cards, vegetable seeds, and packaged snacks. The core idea, as described earlier, was to create employment for the aparajitas by sending them into the compounds where married women were secluded and make it possible for them to buy things from the bag the aparajitas carried. The project was the brainchild of two young

Muslim men with training in marketing and economics, Saif Al Rashid and Asif Ahmed, who are two of the most dedicated feminists I know.

As the aparajitas sold products to the women in seclusion, they learned what was most desired and most difficult for their customers to come by. One of the first things, as you might guess, was sanitary pads. The women wanted them, but the men, on whom they depended to buy everything, would not be caught dead buying sanitary pads. The women in the compounds also wanted a contraceptive that they could take without the men knowing. (It is possible to buy oral contraceptives without a prescription in Bangladesh.) And they wanted bras.

The aparajitas began to change what was in their bag of goods. They continued to bring the usual things, as well as those items their customers requested, but they also added little items they thought might delight and surprise. Sometimes, at the end of an interview, we would ask the aparajita whether she would show us the contents of her bag right at that moment. They were usually happy to comply, and it was fun for everyone. There were hair ornaments and little sachets of fragrance. My favorite was a strawberry condom.

But the aparajitas were also selling one item that had the potential to bring the whole system crashing down. Unilever, a supplier to Jita, provided the aparajitas with Fair & Lovely, the world's best-selling brand of skin lightener. The system was already crossing a line by having poor people sell things for businesses, as well as by selling consumer products, which Westerners often broad-brushed as "stuff the poor don't need." Jita was working very well to alleviate poverty, and it could be scaled up to help thousands, but Western writers and donors can be shockingly judgmental about what poor women are "allowed" to have.

The morality of consumption—who should have what, what things are forbidden, and what can or cannot be displayed—varies greatly from place to place, as does the very notion of what is a necessity and what is a luxury. Volumes have been written about these judgments, the best in my view being Mary Douglas and Baron Isherwood's *The World of Goods*.[5] In the West, press and donors (and government officials and some old-style NGO people) act like we can all agree on what is a moral or immoral product. I know people who think cosmetics are immoral and even some who claim they're an addiction, like drugs or alcohol. Personally, I am a lot more offended by guns, yet I grew up in Texas, where people think it is their moral and civic right to own as many guns as they want. The global health community considers itself on a moral crusade to dispense condoms as widely as possible. Yet many Catholics throughout the world still think condoms are immoral.

I was humiliated one day in Malaysia after I made a judgmental remark about skin-whitening creams. The woman who humbled me said, in front of other people, that there was no difference between skin lighteners and tanning creams. Embarrassed, I realized that she was right, and never objected again. Clearly, the global community does not have a consensus on what is a moral product, and it probably never will.

The same is true of what is deemed "necessary." Usually the obvious necessities in people's minds are the things Douglas and Isherwood refer to as "those we have in common with livestock," dismissing the assumption as a "grossly veterinary approach."[6] But reducing people's needs to what is strictly necessary to stay alive is dehumanizing. In that kind of world, we would have no music or books or art, for instance, because you do not need them to stay alive in the same way that a cow needs food. One might argue, however, that these are things that "make us human" or "make life worth living." When you are doing work that provisions a community, you need to think beyond cattle feed.

Some of the fortunate assume the poor are so focused on survival that they don't notice these more "superfluous" things. Or maybe we think the poor suffer so horribly that they can no longer be moved by beauty. Or maybe—and I fear this is the truth—we think the poor should focus only on survival and have no right to pretty things. We underestimate the positive effect on humans that pretty things have, as well as the large impact small objects of beauty can have in an otherwise difficult life.

Despite their poverty, even the world's most marginalized people still feel and want pleasure, still have a taste for adventure, and still have a sense of humor. The worst thing that can happen in an impoverished place is for the people to fall into despair. At that point, it becomes extremely difficult to help them because they have lost the desire to help themselves. When you see they are still experiencing joy and pleasure, when they can still laugh and enjoy trying new things, you know that their humanity and hope are intact.

As the Jita staff watched their system roll out across Bangladesh, they noticed something poignant. The women normally wore shades of blue. The Jita staff explained to us that the men bought all the fabric for these women's clothes, and blue was their preference. However, as the aparajitas established themselves, the color palette of their clothes changed from blues to a spectrum of colors and patterns—enough for the NGO to notice. The women were, for the first time, choosing their own clothing and so were able to express their identities where there was once only a message about control.

Knowing that the Jita staff had observed that change, we asked about clothing in our interviews with the customers. We saw a marked difference between the younger and older respondents. The younger ones asserted that they dressed to please themselves rather than their husbands, while the older ones said they dressed only for their spouses. One young woman said her favorite color was black. "It looks smart," she said. "Black goes with everything, can be dressed up or down, and is good any time of the year." She sounded like the fashion editor of a glossy magazine. I asked her about a pair of trendy shoes under her clothes rack. She said shoes were her favorite fashion item. Sound familiar? This won't: when she goes out in her burka, the shoes are the only way she can express herself.

Though it had not been common to see women in burkas in Bangladesh, they became more visible as conservatives pushed women to cover up what they saw as the rising immodesty of the clothes underneath. (Has there ever been a culture where old men did not think young women were dressing immodestly?) Some responded in amusing but pointed ways. Instead of wearing a dark monotone burka, one young wife made herself a sky blue one and bought a pair of matching shoes. Apparently her husband loves her in sky blue and he was delighted. She was inspired to make several more, each in a different color, with shoes to match. Her styling was a flippant retort to the mullahs.

The Bangladeshis are especially fond of color and pattern. They paint their trucks and rickshaws as if for a carnival. In the Jita villages, most of the homes were very austere, made of corrugated metal on a concrete slab with wooden beams. But the support beams for the metal roof and walls always had a pattern. Sometimes it was a vine; sometimes, a diamond shape. Occasionally, the residents painted them a pretty color. The grilles on the windows were often a bright shade, like turquoise. A red circular design with a flower in the center appeared often on the floors just inside. I thought that it might be a religious symbol, but I was assured that it was there only because it is thought to be pretty.

Through the example of Jita, we can see how consumption not only expresses but also is formative of identity, morality, and aesthetics. We can see a single category, dress, being used to express disapproval, conformity, ownership, and loyalty, as well as rebellion and even flippancy. We have people building environments for themselves that don't just keep the rain off but also lift their spirits. Here again, often the person who buys has a disproportionate impact on how things look, how they are kept, whether a family member conforms or rebels, and so on. That person is usually the keeper of culture and family; in Bangladesh, it's the men who have that influence.

But as a country shifts from low income to high income, women take on more and more of the provisioning role. Figure 29 shows the percentage of consumption controlled by women along with GDP per capita.[7] As countries get richer, women command more of the spending. In the developed markets, women punch above their weight on consumer spending. Even though they earn less, women spend much more, because they use family funds to buy things for children and men. So, it's not appropriate to think of women's spending on clothing, for example, as covering only the things they buy for themselves. Women buy nearly all the children's clothing and a great percentage of the clothing men wear, too. The same applies to other purchases, from food to sports equipment.

Women actually control the purse strings for many market segments that may appear to be independent. For example, marketers make a big deal out of the "youth market," but while adolescents certainly have more say in what they wear or eat than toddlers do, their mothers are usually the ones who approve the purchase, pay the bill, and place whatever restrictions there will be on the object's use.

WOMEN, CONSUMPTION, AND NATIONAL WEALTH

	GDP per capita (thousands of US$)	Consumer spending controlled by women (%)
U.S.	46	73
CANADA	37.9	75
U.K.	37	67
GERMANY	36	70
FRANCE	34	71
SPAIN	33	60
JAPAN	32	63
ITALY	32	57
CHINA	7	50

FIGURE 29. Women tend to have more control over consumer spending as GDP per capita rises.

Sources: Michael J. Silverstein and Kate Sayre, "The Female Economy," *Harvard Business Review*, September 2009, for consumer spending; World Bank Database for GDP per capita

Yet women still purchase less than men in some categories. Men buy and smoke many more cigarettes than women do, and they also buy more alcohol. Women are much less likely to blow money in casinos. This is why women's economic empowerment helps children, and it is also the reason that the commonplace belief that men are more rational buyers is patently absurd.

Buying for larger social purposes, such as choosing "green" or fair-trade products, has become much more important in the past two decades, and women are considerably more likely to buy according to such social and environmental goals than are men. Evidence suggests that they are also very keen to buy in support of other women. Cause-related marketing campaigns, such as the one Pampers and UNICEF did on maternal and neonatal tetanus, are mostly aimed at women,[8] and some of them have been extremely successful. I think this socially proactive spending suggests women could be organized along consumption lines, perhaps more productively than through strikes and other traditional protest measures, and with more impact.

In 2017, there was a general strike for women's rights in the United

States, in which women were asked to stay home from work to protest the Trump administration's attitudes toward women's rights. But a strike doesn't work for women because they are not present in the economy in the way that men are. Many are at home, and most of those who work are clustered into industries where their coworkers are also female. Women are disproportionately in jobs that are insecure and so are more vulnerable to being fired.

The organizers of the "Day Without a Woman" strike suggested that women who didn't work outside the home should not do care work that day. Yet there is no way women were going to refuse to care for children, especially small ones, for even one day. And who would notice, really, if they didn't sweep the kitchen floor one time? That idea also presumed that everyone was in a heterosexual relationship, so those who suffered would be male. It also assumed that no striker's male partner was on her side, which seems out of touch. There were lots of stories in the news that quoted women saying they did not feel they could strike because it would only shift their workload onto other women. One response illustrated perfectly why strikes don't fit women the way they do men: a woman said she had watched her mother fight for the right to work, so she did not feel right striking against it.[9]

Seeking an impact through consumption, like the 80 percent Christmas strategy, could be far more effective. Purchases are usually done solo, so there is less chance of being observed and enduring retaliation. Everyone can participate. Few of us will be hurt by spending a little less for a holiday. Most companies want to steer away from anything that gets them in trouble with female consumers. But they sometimes forget that they have women among both their target market *and* their workforce. Let's remind them.

11 | MONEY BULLIES

had been engaged for weeks in a struggle of wills with the curators
of the coin collection at the Ashmolean Museum in Oxford. We were
planning the 2014 Power Shift Forum for Women in the World Economy, and the theme was finance. The opening reception was to be held
in the anteroom of the Ashmolean coin exhibit, and the curators were
to give a guided tour of the display. What I wanted was for them to talk
about women's inclusion in the money system.

The curators were first flummoxed by my request, then insulted. Nu-
mismatics, they harrumphed, does not study such "political" questions.
Politely, I pointed out that the exhibit spoke of kings, conquests, and
economic policies. Weren't those "political"? No, that was just history, I
was told. Smiling to soothe me, they asked again if it wouldn't be nicer
just to show the Power Shift ladies the lovely coins with goddesses on
them.

Silence about women is typical in disciplines where the scholars
remain almost all male. Anthropologists ignored women as a topic of
study until the 1970s, as did archaeologists until females entered their
discipline and asked the "political" question. Historians used to write
as if the only things that mattered were kings and war. So I knew it was
possible that the omission of women from the historical record of the

financial system could be just another of those blind spots. This time, however, I had another theory.

Everywhere in the real world, it seemed, I was observing a deeply rooted moral attitude that insisted money was off-limits for women. Ideologies claiming women couldn't or shouldn't manage money were remarkably consistent across cultures, were virtually unchanged from village lenders to venture capitalists, and echoed uncannily what I had seen in my mother's and grandmother's generations. And the practical barriers hardly varied at all. I concluded that every population of women I studied—from nineteenth-century housewives to the women in the compounds of Bangladesh to female entrepreneurs in London— was being excluded from the money system as a whole, and not just from paid work or the top jobs.

The gulf between women and the financial system became highly visible in the early 2000s with the rise of microfinance, a practice that makes very small loans available to the very poor. Muhammad Yunus, a Bangladeshi banker, had won the Nobel Peace Prize for this innovation in 2006. The main customers for microcredit were, and are, poor females in developing countries. From the beginning, despite the fact that these lenders charged extortionate interest rates, women rushed to microfinance, largely because they couldn't get credit from any other source. The women used loans in prosocial ways, producing measurable benefits to families and communities, as they virtually always do.

Global charities began setting up microfinance programs. There were a lot of problems, however. One of the first and most troublesome was the violent backlash from men in villages where microcredit was introduced: any bank that loaned money directly to females was a threat to male dominance. Men often expropriated the cash women borrowed, refused to pay it back, and enforced their decision through violence. Since that time, it has become standard practice to have a domestic violence response plan in place for a program involving financial inclusion for women.

Even though the microloans were small, some women fell into debt spirals because of the astronomical interest rates of 25 to 50 percent or more. To the world community, the risk of over-indebtedness seemed to demonstrate the inherent corruption of the banking system and also to underscore a commonly held belief about women—that they are incapable of financial responsibility.

Worldwide, men and boys consistently score higher than women and girls on financial literacy tests, even after specialized instruction, which usually leads researchers to conclude that there is something about females (perhaps "inferior" brains) that makes them less able to absorb financial information. However, it is crucial to remember that cultural practices have an impact on the life skills developed by males and females especially through the process of building the connectome. Males usually have more experience with financial issues, even at a young age, precisely because females' access to the money system is often severely restricted. Boys are brought up with the expectation they will deal with money and are often involved in business matters at an early age in a way that girls are not. Girls have fewer opportunities for informal learning when it comes to money, and sometimes believe weird ideas like "money is dirty," a mantra I have heard repeated by Bangladeshi women, feminist theorists, and my own grandmother.

Proof that familiarity with money may be more effective than special instruction is offered by the NGOs' experience with women's savings groups, which have been set up in impoverished areas since the mid-1990s. The procedure is as follows: A group of women meets periodically, in a females-only private space. Each deposits a small amount of money into a lockbox. As the pool of cash grows, they make decisions about what to do with the funds, without men to interfere or take the money away. The groups I have known set aside part of the funds for emergencies, and they keep a portion for community needs, such as supporting HIV orphans. The balance is loaned out to members of the group to use in income-generating projects, like raising chickens or making saris. Interest is charged for the loans, usually at a high rate (20 percent or so), though not as high as the rate charged by microlenders.

At the end of a year, the usual practice is to liquidate everything and pay each member a share of money earned by the group, so that every woman benefits from the others' success. With the advent of microfinance, the women could also borrow money from formal institutions and repay it with the income from their investments. Despite the high interest, the repayment rates for these loans have been 98 percent or more, which is an exceptionally creditworthy result.

NGOs encouraged women's savings groups because the benefits were immediately clear: as the women's income increases, families get better nutrition, children are more often in school, and housing improves. All these outcomes reduce poverty. We can infer from this record, consistent across groups and countries, that women *are* capable of acquiring financial acumen when they are allowed to have money and experience managing it themselves. Women also report having increased self-confidence, as well as feeling more valued in their households, as a result of being involved in savings groups, which foster a sense of sisterhood, too.

Educational differences among the women, however, sometimes make the process unequal. For instance, I observed one group in which there were two teachers and a woman who had never been to school. One teacher opened a bank account for the group, and both teachers would discuss the monthly statements with the other members, but the unschooled woman, being both illiterate and innumerate, was unable to grasp what was going on. She became caught in a debt spiral and felt alienated from the group, losing trust in them because she could not understand either the financial consequences of her borrowing or the explanation of the banking statements.

Another group chose as their leader the only woman among them who had a middle school education. She decided to conduct all transactions in cash, because the women who had no schooling were able to understand coins and bills. By keeping all transactions in a concrete form, she maintained the trust within the group.

These two examples illustrate that the basic educational exclusions women have endured have lifetime effects on their financial literacy that cannot be resolved by a specialized course. Methods must be adapted to fit their circumstances.

In the past five years, NGOs have been under pressure from their donors to increase the number of people in savings groups. Their response has been to assemble mixed-sex groups, but unfortunately, men often try to take over, demand larger loans, don't pay their loans back, and expect lower interest rates or none at all. They often refuse to set aside money for emergencies—a very important practice for communities that live on the edge—and are reluctant to use money for charitable goals like helping orphans. The men engage in riskier financial behavior, but insist that women don't know anything about business. The loss of privacy from accepting men into saving groups can be devastating. Being able to save money privately is the single most urgent financial need of women in poor rural communities. If men are in the room, the women may as well be conducting their business in a fishbowl.

The first of the mixed-sex groups I visited had only two men. When I walked in, the women were seated on the floor with their shoes off, while the two men were sitting in the only chairs with their shoes on. Sitting in a chair and leaving your shoes on indoors are both indications of status in the everyday etiquette of the rural poor. The men led the meeting, looking through each woman's savings book before recording the day's transactions, with the women looking up at them from the floor and obediently answering questions.

I could quickly see that the key factors leading to the success of women's savings groups had disappeared with the admission of just two men. Privacy over the transactions, group solidarity, independent decision-making, female dignity, and an open atmosphere free from male bullying had all vanished. By arbitrarily demanding an increase in numbers without understanding the gender dynamics, the donor had compromised the most effective poverty alleviation device of the past thirty years.

I did observe an exception, however. One mixed-sex group, part of a network organized by CARE International, made financial decisions in a respectful, collaborative way, and—probably as a result—their financial gains outstripped every other group in the network. Married men and women in the group told me that the other villagers envied their marriages because they were free of violence. The men tried to tell other males that the respectful ethic for managing finances had reduced tension in their homes, but their buddies did not want to risk their dominance by adopting a new attitude. Despite this exceptional group's performance, however, CARE stopped organizing mixed-sex groups in the area; the predatory financial behavior of men overall had been too destructive.

Another key lesson of the past decade is that women's economic empowerment must not stop at helping them earn—the women must also be able to hold the money securely and privately, in order to control how it is spent. If the women do not have control, you cannot expect to see poverty reduction from their constructive spending. Instead, the money goes to the men and, because it feels "free" or like found money to them, it is more likely to be spent frivolously.

Unfortunately, banks make it difficult for women to save money. I came to understand how financial institutions restrict women's control over their earnings through a project in Uganda I am doing, also with CARE, which is funded by the Bill and Melinda Gates Foundation. This project is testing two interventions: a mobile banking service designed to give women control over their own money, and a family counseling course designed to equalize their participation in household decisions. The theory behind this project is that by making it possible for women to control their own money or have more input at the household level, there will be an increase in poverty-fighting outcomes.

Attitudes and practices within banks, however, made implementation of the project difficult. Until recently, Ugandan banks would not open an account in a woman's name unless her male next of kin accompanied her to give his permission. Though this rule has been legally changed, the banks continued to make women's financial inclusion difficult. For instance, they still demanded documentation such as birth certificates before opening the account; often females are not even recorded at birth. In fact, women's restricted access to formal IDs is a major barrier for their economic inclusion all over the world. Getting proof of identity requires poking around your home village asking if anybody remembers when you were born. Of course, if what you are trying to do is set up an account so only you can access the money, asking everybody to vouch for your identity lets the cat out of the bag. To make matters worse, the bank sometimes requires a letter of approval from the local chief, who usually feels morally obligated to tell the husband his wife is opening a bank account—but he does not feel the same obligation to inform the wife when her husband opens an account. All this means that the normal process of opening a bank account counteracts the goal of maintaining private control over funds, instead helping male heads of household maintain total power by controlling money.

To complicate matters, rural areas have so few banks that the distance from the villages is a barrier, especially because the women often have to walk. Since women need permission to leave home, they cannot go to a bank without the male head of their household knowing.

Mobile banking access offers a potential solution. The technology closes the distance to a bank and offers a better chance at privacy. Women can deposit or remove funds from small kiosks close by. But women are much less likely to have a phone (not thought "necessary" for them), and the registration still requires identification. However, if money could be deposited through the savings group, privacy and control could be achievable. And if a woman did not have her own phone, she could access her account by borrowing one from another member. That is why we delivered both interventions through the savings groups—with their permission, of course.

While the mobile banking intervention is intended to grant women independence and privacy, we hope that the family counseling will achieve the same ends by instilling a more collaborative family environment. The course is intended to persuade the male head of household to include his wife as an equal partner in decision-making and recognize her goals as equally important to his.

Women in the villages where we are working customarily give all their cash earnings to husbands. Men then give back an allowance for daily "necessities" (like vegetables but not toilet soap), while they deal with the rest of the money as they please and usually do not report how it is spent. When we came in, we found that most men already had bank accounts, but many wives did not. Men told us they used the funds for their personal needs. The women also usually did not know that their husbands had bank accounts, what they earned, or whether they had any savings. Wives were left with no idea whether their family had provisions for an emergency. So they surreptitiously withheld a little cash when they paid their husbands and then hid it as best they could. If the husband found his wife's hidden cash, he often simply took it.

Plenty of women had abusive husbands, alcoholic husbands, or husbands on the verge of desertion and desperately needed a way to privately store as much money as possible. From any perspective, there were legitimate and even urgent reasons for women to control money privately, but the prevailing morality held that women should not be allowed do this.

You can imagine how vulnerable these women felt—and how vulnerable they actually were. A woman who did not know the status of her household's finances would worry about an unforeseen disaster and try to save against it, whether or not her husband was a drunk or a philanderer. The women also knew that if their husbands died, they would be vulnerable to the subsequent horror of property confiscation and wife inheritance.

By including standard psychological scales in our research, we learned that women who were in the dark about their husband's money were far more likely to be anxious and depressed than women who knew.[1] Predictably, women were overall more likely than men to suffer from anxiety and depression. Men scored much higher than women on the Pearlin Mastery Scale, which measures a person's belief that they can affect their own destiny.[2] Most importantly, however, women who had their own income stream, bank account, and mobile phone had a greater sense of mastery, as well as less depression and anxiety, than women who did not have these things. These results showed we were moving in the right direction by revealing the emotional distress that unfair financial arrangements produce and by demonstrating that steps to empower women economically could reverse that impact.

We also assessed the impact of patriarchal beliefs.[3] People of either sex who agreed that men should dominate institutions and governments were less likely to believe in their own ability to affect their future. Even though men were far more likely than women to believe in this kind of patriarchal dominance, they were just as vulnerable to feeling disempowered by the system. Women were less likely to share the patriarchal beliefs, but were more negatively affected by them.

While I was doing this work in Uganda, other fieldwork showed me how these basic family and institutional practices built into a formidable barrier for women who own small or medium-sized businesses. In 2017, I evaluated activities related to women's entrepreneurship carried out under a World Bank investment lending operation in Moldova, an Eastern European country that was once part of the Soviet Union.[4] Other studies I reviewed in preparation suggested that Moldovan men were controlling the assets of their households, regardless of where those assets came from, and making all the financial decisions except for those involving small household purchases, despite the fact that Moldovan law held that household assets were jointly owned.

The most telling evidence of these family financial practices was the fate of the property awards made by the Moldovan government at the time the Soviet Union failed. In Moldova's "privatization" process, land had been divided equally among men and women as individuals. At the time, the World Bank had expressed concern that females were disadvantaged in this attempt at equitable distribution because of their more limited knowledge of land rights. Furthermore, because men, as the heads of household, would have decision-making power over their wives' land, it would be difficult for married women to maintain control over the land they had been given.[5] Twenty-five years later, despite the initially equitable distribution, males own ten times more land than do females, and 90 percent of the agricultural equipment. As we have learned repeatedly in women's economic empowerment, "gender-neutral" programs end up benefiting men because they ignore the special disadvantages experienced by women.

In the evaluation I did for the World Bank, I saw that Moldovan men were increasing their wealth exponentially. Men not only owned more of Moldovan businesses but were also expanding their holdings despite their rather mediocre performance in business, as compared with women's. Male business owners were given a boost by a banking system that awarded them preferential treatment. Women-owned businesses grew more slowly, despite otherwise superior business performance, because of their restricted access to capital and the punitive terms banks offered them.

Around the world, women-owned businesses grow slowly. Cross-cultural studies of entrepreneurship frequently conclude that a major reason for women's "underperformance" is that females are reluctant to pledge family assets as collateral for business. This conclusion is invariably delivered as evidence that women are at fault for their own economic disadvantages, but none of these studies ask the obvious question: *Why* don't women pledge family assets as often as men do? Analysts conducting these studies buy into the notion that financial practices are neutral, and so are not prepared to consider that circumstances for men and women differ consistently. So any negative outcomes they find for women are thought to be caused by inherent female inferiority.

Within the financial sector, most pronouncements about women's business ability are made without any basis in evidence. A 2015 study by the Global Banking Alliance for Women, Data2X, and the Inter-American Development Bank discovered that no central bank collects sex-disaggregated data (that is, data separated by sex) about its business customers, and neither do individual banks. The banks interviewed did not believe women were either good customers or a significant part of their business. Therefore, they did not think the exercise of breaking out data by sex was worth the effort and refused to do it. Data drawn from potential customers, rather than from the banks, such as that collected by the Global Findex study, consistently shows that women are less likely to have accounts than men, though nearly everyone in developing countries remains "unbanked." The World Bank has meanwhile initiated a call for banks in developing countries to begin submitting sex-disaggregated account data; the first wave of those submissions came in during 2018.

In most Western countries, however, 1970s regulations forbid banks from having gender identification markers in their customer records. This stricture was intended to stop banks from discriminating, but fifty years later, it is clear that the regulations instead made it possible for banks to discriminate without fear of accountability. Business loan applications are initially made in person, so the loan officer *knows* when the owner is female. If the bank has no field for the sex of the applicant in its customer records, there is then no way to assess whether the overall institution is engaged in a systematic pattern of discrimination; the bank could be making 95 percent of its business loans to men, and no one would ever be the wiser.

That was the finding of a study conducted in 2014 by the U.S. Senate Committee on Small Business and Entrepreneurship.[6] Despite fifty years of supposedly gender-blind banking, the committee found that 95 percent of conventional business loans and $22 of every $23 loaned by a bank to a business went to men—in other words, men not only received more loans by a considerable measure but also got bigger loans. Women own about a third of small-to-medium businesses in the United States, generate $3 trillion annually for the U.S. economy, and employ the equivalent of 23 million people.[7] Given the sheer size of these numbers, allowing banks to starve female owners for capital must produce a powerful undertow on national growth. Getting a handle on the problem by looking at gender-disaggregated data would definitely be worth the work.

BLC Bank in Lebanon has become a favorite exemplar to show the power of gender-disaggregated customer data.[8] In 2014, this bank painstakingly pulled apart its customer records and found that women were a small but highly profitable and low-risk part of their business. Women owned about a third of all small-to-medium businesses in Lebanon but held less than 5 percent of conventional business loans. In other words, the segment was a big one but was being ignored and therefore underserved by Lebanese banks. Since no other banks in the country were trying to attract female business owners as clients, the market segment was wide open, and since the Lebanese financial market was stagnant, serving women was one of the few opportunities for the bank to grow. BLC Bank decided to go all out to become the bank of choice for women.

Assisted by the International Finance Corporation (IFC), BLC Bank did extensive market research among female business owners, including focus groups and interviews. After listening to the women explain their business needs and preferences, the bank designed and adapted products and services to suit them. For instance, Lebanese women who own businesses experience severe time poverty, meaning they wanted the bank to provide longer business hours, closer locations, and streamlined application processes.

Through this research, BLC Bank also learned that Lebanese women were sensitive about the negative way in which bankers treated them. The bank would have to communicate directly that it accepted this criticism and would treat female customers with respect. That meant the messaging to women could not be disguised as a gender-neutral communication about new products and services. Changing products to appeal to women but offering them in a "gender-neutral" way is a frequent strategy of banks, which insist they must hide gender appeals to avoid "offending" their male customers. If true, this excuse says unpleasant things about their client base, but it seems more likely that these financiers just don't want to be known as "the pink bank." It's a cowardly tactic that speaks to the central problem: the disrespect bankers consistently show for women.

Instead of hiding its intention to court women as customers behind gender-neutral imagery, BLC Bank addressed the problem head-on. The bank produced a series of humorous commercials, dramatizing the problems women usually have with banks. It retrained all its employees to avoid biased behavior and put incentives in place to reward them for recruiting female customers. In a laudable effort to walk the walk, BLC Bank also changed its personnel policies in order to increase the number of women at higher ranks within the bank. And it began posting YouTube videos in which employees acted out their own skits to teach lessons about gender discrimination in the workplace.

Not surprisingly, BLC did become the bank of choice for Lebanese women; the increase in female customers was substantial, as were the number and size of loans made and the number of accounts opened. Women usually buy all financial services from one supplier, and the new BLC customers did the same, making these female customers more profitable than male customers. The women also exhibited much lower default rates. Finally, the bank's customer surveys showed that both men and women applauded the bank's progressive steps to include women. BLC Bank had successfully captured a profitable, low-risk customer segment in a stagnant market. The only thing stopping other banks from doing the same is their own prejudice.

The unwillingness of most banks to respectfully and fairly serve female customers has important economic policy implications for international development. In a 2019 study by the World Bank, developing country banks have a $1.46 trillion gender credit gap.[9] Denying women credit blocks national growth as surely as does keeping them out of the labor force. This practice also depresses household livelihoods, with all the attendant consequences we have seen, only magnified to the tune of a trillion dollars. The Women, Business and the Law group, also at the World Bank, further reports that nations doing a better job of "banking" women have greatly improved economic stability.[10] Once again, excluding women comes at a dear price, and including them is to everyone's advantage.

Unfortunately, unsavory practices intended to scare women off are often used. A 2014 case study I wrote with Jiafei Jin from the Southwestern University of Finance and Economics in China demonstrates this reality and further illustrates how groundless bankers' justifications for excluding women can be.[11] Officers at the "Bank of Chengdu" (a pseudonym) claimed there were no women-owned businesses in their loan portfolio, except for those owned by one-child-policy heiresses who left their late fathers' businesses in the control of their fathers' male managers.[12] They claimed that women who had businesses of their own never applied for a loan, though they were not tracking who came in the door, who got fed up and left, who stayed long enough to apply, or who was rejected or approved. Despite a total lack of evidence, the bank officers could rattle off a litany of reasons why women were not good bank customers: they ask too many questions; they look too closely at interest rates; they are risk-averse; and "they have children and are therefore not serious." Since asking questions, being vigilant on interest rates, and showing caution about debt are all indicators of a creditworthy customer, it made no sense to reject female customers for these reasons.

In truth, the Bank of Chengdu had no idea whether women were good customers, because it had no experience with them. But we can't conclude that the problem here was unconscious bias, since the bankers were vocal about their prejudices and confident that their beliefs about women were true, despite the absence of evidence. They were also engaging in a social ritual that they *knew* had the effect of scaring women customers away, a ritual I was keen to expose in this study.

Months earlier, I had been in Zhejiang interviewing three female entrepreneurs who had just graduated from Goldman Sachs's 10,000 Women training program. When I first asked them about the biggest barrier to their success, they said it was training. But you have that covered now, I said, so what's the next barrier? I fully expected them to say childcare. Instead, they looked at each other, turned to me, and said, seemingly in unison, "Karaoke." Whaaaat? They explained: In order to get loans from a bank, you had to be willing to go out for long, boozy dinners with the loan officers. After dinner, the men would want to drink more and go for karaoke. After that, it got dangerous. No woman who cared about her safety, her reputation, or her marriage wanted to expose herself to this risk. It was this revelation that led me to ask Jiafei Jin about partnering on some research into banking and women.

Sure enough, the Bank of Chengdu was devoted to the karaoke ritual. Client evenings usually ended in visits to prostitutes, after which the men would take limousines home because they were too drunk to drive. The practice was expensive for the bank, and not particularly healthy for the loan officers, who were expected to do this with all their customers. Since these evenings usually occurred during the week, bankers were probably hungover during the next working day, which would have affected the accuracy of their financial work, and one can only imagine the impact on their families. The bank had few female executives as a result—how could they be part of this culture of debauchery?—and did indeed use female entrepreneurs' refusal to participate as justification for having no female customers, saying there was no way they could "build trust" with someone who would not get sloppy drunk with them.

The reality is that every financial center has its karaoke ritual. In London and New York, it's getting lap dances. In Eastern Europe, it's the sauna. Whatever the specifics, the sexually dangerous ritual used to bar women from the money system is ever present. Given these kinds of attitudes and practices, you might be able to see why offerings designed to be "women-friendly" but made available to both women and men typically do not have an impact on women's financial access: regardless of the intention, prejudicial practices make the offering more readily available to men.

When I asked the three women in Zhejiang what would make access to banks easier for them, they answered quickly and unanimously: they wanted more female bank officers. I have heard this answer many times, but it's not a likely solution because the financial sector also excludes women by barring their career advancement.

In Britain's Equal Pay Scandal of 2018, the banks' results were even worse than the airlines, the gambling houses, and the meatpackers. Not only were their gender pay gaps larger across the board, but women had even less presence in the highest-ranking, best-paid jobs in these industries. At Goldman Sachs, only 17 percent of the highest-paid quartile were female. Barclays reported that women held only 19 percent of the top-paid jobs. At HSBC, 34 percent of the highest-paid employees were female, but 71 percent of the lowest-tier jobs were held by women.[13]

Across the entire financial sector, high-ranking females are rare birds. You can probably guess that the explanation usually offered for their low representation is the "gender math gap."

In 2016, I had a direct encounter with this brain bigotry. I was working with colleagues to put together a training program for the IFC. The program would be used to persuade IFC-affiliated banks around the world to be more welcoming to female customers. In our very first conference call, the IFC representatives told us they needed "something about brain differences" to be put in the curriculum we were designing. I explained that it was now well established there were no brain differences between men and women. I thought the question was resolved, but as we proceeded to develop the course materials, they kept bringing up the matter.

Eventually, I could see that we would never close out this job if I didn't sit down to write a literature review on the topic of brain differences by sex. So I synthesized the scientific studies showing why it was no longer the expert consensus that "sexual dimorphism" in brains caused cognitive performance differences. Our clients at IFC were delighted. Only then did they explain to us that the main resistance tactic they were experiencing from bankers was an aggressive assertion that women's brains were incapable of doing math.

Another tactic is brazen sexual harassment. The treatment of women on Wall Street has led to a number of confessionals in the media about how both women and men feel about the juvenile and debased "bro talk" that typifies investment houses. Maureen Sherry, formerly a managing director at Bear Stearns, a casualty in the crash of 2008, recalled a trading-floor ritual in which a stuffed beaver was thrown overhead to any man who had a big win. Writing in a *Fortune* article called "The Brutal Truth About Being a Woman on Wall Street," she recounts, "He had been a gift, a wink, from one trader to another in admiration of a well-executed trade. Sexual connotation was the point: The guy was getting some beaver . . . The few women I worked with didn't allow themselves to feel revulsion. We all knew we were lucky to have our jobs, and the ones who didn't left."[14]

Sam Polk, in a *New York Times* article, "How Wall Street Bro Talk Keeps Women Down," says what goes on when the women are not around can be worse. He recounts going to a Brazilian steak house with a managing director and an important client, both men. When the waitress walked away from their table, the client said, "I'd like to bend her over the table, give her some meat." Sam forced a smile, but later felt furious with himself. "I was troubled by the comment, and disgusted by the man who said it . . . Why hadn't I said anything?"[15] Polk failed to speak up for the same reasons that the women grit their teeth and try to endure it: you cannot keep your job or advance if you don't tolerate this behavior.

Once again, it's the band-of-brothers "chest bump."[16] Men who participate are "liked" and generously rewarded, while men who object are punished. The most precarious men act like watchdogs, sniffing out dissent.

The bro talk reinforces the bonds between men but also acts as a signal to women that they aren't welcome, a reminder of their status as objects. In an environment like this, you can see that the women would be kept to the lowest rung. Imagine how it plays among the brothers whenever a woman is promoted—to advance a female necessarily means one of the buddies gets passed over. That can mean trouble, as the forsaken candidate may retaliate in anger. When we look at how hard it is for women to push *up* into the higher levels of finance companies, we should ask whether the brotherhood is pushing *down* against them.

The band of brothers never limits itself to terrorizing women; the forced buddy behavior is also how they keep other men in line. In summer 2018, newspapers were reporting yet another shocking incident in the financial sector. This time it was a senior banker at Credit Suisse who had a history of bullying behavior so bad that he had been barred from recruiting efforts, but he had nevertheless risen in the ranks. This time, he physically attacked a male intern and was dismissed. There had been a long series of formal complaints that Credit Suisse had chosen not to act on, allowing the man's behavior to continue unchecked. All these companies, as both Sherry and Polk point out, have showy antidiscrimination training and adopt diversity-recruiting programs, but this offensive behavior, which uses the most primitive bonds among men to keep women out, is never seriously addressed.

Institutions perpetuate this toxic environment through toothless complaint procedures. Furthermore, there is a propensity in very male-dominated environments for the bullies to rise to the top, not in spite of their behavior but because of it. Excessive aggressiveness is, after all, exactly what *makes* a man an alpha male. The guys at the top are no better—and maybe worse—than the ones on the trading floor. If they weren't admired by the brotherhood, they wouldn't be the ones in charge. The leadership often blames "thin-skinned" women for making too much of these offenses and they quash complaints with disciplinary processes that are designed to go nowhere. Many gripe about the lack of due process for males who are accused by the #MeToo movement, yet complaint procedures have denied women due process for decades.

None of this sexually inappropriate behavior counts as "unconscious bias." In the upper echelons of the financial sector, virtually everyone comes from a privileged family, went to a prestigious school, and is required in their private life to attend elite events and behave like they weren't raised by chimps. Their ability to compartmentalize tells us that the bullies know what they are doing—and they are able to shut it down when they have to. Just as wife-beaters can look like nice guys in public and be monstrous at home, bullies in the financial sector know they can get away with things at work that would be forbidden anywhere else.

This rash conduct has no place among twenty-first-century humans, never mind in the institutions that most affect the future of the world economy. Why are we letting it persist? These guys argue that the economy, the business world, and the financial sector are jungles where only the fittest can survive. By making everyone work in this bizarre environment, they say they ensure that only the best remain—as if base behavior were a proxy for merit. Often the top managers in this sector go so far as to suggest that allowing more women in would lower standards.

So what is the evidence that this band of brothers is better at finance than women? Ironically, the available data strongly suggests that the "macho" environment typical of finance reduces males' ability to make good decisions and, as a result, makes the world economy more volatile.

A significant body of research shows that men, when they are in the all-male company of the brotherhood, are prone to making reckless financial choices: they take unwise risks, become trigger-happy in trading, and fall victim to herd thinking.[17] Rising levels of testosterone and the stress hormone cortisol explain what happens: The dominance-seeking behavior of some males raises the level of testosterone across the whole group, making all of them more competitive and aggressive. The more aggressive the behavior gets, the more the testosterone ratchets upward. Each individual's need to prove he is a manly member of the brotherhood makes everything worse. The willingness or ability to mentally step outside the chaos and assess the big picture is lost. Eventually, the interaction between the hormones, the male-dominant setting, and the stress has its tested effect—it produces overconfidence and increased risk-taking, simultaneously impairing judgment and reducing the ability to make calculations that require thought, all the while dampening the inclination to control impulses or act independently. On a macro scale, this phenomenon is what makes market bubbles, which occur when stock prices are pushed above reasonable estimates of their value. Bubbles are caused by traders who are not thinking critically, but instead are just running with the herd. So the suggestion that the bro culture of Wall Street ensures excellence is ridiculous. In fact, it's frightening to think that the monetary system is being operated under these conditions.

Women also have testosterone, of course; rising levels of that hormone make them more confident, too. However, for whatever reason, the interaction between testosterone and cortisol does not impair thought and judgment in women as it does in men. And, of course, women's outsider relationship to the brotherhood excludes them from the ritual of membership. Women, therefore, are better able to keep their heads in financial trading.

Many studies of financial behavior have now connected the dots between gender behavior and financial decision-making.[18] Usually, women come out with the better record: they are more likely to do their homework, they are more realistic in their estimates of both upside and downside risk, they think more big picture and long term, they are less subject to herd influence, and they think outside the box more often.

All these factors produce better financial outcomes. It's important to note, however, that the best performances come from mixed-gender teams. The investment tendencies in males and females complement each other; gender-balanced work environments also keep unwanted brotherhood pressure from distorting decisions.

With the image of the testosterone-crazed trading floor in mind, pundits writing in the aftermath of the crash of 2008 asked rhetorically whether the collapse would have happened at all if the financial sector were dominated by females instead of males. Women who already worked in the financial sector began to question the stability and direction of the world's monetary system. These women started forming groups to brainstorm ways the financial system might be harnessed for good, especially for the benefit of women. A core concept that emerged was gender-lens investing—an investing philosophy where the goal was to support and value women.[19]

One of the leaders in developing this radical idea was Joy Anderson, who founded Criterion Institute, an organization dedicated to supporting financial innovations that benefit women. The first thing anyone hearing about "valuing gender" has to overcome is the notion that financial indicators are measures that have divine status as logical, necessary, and objective. Joy, who has a Ph.D. in history, brought the house down at Power Shift when she explained how arbitrary these measures really are: "I am a historian. I can tell you the exact dates we made that shit up."

So the task is to "make up" *new* financial indicators that reflect the realities of gender—and calculate the benefits that come from addressing those realities. An example would be that if you were rating a bond to build a municipal subway system, you would evaluate the project more positively if it had better structures to keep female commuters safe at night. Better safety for women would reduce costs attached to police and medical responses, as well as raise productivity, both of which would add financial benefits to the city's project, thereby raising the value of the investment. The concept has begun to catch on: a Gender-Smart Investing Summit in London during fall 2018 was packed to the rafters with investors wanting to adopt investment strategies that benefited women. Gender-lens investments can be selected using any number of criteria, from women's representation on boards to female-friendly product design.

The gender-lens investment approach was considered implausible until recently. But when Bloomberg tested its new Gender Equality Index in 2017, the concept had clearly moved into the mainstream. Bloomberg provides investment information to 325,000 financial institutions around the world. Its base of investors had asked it to create a gender rating system, apparently believing that the stocks of companies with better gender inclusion would outperform other indexes. Turns out, Bloomberg's investors were right.

The gender-index prototype Bloomberg initially tested was very basic, rating companies on things like the number of women on the board, the number of women in top management, and whether the company offered maternity leave. The first-year test was conducted only on financial services companies—the very institutions we are looking at in this chapter—and the outcome that year was that financial firms with better ratings on gender issues consistently outperformed their peers, but only by a small amount. However, in the years that followed, the Gender Equality Index for financial companies increasingly outperformed the Bloomberg Financial Services Index, as well as the MSCI financial indexes. By 2019, the Bloomberg Gender Equality Index was 50 percent higher than the other two (Figure 30).

In 2018, Bloomberg added data from more companies, 230 corporations that cooperated by supplying additional information. Adding these new firms allowed the index to reflect gender equality across several industries. By the third quarter of 2019, the expanded Gender Equality Index had been outperforming the MSCI World Index and the MSCI All Country World Index every month.

The Bloomberg Gender Equality Index offers something important to women's economic empowerment. Using this index, Bloomberg subscribers will be able to choose to buy individual company stocks from a gender perspective, and can watch how the gender-friendly companies as a whole perform financially. So far, the index shows a positive connection between a company's gender performance and its financial value: gender-equal companies are simply better investments than companies that are not women-friendly. Therefore, investors will be motivated to buy more stocks from companies with good gender practices, which will likely push up their stock prices—and companies that don't do well on gender will be incentivized to change their ways.

Another rising force is the influence of wealth in women's own hands. Though women still control a much smaller slice of the world's wealth than do men, changes in inheritance laws as well as women's own business successes have created a growing cache of individual wealth among females. Importantly, research shows that wealthy women are much more inclined to choose socially and environmentally responsible investments, as well as to give more to charity, than their male counterparts. They are also more attuned to the long-term impact and benefits of an investment, rather than the short-term payoffs that the financial markets have traditionally chased.

Unfortunately, women with funds to invest are chronically underserved by the financial sector. Wealth advisors consistently assume that women don't know anything about finance and have no real financial goals or plans. They present women with "safe" and "standard"

BLOOMBERG GENDER EQUALITY INDEX FOR FINANCIAL SERVICES COMPANIES VERSUS OTHER FINANCIAL INDEXES, 2016–2019

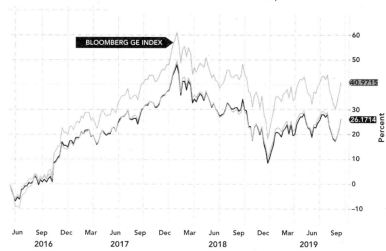

BLOOMBERG GENDER EQUALITY INDEX (ALL INDUSTRIES) VERSUS COMPARABLE INDEXES, 2019 (YEAR ONE)

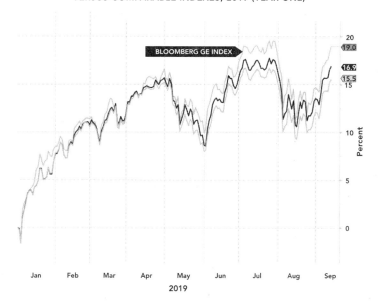

investment options, holding back more innovative vehicles. They insult women of wealth by communicating with their husbands, even when a portfolio belongs to the wife. The advisors also underestimate women in subtle ways, such as referring to a portfolio as "family wealth" even when the woman earned the money herself.[20]

Sexist financial advice is also hurting national economies. Research conducted by Sylvia Ann Hewlett and Andrea Turner Moffitt among six thousand wealthy individuals in the United States, the U.K., India, China, Hong Kong, and Singapore showed that women were so unhappy with financial advisors that a very large percentage were working without one. A great many of these women were, as a result, leaving their money in cash rather than investing it.[21]

If a significant portion of wealth in women's hands is lying around in cash rather than invested, it reduces their country's ability to grow its economy, to create jobs, and to support innovation. Given the higher propensity women have for investing in firms with a positive social and environmental impact, this problem also reduces the resources available to combat intractable problems. Even the wealth management companies would earn more money if only they would treat women with respect. Instead, by clinging to their gender prejudices, they choose an economically irrational course that hurts women, hurts their country, and hurts their own pocketbooks.

FIGURE 30. (opposite) The top graph shows the performance of financial services companies included in the Bloomberg Gender Equality Index from 2016 to 2019, as compared to two other indexes that monitor financial services companies, the MSCI World Financials Index and the MSCI All Country World Financials Index. The Gender Equality Index performed slightly better than the other two for the first year, then began to outperform them dramatically about mid-2017. The gap between the Gender Equality Index and the comparative indexes widened for the next two years until the Gender Equality Index was clearly delivering superior returns.

In the bottom graph, we see the new, expanded Gender Equality Index performing during the first three quarters of 2019. As with the trial version that included only financial services companies, the Gender Equality Index is showing a slightly better result compared to other, similar indexes in its first year.

Source: Bloomberg Finance L.P., 2019

Both men and women in Hewlett and Moffitt's study expressed a desire to invest their wealth in a way that had a positive impact on society, as well as to support organizations with diverse leadership. This is the same impulse that is driving demand for indexes that reflect positive social, environmental, and gender behavior from companies. It's encouraging that so many people want to engage with the investment world in a positive way, rather than just seeking to make profits any way they can.

These trends indicate the potential for radically changing the spirit of the global economy. As responsible investing continues to outperform the old rape-and-pillage approach, as more investors demand opportunities to make sustainable investments, and as international institutions work to insinuate a different gender ethic into finance, we can hope the financial world will outgrow its Genghis Khan mentality.

12 | OWNING IT

Fear of the Nazis made Vera's Austrian parents send their five-year-old daughter to Great Britain in the Kindertransport, the "orphan train" that brought roughly ten thousand children to safety just before the outbreak of World War II. These young refugees were raised in ordinary homes and, by the end of the war, were often the only survivors in their families.

Vera, like so many other young evacuees, remained in England and built a life there. She was interested in mathematics from an early age, but since the girls' school she attended taught neither math nor science, she obtained special permission to go to a boys' school for instruction. She chose not to attend university because botany was the only science women could study, and she was not especially interested in that. Instead, she went to work for the Post Office Research Station at Dollis Hill in London, where she, the lone female among two thousand programmers, built computers from scratch and wrote code in machine language. "When I first started, I was patronized, as women were, but when I began to make it clear that I was pursuing a vigorous professional career, then it became a more entrenched position to keep me out."[1] She went to night school for a degree in mathematics and, at age eighteen, became a British citizen and changed her name to Stephanie.

Stephanie was forced by her employer to quit her job when she married a physicist, Derek Shirley. Though she managed to find new work for herself, she hated seeing other talented women around her being pushed out because of marriage or pregnancy, too. One fateful day in 1959, she decided to do something about this unfair and wasteful practice and used £6 to found "freelance programmers" (a company name she would always have printed in lowercase, because the enterprise had no capital), a new kind of company where women could be wives and mothers, as well as software developers. Everyone could work at home and decide their own hours, as long as their output was error-free and on time.

Stephanie's husband had to go with her to open a bank account for the new business, and when she began sending around letters to solicit sales, she was advised to sign her name "Steve" instead of "Stephanie." With her typical flair for irony, this 1960s tech pioneer actually began using "Steve" as her name. Despite these inhospitable conditions, her business took off, quickly earning a reputation for superb programming. Meanwhile, the business modeled a way of working that was "family friendly in the extreme." As Steve explained many years later, "I recruited professionally qualified women who had left the computer industry to marry or have children and structured them into a home-working organization."[2]

By 1975, the company employed three hundred people and was involved in a number of high-profile, high-security innovations, such as programming the "black box" for the Concorde. By the 1980s, it employed thousands of people and was doing work for the top businesses in England. When the company was floated on the London Stock Exchange in 1996, it was valued at £121 million (US$160 million). Because Steve had given away many of her own shares to employees, seventy of the people she hired became millionaires.

Steve Shirley became one of the U.K.'s richest women. A tireless servant for her country, she has also been one of its most generous philanthropists, giving away nearly all her wealth by the time she reached her eighties. She often reflects on the circumstances of her entry to Britain: "Without my being fully aware of what was going on or why, a large number of good-natured strangers took it upon themselves to save my life. It took me some years to digest this fact and its implications. But, once I had, a simple resolution took root deep in my heart: I had to make sure that mine was a life that had been worth saving."[3]

By the time I met Steve—now "Dame Stephanie"—for tea in Oxford, she had already been an icon for more than thirty years. I was there to engage her in a different project: helping empower other women throughout the world to become entrepreneurs, just as she had become. I wanted her to tell her story at the opening of the first Power Shift Forum for Women in the World Economy. Her tale was a perfect parable for the constraints female entrepreneurs face, the creative ways they cut through them, the liberation they often experience as a result, and the legacy they can leave behind.

The continuing disadvantages women experience in formal employment are due, in large part, to the fact that men own the companies that employ them. Women who own businesses are more likely to hire other women, to give them training that improves their job marketability, and to promote them. So, a beneficial strategy that should run alongside other efforts to improve women's working conditions is to create a foundation of female employers. Unfortunately, *all* the constraints that the Double X Economy faces in other parts of the economy come home to roost in entrepreneurship. Here I will show you three examples to illustrate the potential and the problems: poor black women's experiences selling Avon in South Africa, the Moldovan government's interest in stimulating women in business, and the positive contribution that women investing in women-owned businesses could make in Britain.

The idea for my Avon in Africa study grew out of long hours spent reading old women's magazines in the stacks of the University of Illinois library when I was researching my book *Fresh Lipstick*.[4] I noticed that many ads between about 1880 and 1920 wanted women to sell various goods as agents. In those years, married women were not yet in the formal workplace, but they would have been able to work near home as agents, just as the aparajitas do in Bangladesh today. Networks of female agents did emerge across the United States at that time, and by carrying goods from a central source out to rural areas, these webs of women built the formidable American consumer market, still one of the U.S. economy's most enviable assets. These sales agents also benefited from the opportunity to earn and to be part of a network of other women.

I wanted to see whether this kind of network system could benefit and empower poor women in developing nations. Most of the companies I saw in the magazine advertisements were long since defunct, but one of them, Avon, had become a global giant. Begun in the late nineteenth century as a perfume company, Avon was still very much alive, had never changed its distribution system, and now did most of its business in developing countries. There were press reports of Avon reps selling up and down the Amazon River. That was exactly what I wanted to study.

When I moved to Oxford in 2006, I believed the more global orientation of the university would give me the opportunity to pull this off. I wrote to Avon's global CEO, Andrea Jung, and asked if I could study her operation in Africa. What the hell, I thought, clicking "send." She wrote back within an hour, not only giving permission but also introducing me to the head of the South Africa office. I was astounded. In Johannesburg two months later, I was introduced to the district managers who could connect me with the poor black women I wanted to research. Then the company cut me loose. Over a three-year period, Avon did not once attempt to interfere with my research, nor did it ever ask to see anything I wrote in advance of publication.

That visit to Johannesburg was my first trip to Africa. So I knew I needed someone with African experience to team up with me. Catherine Dolan, a specialist in Africa, anthropology, economic development, and gender—who had also just arrived in Oxford—agreed to work with me, the first of our many collaborations.

In 2007, the U.K.'s Department for International Development issued a public call for proposals through the Economic and Social Research Council, the main government funding arm for social science research. The call requested innovative ideas for fighting poverty in developing countries. When I went in to float my Avon concept, the ESRC guy laughed loudly in my face and said, "Well, we are looking for new and crazy ideas, so you may as well submit yours." Against the odds, we got the money and started our study.

Avon sells through a catalog rather than through advertising, so people don't usually realize it is the fifth-largest cosmetics company in the world. Four Avon lipsticks are sold every second. There are 6.5 million Avon reps, 99 percent of whom are female, in more than 100 countries. More than 600 million Avon catalogs in twenty-five languages go out to 143 countries each year—that's six times the number of Bibles printed.[5]

When Western women went to work in the 1970s, however, the door-to-door selling that built Avon hit a block—now no one was home to open the door! So the company began experimenting with expansion into developing countries. For instance, after the fall of the Soviet Union, the company set up in the former satellite nations, where women were struggling even more than men to find a way to survive economically. As a massive international corporation that requires no capital, training, or office space to give a woman an income, Avon threw a lifeline to the displaced women of Eastern Europe. A staggering fourteen thousand women showed up to the very first recruiting meeting in Ukraine. The man who was head of that operation told me, with a little embarrassment, that women would come up to him crying tears of gratitude into his chest until his tie was wet. Since that Eastern European experience, Avon has extended into developing countries with consistent success. There are, indeed, "Avon ladies" paddling up the Amazon hawking lipstick. Some say there are more Avon ladies in Brazil than that country has people in its military, and I would not be the least surprised to learn that's true.

Avon agents are not employees, but independent contractors or "entrepreneurs," loosely defined. The 20 percent commission they receive is generous for this kind of work, but agents can make still more money by recruiting other women to become reps. Since the newer recruits are encouraged to bring in more women themselves, another group forms a third level. And then another and another, eventually creating a web of relationships in which clusters of women are related to one another through the person above them—their "upline." If you drew a picture, it would look like a family tree. So, women recruited into Avon instantly become part of a community of peers.

Because the system grows organically and the women work from home, Avon is easy to set up in a new location, compared with the store distribution systems of other cosmetics companies. When it starts up in a developing country, Avon grows really fast, multiplying as if it intends to take over the world. As the network of agents develops, each upline is responsible for managing her immediate "downlines." She trains them, advises them on business matters, encourages them, adjudicates disputes, and mentors them. For that, she gets a small commission on every downline's sales, as do all the uplines above her. If you have a lot of downlines, it can represent pretty good money. Indeed, it's an income that can close the largest inequality gap in South Africa: between black women and everybody else.

Most people think the main axis of inequality in South Africa is race, a perception that is true, but only to a degree. Blacks constitute 80 percent of the country's population. Whites are only 9.2 percent of the population, but 79 percent of them earn in the top income quartile. Less than 10 percent of blacks earn that much. By far, the vast majority of government benefits and remittances go to black households.

Blacks are unquestionably the poorest people in South Africa, but within that community, the women are far more disadvantaged than the men. At the time of our study, the poverty line was 645 rand (US$48) monthly. About 70 percent of black men earned at least 1,000 rand (US$75) a month; only 53 percent of black women earned that much. Furthermore, black women, when compared with black men, had higher unemployment rates, lower incomes, lower education levels, higher involvement with unregistered businesses, and lower use of financial products. They were the population segment most likely to be self-employed, but 94 percent of their businesses were informal efforts to sell produce and handicrafts.

Women's inequality is perhaps most visible in gender-based violence. South African women die from intimate partner violence at six times the global average. A study appeared during our work that showed 25 percent of South African men admitted to raping *at least* one woman, and half of them said they had raped between two and ten. Local writers like Redi Tlhabi have written harrowing accounts of rape within the black community. Because coercive sex is so prevalent, five South African women for every two men have HIV/AIDS. Yet a 2009 article in *The Lancet* reviewed research on violence against women in South Africa and concluded that "there has been a conspicuous absence of government stewardship and leadership" in addressing this issue.[6]

Since our grant was intended to focus on poverty, our sample was composed entirely of poor black women. We found that their average monthly earnings from Avon were 900 rand (US$67), a figure that put them in the top half of black women in South Africa as a whole, and in the top 10 percent of self-employed black women, within shouting distance of the average for men, and significantly above the poverty mark. When we compared the average Avon earnings with the cost-of-living expenses provided by the South African government, we saw that a woman who stayed in the system for sixteen months and made average earnings could cover most living expenses for a family of four, but could not cover housing.[7] So an Avon agent with a family might have to live with others or have another job.

Among our respondents, 68.6 percent were either the female head of their own household or lived with another adult female with whom they shared expenses. Few had a man to help, and children were nearly always present. In South Africa, 41 percent of households are headed by a female, a very large number compared to the global average.

We were particularly interested in comparing selling Avon with the microfinance schemes that were then spreading around the world. These usually just provided the funds for women to sell something of their own making or choosing. There were a few Avon-like systems that sold durable "good for the poor" products, like solar lanterns or clean cookstoves. These entities ran into trouble because the products were big-ticket, heavy to carry, and a onetime purchase for the customer. Once women had sold one to everybody in the village, there was nothing else for them to offer as a means of earning income. What was really needed were products that were low in price and light to carry—and were periodically repurchased. Microfinance programs had also found that women need more than money: they need help and advice, a little training, and a lot of encouragement. Advisory services and training courses were expensive to set up, and most performed poorly. By far, though, the high interest on microloans was the main problem.

Avon comes prepackaged with solutions to all that stuff. The company, for instance, has a credit system that is vastly superior to microfinance. Avon lends only inventory, rather than cash, and the agent must pass a credit check to get her first products to sell. The company has also devised a credit-scoring system that even very poor women can usually pass. A woman who passes can take out a small amount of inventory initially and build up her credit as she expands her customer base. If a new rep can't pass the credit check, she can still buy inventory with cash and build a record over time. If she does not have the cash, another Avon rep often offers to lend it to her.

The value of the inventory has to be repaid whenever a new catalog is issued, about every six to eight weeks, so there is never the buildup of debt that has haunted microfinance. Avon does not charge interest. The system is very forgiving, though tightly managed. If a rep defaults, she can always earn her way back in.

Avon further insists that women use bank accounts for payment. There are numerous efforts to "financially include" women in poor countries by helping them get bank accounts—and it's a struggle, as you now know. But Avon comes into a place and, bang, they're all banked. Ninety-two percent of our respondents had accounts in their own name.

The microfinance schemes that were being used as poverty-alleviation strategies normally did not have job creation as a goal, but were focused on providing subsistence for one woman and her family. Job creation is often a priority for governments, however. Unfortunately, women-owned businesses typically employ very few people—fewer than four, as a worldwide average. But in our sample, the Avon group leaders supervised an average of 137 reps (the range was 10 to 817). The human resource management experience these women pick up at Avon is a marketable skill. Other basic business management methods are also taught, forming a toolbox that Avon reps recognize they can use to get another job or start a different business all their own (89.9 percent said their Avon skills were transferable to other work or another business).

In essence, Avon acts as a low-cost bank and credit management service, as well as a supplier, trainer, and marketing arm for its network of agents. By the time Catherine and I had finished the project, the agent networks that became typical of microfinance were sprouting up all over Latin America, Africa, and Asia—and failing just as fast as they appeared. Economic development experts were eyeing Avon's 125-year-old, worldwide agent system and asking how the company did it. Our report could not have had better timing.

Back in Oxford, however, many of our colleagues still thought we were completely nuts to be doing this work. And, predictably, some colleagues, as well as some media critics, expressed "moral outrage" that we were looking at this system as a means of fighting poverty. Avon, they huffed, shouldn't be selling things to the poor that they don't need.

These comments were so off base compared with what we observed that it was difficult to respond calmly. Avon reps make a point of selling outside their own communities and targeting wealthier customers. Our data confirmed this was indeed happening and also showed that poor customers mostly bought staple items like lotion and soap. When the poor did buy small luxuries, they waited until Avon put them "on special," which usually meant a substantial discount. They also bought gift sizes. These small purchases brought a little joy to lives that were otherwise pretty bleak. The moralists back home were imposing their own country's judgments on a distant and vulnerable population who had a very different consumption ethic. The disapproval from the U.K. came from a colonialist perspective, to say the least.

The products were seen by the reps themselves as a strength. We asked our respondents to compare selling Avon with selling agricultural produce or curios and were told that Avon products sell faster, offer variety, have good margins, sell again in repeat purchases, are not perishable, and do not require the seller to sit by the roadside all day under the hot sun. Selling Avon is seen as a more dignified way to earn money. Its market muscle is also a big plus. Avon's algorithms read the relevant market for the reps, select the right products and prices, and put together a glossy, tailor-made, handheld selling tool. If something special is needed for a particular marketplace, such as a different range of makeup shades, Avon will design or try to find a product that fits. Having been the first major U.S. cosmetics company to offer makeup for black skin tones, it had decades of experience suited for the South African market.

The need to interact with strangers in order to sell was the real drawback of Avon in South Africa. Violent attacks occurred often. We knew women who had been robbed and raped while on their sales rounds. Yet the attacks on women at home were just as bad, and, in fact, more frequent. We were told several stories about reps who had been beaten by their husbands because they resented their wives' success. The narrative invariably ended with the woman saving enough money to take her children and leave. Indeed, some reps purposely recruited women at risk of domestic violence because they wanted to help provide a way out of an abusive home.

Avon encourages women not under immediate threat to set personal goals, suggesting that they should not spend all their earnings but instead try to save capital for financial achievements. To that end, the uplines tell the downlines to cut out a picture of something they dream of—something big, like a house—and put it where they can see it every day, as a reminder of the goal. Then they each make a business plan for how they are going to reach their dream. They all know one another's dream, so there is social pressure to stay committed. The women are usually proud of the things they have planned and achieved, as well as the plans they have made for the future. Indeed, the fact that they *can* plan, instead of just surviving each day, is very important to them. Quite a few had purchased homes, put children through college, bought nice cars—all the hallmarks of a middle-class existence.

Their achievements were particularly impressive because most had started with nothing. Literally nothing. Some had been refugees. HIV orphans. Women on the run from domestic violence. A single mother who escaped the refugee camps said:

I did have a problem . . . my uncle he raped me . . . I couldn't cope with school and the pressure and living with the same man . . .

Then I found out I am HIV positive [from my uncle] . . . I didn't do anything, I didn't care, I didn't want to know . . . I was just waiting for my dying day because I didn't have the guts to kill myself.

I just don't want to die anymore, I want to see my [Avon] business grow . . . I want it to be big at a high level. I left school at an early age. I don't think that there is another way I can survive except to stick [with Avon]. To put all my dedication to this because now I can feed and clothe my kid . . . like [my upline], have a car and drive around, take my kids to town and buy them everything—that is my dream . . . Because I didn't go to school, I won't find a job. I have to think of Avon as my job, like raising a child—it's my baby, I have to raise it.

At least when I die I know I left my kid something. I don't want him to say, "My mother didn't have work" . . . I am planning to stay with Avon a very long time, as long as I am still with my son. It was the best job that came into my life. Before I was sad and miserable.

Every woman we interviewed knew what it meant to worry about feeding her children, and I would guess that most of them had experienced hunger. Many had survived severe traumas and most were old enough to remember apartheid. There seemed to be abandonment, rape, disease, or some other horrible thing behind every face, yet their faces were smiling. I used to joke to Catherine that the women in this study talked about Avon like some folks talk about Jesus. We heard "Avon saved me" over and over. Our first article, titled by Catherine, was called "Lipstick Evangelism."[8]

The one topic that made these voices turn bitter was the legendary unwillingness of their men to provide for children. As one respondent told us, "Culturally, the black community and the Indian community have the perception that the women's role is to raise the kids. 'I am the man of the house and I will go and hunt, [be] the hunter and the gatherer, and you will cook and feed.' [But] not many black men support their children. It's a known fact." The injustice of being left alone to provide for children is even more shocking in a country where such a high percentage of homes have no men at all.

And the burden didn't stop with the children. Our respondents had as many as eight dependents, and a number supported diseased or disabled relatives. Practically everyone was sending money to family in the villages, and many were educating other people's children. As women seem to do everywhere, they did their best to help others who were even worse off than they were, especially other women.

Avon reps are expected to use the products themselves and to present an attractive, confident appearance when they are selling, though they are not at all pressured to use the makeup or to present themselves in any particular way other than clean, groomed, and confident. I never heard anyone complain about this; quite the opposite, most of them were proud of their new grooming expertise and somewhat disdainful of those who did not make the same effort. (One woman grabbed my chin, looked closely at my cheeks, and said, "Ooooh, honey, your skin is a mess. Let me help you." I got multiple offers for a free makeover, and it was made clear to me that I needed one.) The women insisted their own appearance gave them a confidence that they hadn't had before. The overall "look" was more than grooming; it was a head held high, a purposeful stride, a straightforward gaze, and direct speech. Eighty-eight percent of our respondents said their experience with Avon had made them more self-confident.

South Africa is a very stratified society, by class as well as race. The outcome that impressed me most was that these poor black women, the most disadvantaged and excluded people in a suffering nation, claimed to have lost the fear of those who were, in their own words, "higher" than themselves. Seventy-four percent agreed with the statement "Because of Avon, I am no longer intimidated by people I thought were 'higher' than me."

Were they empowered? There's no question that they thought so—and said so to us in so many words. You could not say, however, that Avon reps own the means of production, and many business experts would not even see them as entrepreneurs. Still, the women consistently told a story of past suffering so intense that they had lost any sense of control over their destinies. The ability to command the means to make their own living seemed to me the first crucial step on the path to autonomy. I don't think such an achievement should be diminished.

As I found when trying to figure out how women farmers in the mountains of Uganda could earn more, it is nearly impossible for people living under such material scarcity to come up with new value-added product ideas, let alone buy the packaging, arrange the transport, and so on. Avon comes in and provides all that on a "just add hot water and stir" basis. It teaches these women job skills, helps them manage their money, and builds their confidence. That whole system, when put to work in support of poor black African women, was a blessing. People in economic development, as well as academics, quite often feel that governments should be the only ones to work on poverty. People who say this usually are thinking of the governments of rich nations, which have the means and, to some extent, the willingness to be the savior of their citizens. However, many countries have not stood up for their female citizens and do not appear likely to do so anytime soon.

In the case of South Africa, the failure to deal with the economic exclusion of black women is dragging on the economy like a huge stone. Nearly half the households rely on a female to provide. Yet, even though the laws of South Africa technically make women equal, the tribal rules, the violence, and the burden of care ensure that they are systematically precluded from providing for their homes as even poor men do. South Africa will never pull out of poverty until it focuses its attention on equalizing the economic circumstances of black women—who have the strength to turn that nation around, if only they are given the support.

At least the government of Moldova is trying to help its women. Moldova, the poorest country in Europe, is still suffering from the economic shock of the Soviet Union's failure in the 1990s. Formal employment is limited, labor productivity is low, and corruption is rampant. Meanwhile, outward migration is reducing the labor supply: the men go to Russia to work jobs that do not require much education, while the women—who are more educated—migrate west to Europe. Fertility has been in a steady decline since 1960; the number of children born to a woman in her lifetime is now 1.25. The combination of low fertility and outward migration is causing the population to decline every year.

Women's labor force participation, at 39 percent, is very low, yet 30 percent more women than men enroll in higher education. Females dominate in technical and professional jobs, yet there is a large gender gap in pay. Moldova has one of the highest proportions of female-headed households in the world (about 40 percent, similar to that in South Africa), yet there is no childcare for children under five. There is also a great deal of violence against women in Moldova, and trafficking in females is one of the country's biggest problems.

Today, the Moldovan national government wants to encourage both employment and entrepreneurship among women for the same reasons that other governments do—to stimulate economic growth, create jobs, and so forth—but also for more gender-specific reasons. Moldova's "brain drain" is female; its fertility rate is mostly a function of poor economic prospects for mothers; and the problems of violence and trafficking, here as everywhere, are rooted in female economic vulnerability. The government hopes that female business owners will create new jobs and also hire more women into those jobs, pay them equally, and promote them.

In 2017, I was invited by the World Bank to evaluate activities supporting women entrepreneurs in Moldova that were implemented under an investment lending project.[9] I saw that Moldovan women represented about 25 percent of all business owners, less than the global average of 30 percent. Their businesses appeared to grow less quickly than those owned by men, despite the gender equalization of capital that took place after the Soviet Union collapsed. Men also started more businesses than females did. However, men's businesses appeared to fail three times as often, usually in the earliest stages of development (Figure 31). As a result, women-owned businesses had been running, on average, twice as long as men's.

In about half of all industry sectors, Moldovan female-owned businesses produced higher sales and showed greater productivity. Women-owned businesses also employed more people across the whole economy. And they not only employed more females than men did, but also pro-

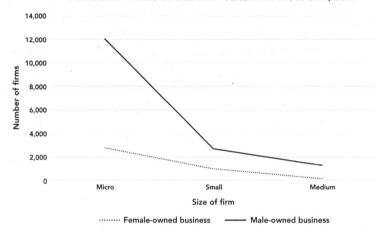

NUMBER OF FIRMS BY SIZE AND GENDER IN MOLDOVA, 2017

FIGURE 31. In the graph above, male- and female-owned businesses are graphed by size. Men start businesses much more often than women do, but a large number fail in the early stages. At the last stage, men buy the businesses owned by women, which not only accounts for the difference in the number of firms owned by each sex but also improves the performance of male-owned firms considerably.

Source: Supporting Women's Enterprise in Moldova, 2018

vided training more often and promoted women in greater numbers. Women were far more likely to occupy top management posts and to have shares in businesses owned by other females than in companies owned by men. In fact, in every district, in every industry, in every way that you could measure it, the women made better employers for other women than the men did. On the surface, therefore, the potential for female entrepreneurs to fulfill the goals of the Moldovan government seemed good. But when you began looking at how the firms were financed, the disadvantages that the Double X Economy carries inevitably rose into view.

Men much more often reported that they had acquired their firm through purchase, which pointed to their having accumulated significant capital. They could fund their businesses through personal means and family support, largely because household capital was seen as theirs. As a result, they had much less need to take on debt in order to expand the business, update equipment, and innovate.

Women, on the other hand, more often used bank credit, in particular to capitalize at startup. Financial institutions were charging women higher interest rates than they did men and demanding more collateral. The end result was that women struggled with debt and were less able to reinvest. As the firms they had founded became larger, women lost control of their businesses, while men did not lose theirs. The shift appeared to occur because the women with growth businesses did not have enough equity capital to expand, got maxed out on credit, and were forced to sell more shares in order to keep scaling up. At that point, they had to sell to men because that's who had the money to buy. Once a woman sold a majority of shares to a man, her firm became a male-owned business for the purposes of counting in the studies of the World Bank and other international data collectors. Since the men were buying women-owned businesses that were outperforming their own, the shift made it look like the men overall had healthier businesses than the women did. At the same time, the best businesses were removed from the women's numbers, which made them look less robust as a group. The end result was misleading because men were given credit for the achievements of the women.

Two exceptions, however, illustrated the upside of equalizing capital access. In the hospitality sector, the women were older and had been adults during the privatization of the Moldovan economy. They had received land as part of that gender-equal redistribution, had held on to it, and had used it to start a hotel or restaurant. Thus, unlike most other Moldovan women, they had equity capital and did not have to rely on debt. Moldova is a pretty country, but it is not yet a big tourist destination; even so, these women were doing very well in their businesses. Furthermore, as old age approached, these hotel and restaurant owners would be in a much better position than their peers; the support of elderly women is a problem the Moldovan government sees approaching fast.

The other exception was wholesaling. In this sector, a surprising percentage of the women had inherited their businesses, so they began with equity capital and did not have to take on debt. They were running circles around the men when it came to revenue and productivity. Female wholesalers, however, were alienated, and it did not take much digging to find out why. The data showed that these women were being visited by tax inspectors at an unreasonable frequency, and they were being asked for some kind of bribe on almost every visit. Customs agents were also a problem for them. The male wholesalers were having no corruption issues at all. Indeed, across the whole sample, extortion was a problem for women, but seldom for men. Given the Moldovan culture of violence against women, I feel certain that the "gifts" being extorted from the female wholesalers were frequently of a sexual nature.

At the end of this work, I made a presentation in Chisinau, Moldova's capital, outlining recommendations. Government ministers and heads of NGOs were present, and they were very receptive. I came away feeling good about the prospects for the government to do something effective for the women. I was also optimistic because supporting these women would help Moldova solve some of its most intractable problems, from low fertility to human trafficking. That's because the Double X Economy always pays off investments with more than just money.

Global data shows that women prefer secure formal employment—with benefits and pension plans and so forth—and will choose to stay in those jobs when they can, rather than start their own businesses. You will probably see by now that this preference is completely in keeping with the Double X Economy's usual ethic and goals: women tend to want long-term security and consistent provision for their families. But in the United Kingdom, women's formal labor force participation has stalled out; instead, women are starting their own businesses.

Women who start businesses in the U.K. list motives that emphasize personal autonomy and self-realization over getting rich, which is the goal British men prioritize. These women do seek the ability to balance care with work, but that is not their primary purpose. They seem to be looking to be independent as well as secure, and possibly to escape sexist attitudes in the formal workplace. However, they are also keen to make a positive contribution to society.

Given the educational profile of British women, which, like that of their American cousins, emphasizes business and medical or biological science, we should not be surprised that the businesses British women most frequently start are professional offices, like doctor's offices and accountancy practices. This kind of business is actually the most profitable and stable of all industry types in the U.K., and there is growth in these sectors. However, such businesses do not usually employ a lot of people, and they do not exhibit the kinds of growth rates you see, for instance, in tech. Of course, they do not exhibit the high failure rates, either.

As elsewhere, government and business leaders in the U.K. are convinced that women are off studying art somewhere and need to be encouraged to study science so that they can become tech entrepreneurs and achieve spectacular growth and profits. So there is a lot of hand-wringing about why girls don't like science, can't do math, and all the rest of it. (For all their rattling on about math, none of these people seem to be able to read hard data themselves.) These leaders have been blinded by stereotypes, but also by the myth of spectacular entrepreneurship.

Currently, British culture glamorizes entrepreneurship as a hyper-masculine, high-risk, high-reward environment. An example is the popular U.K. television series *Dragons' Den*, which features small-business owners seeking investment from male venture capitalists (VCs), the eponymous "dragons" who snarl before blasting the supplicants' ideas and, sometimes, condescending to offer them deals. (*Dragons' Den* is the British *Shark Tank*; both originated with Japan's *Tigers of Money*.)

This theatrical scenario has come to stand for the world of enterprise in British public discourse, grossly inflating the role this kind of experience plays in the U.K. economy or in the lives of real entrepreneurs. Venture capital really funds only 1 percent of British enterprise and, of those who apply, only 2 percent are actually awarded investment. The gender bias in these decisions, however, is truly outsize. Ninety-three percent of VCs are male, and only 10 to 15 percent of their investments each year go to female-owned firms. Venture capitalists also strongly prefer technology firms, yet only 9 percent of their awards go to female-owned tech startups, despite the fact that women represent closer to

30 percent of students or employees in that sector. If VCs closed the gender gap in their own practices, the United Kingdom would reap £25 billion (US$30 billion) in domestic production and gain 150,000 jobs.

Virtually all venture capital in Britain goes to tech companies. Yet tech startups are the highest-risk businesses in the U.K.: more than half fail in the first five years, as do nearly all the rest within a few years after that. A venture capital deal accelerates the life of a startup; any desire to help the world or create a good working environment goes flying out the window as the VCs drive the owner toward a "successful exit," which means putting the company up for sale or a public offering as soon as possible. A successful exit means the VCs make a lot of money very quickly, as does the entrepreneur. But just as winning happens very fast, so does failure. Only 27 percent of the young men who get VC money actually achieve a successful exit. The rest are left with only the smoking husk of their idea.

Venture capitalists and the male entrepreneurs they prefer have nevertheless become the swashbuckling image of enterprise in the U.K. The British press covers venture capital awards like extreme sports. Each year, the headlines scream about how little money went to females, and the reports include stories of VCs humiliating and rejecting women who have pitched their ideas. VCs have a terrible record of gender bias everywhere, but it is particularly bad in the U.K.: British males are 86 percent more likely to win VC funding than females.

There is no mystery as to why venture capitalists seldom fund women. As an international investment phenomenon, VCs have been studied often and consistently found to be grossly gender-biased. Two studies that appeared in the *Harvard Business Review* swapped the names and pictures on proposals or staged presentations where a man presented a woman's idea and vice versa. These studies showed that an idea presented by a man will win and the same idea presented by a woman will lose. Another study analyzed two hundred videos of venture capital presentations, including the questions and comments from the VCs, and found that the questions they ask entrepreneurs differ starkly by gender. Men are asked variations of "How are you going to make me money?" while women are asked some variation of "How are you going to keep me from losing money?" The words VCs use in their comments on entrepreneurial proposals also differ by gender. When talking to men, they use *gain, hope, ideal, accomplish, achieve, aspire, obtain, earn, expand*, and *grow*. For women, it's *accuracy, afraid, anxious, avoid, careful, conservative, defend, fear, loss, obligation*, and, especially, *pain*.[10]

VC sexism does not stop at investment selection. Another study analyzed the outcomes using the records of Crunchbase, a huge database of startup statistics, and found that the difference in successful exit rates between men and women was entirely attributable to the gender of the VC. If a venture capital company buys a man's startup and assigns a male partner to manage the progress toward exit, there is a 27 percent chance of success, while a male partner managing a woman's startup has a 17 percent chance of success. Yet when the managing partner is female, the woman's company has a chance of achieving success equal to that of a man's.[11]

The lore on women and venture capitalists is long and ugly. Justine Roberts, founder of Mumsnet, a website for parents, remembers her experience pitching venture capital: "In one meeting, the guy kept turning to the person next to him to ask what my name was. If I got defensive he'd say, 'You look like you're going to cry.' There were references to having sex with me if he wasn't married. You want to prove yourself and your worth, and it was only really after that I was like, 'Why did I sit through that?'" Today, Mumsnet is one of the most visited social sites in the U.K., with 12 million unique visitors a month. Roberts has been awarded a CBE for her service to the British economy, but she still gets investors asking her who runs the business side of her company.[12]

Heidi Zak, one of the founders of ThirdLove, recounts what happened when she pitched venture capitalists: "At the end of the session, a guy told me, 'Sorry, we only invest in things we understand.' We sell women's underwear. They invest in incredibly complex and intricate technology, but I lost him when I said 'bra.'"[13] In late 2018, ThirdLove made *Forbes*'s annual Next Billion-Dollar Startups list; the company is now valued at $750 million.[14]

"When a man walks into the room, it's automatically assumed he's competent. When *I* walk in the room, it's automatically assumed I'm not,"

Kim Taylor says of the gender dynamics of presenting to venture capitalists.[15] Taylor eventually sold her online education company for $25 million, but when she first presented her idea, the VCs wouldn't believe the data in her market analysis. "It became very bizarre to me that I could present people with nationally accepted data or information and they just wouldn't acknowledge it as being true," she said.[16]

But it's not like VCs *don't know* they have a bias. It's that they take no steps to improve themselves even though their prejudice is leading to bad decisions.

Gender prejudice is, unfortunately, typical of the investment climate for women in the U.K. Female entrepreneurs get only 9 percent of available investment funds each year. When a group of 750 female business founders was surveyed by the *Telegraph* in March 2018, 65 percent felt that financial services had treated them unfairly, and 67 percent said male investors would have treated them differently if they had been male. In response to the question of whether they had difficulty being taken seriously when setting up their business, 65 percent said they had. Half had at some point been told they needed a man to run their business. Mothers reported even more unfair treatment. As a result of the nearly complete absence of institutional financial support, 72 percent of these women had opted to fund their own businesses out of savings or on credit cards.[17]

Angel investing is sometimes suggested as a solution to the gender gap in British enterprise funding. "Angels" are the spiritual opposite of the dragons in venture capital. They invest in the entrepreneur as much as in the business idea and hope to support the realization of the dream, rather than burn it up with their breath. They generally use their own money, not a pool as venture capitalists do. Nevertheless, most angel investors are men (86 percent), and they, like venture capitalists, do have a bias for investing in other men, but it is not as strong. While men are 86 percent more likely to get money from a VC, they are 56 percent more likely to get money from an angel.

Aren't there some wealthy British women who could act as angels? A study led by the UK Business Angels Association surveyed and interviewed more than six hundred wealthy women across Europe and found that those who meet the requirements for angel investing often don't know what it is or how to access it. Their financial advisors, who assume that women want safe and standard investments, usually don't mention angel investing to them. These potential angels don't think they have time to do the homework it takes to evaluate an investment of this sort, and they often believe this kind of investment is too risky. However, when presented with the concept of joining a group of other investors who would share the work of assessing investments and spread the risk, the women were keenly interested.

When some of these female investors tried to join existing angel investor groups, however, they found that the men in those groups were unfriendly to them. "I wanted to join an angel network but they were all run by older men. The atmosphere was terrible and I never invested there," reported a Frenchwoman. A Portuguese woman investor said, "Being in a network of mainly male business angels, you have to be aware of the rules—their rules, like how decisions are made. It's a man's world." The report on the study concluded: "Many women investors had had negative experiences in attending male dominated or all-male angel groups across Europe, and there is strong need to establish women-focused/women-friendly groups in the Partner countries."[18]

The obvious solution, said the report, would be to encourage the formation of women-only angel groups. It also recommended that governments offer matching funds for angel groups providing money to support female entrepreneurs, a step that could probably not occur in the U.K. because it would constitute positive discrimination. Any action to form such a group would be seen as "unfair" in Britain, despite the fact that venture capital and existing angel capital are overwhelmingly dominated by male investors and recipients.

Crowdfunding offers another option for funding women-owned startups. Online sites such as Kickstarter and Indiegogo allow people to post proposals for donation or investment to the public. While men are more likely to post proposals on such sites, women are more likely to be funded when they post. This seems to happen because female investors intentionally put money into women-owned startups. Crowdfunding is a way for both the entrepreneurs and the investors to get around the fire-breathing environment of the financial sector. And because everyone simply posts to the public or invests private money, this means of supporting women is acceptable even in Britain.

In any case, though, the emphasis on venture capital and digital technology presents small business in a way that is anathema to women. The *Dragons' Den* scenario should be anathema to governments, too. It is one thing to support high growth and innovation, but if the *whole* economy were being grown on the template of this testosterone-crazed roller coaster, it would be unstable and would not grow very much because the successful tech base is so limited. It's the kinds of businesses started by women that add stability, reliable growth, secure employment, and community responsibility to the national foundation. It is foolish to keep treating the female economic ethic as slow, undesirable, and a reflection of inability. Only weak policy will result from that attitude.

Instead, what is needed is an investment ethic with room for slower growth but less risky business opportunities. Investment portfolios should always have a balance of short-term, high-risk, high-potential vehicles and long-term, low-risk, more realistic investments. There is no reason that a capital program for women based on that philosophy could not be built, but it is unlikely to happen because of the band-of-brothers culture in the enterprise investment community that rewards risky behavior, shuts out women and nice guys, overlooks bad manners, is wanton about incinerating good ideas, and values outsize aggression for its own sake. It may be fun to pump up your cortisol like that, but it's not a responsible way to build a national economy.

My hope is that the women's economic empowerment movement will catch the attention of female investors and encourage formation of a women's investment community to support the reasonable basis for growth that women represent. Doing that will also provide more egalitarian workplaces for women and support communities in a positive way.

Let's return to the story of Dame Stephanie Shirley. She is obviously such an exceptional woman, someone who combined intelligence, determination, and generosity to leave an extraordinary legacy to society. Yet by looking out for other women, she is, I believe, typical of most female entrepreneurs. After interviewing hundreds of women business owners all over the world for the past decade, I am convinced that harnessing that desire to help is one of the most powerful things our women's economic empowerment movement can do to advance the cause worldwide.

13 | JOINING THE GLOBAL MARKET

The women's groups in Papua New Guinea were abuzz with the news: a local businesswoman had brokered a deal for thirty thousand female farmers to supply produce to Stop & Shop. These poor women had been eking out subsistence from small gardens, as so many around the world do. But a locally organized NGO called Mothers Helping Mothers had been training them to supply a big buyer. They learned new methods and how to select the fruits and vegetables that would pass quality control. They figured out how to get their produce to a container ship that would arrive once a week. The deal would solidify a high-quality, reliable food source for Stop & Shop while securing a consistent income for women who were otherwise severely economically limited.

When I arrived in Port Moresby for the 2018 Asia-Pacific Economic Cooperation (APEC) "women's meeting," the question in the air was, How can this be done in other countries to help more women? The obstacles that agricultural markets pose for females everywhere—the lack of transportation, the gender-exclusive cooperatives—had at last been overcome. The global market had been made to work *for* women, instead of against them.

The global market. It sounds like some immense, fantastical beast, but it's just a web of exchanges built from thousands of deals like this one. The global market is put together, point to point, by ordinary people who make the connections, agree to exchange, and work in relationships to make and move objects from here to there. But women are too often excluded from this huge network, because they don't know the right people and the right people don't know them.

Being in the network is also important because, before a deal like the one Mothers Helping Mothers struck with Stop & Shop can be done, a sequence of problems inevitably must be solved: how to get the fertilizer required by the new method, where to get the boxes to take to the container ship. Usually pretty ordinary things, really. Once all the problems have been solved and the connections made, though, you have built a chain of actions and transactions that can keep rolling, pretty much automatically, as long as there is somebody at the end of the chain who will buy. And that can make for a nice income stream for everybody, including the folks who drive the trucks, make the fertilizer, and sell the boxes.

When a large company or a government decides to buy something—anything—in bulk, it's called *procurement*. It could be grapefruit, soap, earrings, or thumbtacks, depending on what sector the buyer is in. If the objects purchased are shipped across national boundaries, it counts as "international trade." And that's it. Nothing mysterious, just a lot of moving parts.

Men hold 99 percent of the procurement contracts in the world, and consequently, they control 99 percent of international trade.[1] So this is a lucrative part of the economy where women are almost totally excluded. The female business owners in Moldova or the startup entrepreneurs in the U.K.—or any other woman-owned business that sells something a big buyer could use—would *have it made* if they could get just one of these contracts. Since those women are better employers for other women, it would also be a good outcome for the women's movement.

The problem is that if you belong to a class of people who weren't allowed out of the house or off the farm for thousands of years, you may not know anybody to sell to or build solutions with, and you often don't know how to do many of the things that are required to participate. That much is true whether you are in Papua New Guinea or Guadalajara or

Aberdeen. So, women's economic empowerment has been moving into procurement and trade, too. Since about 80 percent of international trade goes through multinational corporations, an initiative began to get multinationals to integrate women-owned businesses into their supply chains.

The term *supply chain* is jargon, but the meaning is really very simple. Let's say a company buys uniforms from a garment company; that's the first tier of the supply chain. In turn, that garment supplier buys fabric, machinery, thread, and packaging from other companies. That's the second tier. Those companies in turn buy from textile manufacturers, steel factories, plastic and paper companies, and even lumber companies. That's the third tier. You can see that by the fourth or fifth tier a large swath of industries and a considerable number of people are involved.

Many women work throughout the supply chains of multinationals, so a focus on the supply chain can help a large number of female employees, in addition to entrepreneurs. For instance, when retailers like Primark and Target buy from a factory in, say, China or Sri Lanka, they vet that supplier to ensure that it meets safety standards. When a big customer wants the factory to have something—such as lighted exits—the request is likely to be accommodated so that the factory owner can get and keep the contract. Sometimes, a factory will allow a big buyer to come in with a training program designed to improve social or health practices. Or a big buyer will ask for the factory's gender or race representation, subtly signaling that it prefers to deal with diverse companies. The buyer stipulates what the factory purchases to make its products, whether it's flame-retardant fabric or recyclable packaging. That, in turn, influences the second tier. So, a big multinational can potentially change a great deal in its supply chain by virtue of the first-tier contract and, beyond that, through "soft influence." In all these cases, however, the buyer only *influences* and cannot *dictate* practices, because it does not *own* the supplier. Its only leverage is to threaten to take its business elsewhere.

Beyond the second tier, even a multinational has limited visibility into the supplier firms, as well as reduced influence. And unfortunately, the third or fourth tier, especially in developing countries, may be hiding some dark practices. In particular, there may be labor abuses and even slavery. To combat those problems, the multinationals work with governments, unions, NGOs, and international agencies, as well as the other companies in their own industry, to eliminate corruption and abuse.

If I am talking down to you, please forgive me. I'm assuming you don't know any of this stuff because I didn't either until 2013, when I took on a research project for Walmart.

Walmart had made an enormous public commitment to women's economic empowerment in 2011, promising to buy $20 billion in products from American women-owned suppliers within five years and to double its spending with women in international markets during the same period. Walmart gave $100 million in grants to support projects aimed at women's economic empowerment, including a huge initiative for women in agriculture. It also promised to train two hundred thousand women in developing countries for retail careers, which lead to upward mobility, and it undertook factory initiatives among its suppliers, with impressive results, including achieving pay parity and a reduction in workplace violence.[2]

My role was to figure out how to assess a program called Empowering Women Together (EWT).[3] In the EWT effort, Walmart wanted to help very small women-owned businesses grow by offering the goods they made to Walmart's 140 million consumers, initially via a special portal on the retailer's website and, as the businesses grew, through the thousands of brick-and-mortar stores. This effort was focused not on agriculture, but on small manufactured goods to be sold at retail—anything from sweatbands to baskets. If the EWT effort was successful, Walmart would have demonstrated the feasibility of bringing female entrepreneurs into international trade by integrating them into a corporate supply chain, which, it was hoped, would encourage other multinationals to do the same.

In many different supply chains, Walmart is by far the biggest player. Think about all the products Walmart sells: housewares, jewelry, gardening equipment, consumer electronics, food and beverages, household cleaners—it goes on and on. As the world's largest retailer

(and the world's largest grocer), Walmart probably has the most extensive and varied supply chain in the world—and it reaches into nearly
every country and industry. If you could introduce a women's economic
empowerment objective into that web of connections, you could help a
lot of people. That's why I was keen to be the one who did the study.

Through a University of Oxford research grant that gave me full independence to report and publish findings as I saw them, I undertook
to monitor the EWT effort as it unfolded. At the time our team took up
the work, EWT had chosen thirty female entrepreneurs, including small
firms and startups in North America as well as in Africa, Latin America,
and Asia. The effort crossed twelve countries on four continents, and
the suppliers ranged from two Stanford engineering graduates who invented learning toys for girls to a factory producing felt flowers in Nepal.

Finding those thirty women-owned businesses had been a challenge. No registry of small businesses owned by women existed—not
even in the United States, where efforts to achieve supplier diversity are
the most advanced. Since there was no list, the Walmart EWT team—
at that time led by MiKaela Wardlaw Lemmon—asked around at commercial events and made notes of things they spotted in magazines or
newspapers. The EWT buyer found one of the companies, a manufacturer of environmentally friendly dry-cleaning bags, on *Shark Tank*.

The Women's Business Enterprise Council, better known as WBENC
(usually pronounced "We-Bank"), was founded to solve this problem by
creating a registry of women-owned U.S. businesses. WBENC is funded
by a group of companies, cities, and other organizations trying to find
women-owned businesses to buy from. The U.S. government has supplier
diversity requirements for all its contractors, as do other big organizations, so many American firms seek women-owned suppliers. But before
a business can be legitimately counted for such a requirement, it has to be
certified as actually belonging to a woman. So WBENC also certifies and
does training to help women get up to speed as suppliers to large buyers.

Finding women-owned businesses in developing countries was even
harder. Other countries, including many rich nations, have not taken
the steps toward a diverse market that the United States has. And you

can't just wander around other countries looking for businesses that might be owned by women. It's inefficient and can be dangerous. So, in about 2013, WEConnect International was created to build an international list of women-owned businesses. Founded by a group of seventy-two corporations that collectively spend more than US$1 trillion a year on products and services, this NGO now goes around the world, operating under the protection of governments, to hold large public events where women can sign up to become suppliers. Melanne Verveer, the first U.S. ambassador for global women's issues, and the U.S. secretary of state, Hillary Clinton, were leaders on this important international initiative. WEConnect both certifies and trains the women who sign with it, and has now identified suppliers in over one hundred countries.

There is also an independent WEConnect effort in Europe that advocates for supplier diversity with those governments; the whole concept of supplier diversity is late-breaking in Europe, and it has met some resistance. Particularly in Britain, the idea that you would be trying to include women in international trade leads straight to the objection that you are giving females preferential treatment. This reaction always floors me: Where 99 percent of the business is controlled by males, how can anyone seriously object that giving women a small boost is unfair? What about the unfairness of allowing a monopoly to continue unchecked?

Back in the days of the EWT project, the Walmart team didn't have these kinds of options anyway. They traveled to events and exhibitions seeking out women to buy from. They might go halfway around the globe and still locate only one woman with a product they could sell. Eventually, they engaged two NGOs to help them, Full Circle Exchange and Global Goods Partners.

The people who started these NGOs were as special, and as ordinary, as you or I. The Full Circle Exchange principals were three middle-aged men—the Priddy brothers—from Boise, Idaho. They had made money selling to big retailers and wanted to give back. Using their own cash, they opened Full Circle Exchange in 2012, choosing women's economic empowerment as their mission for the same reason others have: helping women is an effective way to combat widespread suffering. In just a couple of years John, Mark, and Ed Priddy had put together a network from Africa to Peru, and they were brimming with ideas about how to market women's handicrafts.

The two women who started Global Goods Partners, Catherine Shimony and Joan Shifrin, had known each other since their graduate work at the Johns Hopkins School of Advanced International Studies. After finishing their degrees, they both went to work for foundations, awarding funds to poverty-alleviation programs in developing countries and learning firsthand how much good can be done when women have money. In 2005, supported by grants from the foundations where they worked, they opened Global Goods Partners in an old office building in New York. Their mission was to connect female artisans in developing countries with the U.S. consumer market. They began with a small portfolio of women's groups they knew from their foundation work and, with references from their own network of economic development contacts, built a list of forty partner groups in twenty countries.

So, with the help of Joan, Catherine, and the Priddy brothers, as well as *Shark Tank*, the EWT effort had arrived at the list of thirty entrepreneurs. Global Goods Partners would work only with organizations with established programs to help women; for instance, one of their partners was the Maasai Women Development Organization (MWEDO), which helps these indigenous women feed their families by finding a better market for their beading, a technique that has been admired in Africa for centuries. In North America, Full Circle Exchange had partner businesses that gave jobs to female refugees and former felons and that were owned by minority women. In developing countries, their partners were giving employment to some of the world's neediest women.

In many cases, however, the next hurdle almost killed the deal: each woman-owned business now had to pass Walmart's supplier vetting process, called the "ethical sourcing audit." As most readers will know, multinational corporations get a lot of criticism for the working conditions in their supply chains. Most Western companies have taken that criticism seriously, creating standards and procedures to prevent infringements. One way Walmart addresses the issue is to contract only with suppliers that can pass a stringent audit, conducted locally by independent assessors. The criteria include whether there are toilets, fire-safety devices, lighted exits, doors that swing both ways, labor contracts with set hours and wages, no child workers, and the other things we expect a responsible manufacturer to have.

The North American suppliers had no trouble passing the audit because the U.S. and Canadian environments are already set up to meet all these criteria as a matter of law. But the businesses in developing countries found it very hard. Since women usually start with little or no capital, they normally begin as low-cost informal enterprises. That often means the company owner is working from home and pays out of pocket for each piece produced, instead of having a fixed schedule of hourly wages. Neither working at home nor paying by the piece is allowed by Walmart's audit requirements. Some of these operations were in villages with no electricity or plumbing, which precluded flush toilets and safety lights. Sometimes the women worked outdoors, under a tree. Also not allowed. Some women were accustomed to looking after their children as a group while they worked and chatted, which was precluded by rules against the presence of children. The mobility constraints typical of gender arrangements in developing countries meant some women could not punch a clock: in one country, the women could not leave home for long for fear their husbands would punish them, so they had to walk into town, get their craft materials, and then hurry back home before their absence was noticed.

I had the chance to explain all this to a young man on the ethics team at Walmart headquarters in Bentonville, Arkansas. He was surprised that I would question the standards. I totally understood why he felt that way, but people in rich nations think these regulations are an objectively moral standard, and I don't agree. Often, the people making such policies have no experience with women working under a tree, where there is no electricity or plumbing for miles. They don't understand that all the women of the village sitting under the same tree *is* the day care.

I felt there should be a system change that could allow not for corruption or cruelty, but for differences in living conditions. What was needed was a set of international standards that contemplated a business environment other than that in large, Western-standard factories. By restricting approvals to owners with the capital for modern facilities, international policy effectively excludes poor women from trade, reserving it instead for the men who already control wealth.

On occasion, the restrictions turned away the very people EWT was intended to help. For instance, the audit for MWEDO presented an identification issue. The Maasai, a very patriarchal culture, practice child marriage and leave the matter of supporting the babies to their mothers, so there are lots of very young women among them who badly need to work. Since women in rural Africa often don't have birth records, they sometimes can't even tell you their age. Because of malnutrition, an eighteen-year-old might look twelve. So when this organization was audited, many of the workers looked underage and couldn't prove their birth dates—but had their own children with them. Fortunately, in this case, the auditors asked around villages until they could verify the ages of these young mothers. Most auditors wouldn't have gone to the trouble.

The ID problem arises whenever you have a program that requires formal registration, like getting bank accounts or credit or telephones. In the years since I did this project, other companies, like MasterCard, have begun coming into developing countries and partnering with governments to get ID cards issued to everyone, including especially women in the rural areas. So that's another problem potentially solved.

Access to materials is a big issue outside North America. When the women are making housewares or personal items for Western stores, often a new style of fabric or ribbon or bead is part of the design. In North America, you can find nearly any material online and have it drop-shipped to your front door the next day. In the developing countries, some of that stuff is impossible to get.

And then there are really basic things like pigments. Think for a minute about the seasonal displays you see in retailers' windows—the colors in shoes, bags, and scarves often match exactly. The products displayed, however, are probably made by different manufacturers—maybe in several countries—who all work to a standard Pantone color so that when everything arrives at the retailer's warehouse, all the objects match. Our team observed women in Kenya who couldn't get the right pigments to match the color for some woven baskets. They were also trying to dye the raffia using big pots of river water on the same kind of stone "stoves" I saw in the mountains of Uganda—then they dried the straw in the sun by draping it across bushes. Every step they took caused a potential variation in how the dye came out—and so might not pass quality control at Walmart. The women needed assistance procuring supplies as well as technical help. Providing that kind of support would lift another barrier.

The North American businesses were advantaged because of the greater technical sophistication of their markets but also due to the ethic of those markets. For instance, the Women's Bean Project in Denver sells all kinds of things made mostly of a simple ingredient, beans. When pricing or availability changes on any of the beans they typically use, the supplier notifies them well in advance and suggests a substitute or warns of a delay so they can plan. That kind of cooperation is just not there for the women in the developing nations.

In both the developing and developed countries in this project, as well as in others I have observed since, the women needed technical production advice and assistance in everything from materials to manufacturing to shipping. The North American businesses, for instance, usually designed their own products, but then had to find a way to get the design translated into production specs, costed, and contracted to a factory to produce. Some eventually used facilities in the same country, whether the United States or Canada, and others sent the work to a factory in another part of the world. The problem was finding the factory, wherever it was, that had the right equipment to do the job and translating the specs for production. You just have to know someone who knows someone—and women usually didn't know the right someone, because they weren't part of the right networks.

Once the manufactured products are in hand, they have to be tagged and packaged for conveyance to the retailer. This in itself is a big job if you have a large volume. Most of the North American women I spoke to hadn't known there were "fulfillment" companies that do this for you and had spent a painful few months trying to do it themselves. Again, it's just the problem of being excluded from the networks where you find that stuff out.

That learning curve could probably be made much less painful—with the result of more women-owned businesses surviving—if the right people were aware the need was there. In the United States and Canada, for instance, technical advice of all sorts could be provided through volunteer organizations like the Chamber of Commerce or the Rotary Club. In the developing world, such assistance could be delivered along the same lines as the agricultural field agents' work—only given, respectfully, to women.

Shipping and customs add to both cost and risk for EWT suppliers in poor countries. Transportation from the point of production to the export zone is often expensive and difficult to arrange. To make matters worse, the customs agents often demand bribes or change the duties capriciously. An EWT supplier trying to ship the raffia baskets from Nairobi, after all the headaches and unexpected costs of production, brought her wares to the export processing zone only to have the customs agent renege on the original estimate and demand a fee that was more than the value of the order.

Government corruption, especially at customs, is a bigger problem for women than for men all over the world.[4] Women are assumed to be ignorant of the rates and rules for everything, and the agents feel it's okay to lie to them. Of course, women are also vulnerable to sexual bullying. Since most developing countries have only one or two main ports, it should be efficient to station special agents to assist women trying to export goods to make sure they are treated right. If countries want to increase exports from women-owned businesses—which they all seem to want—this would be an important and comparatively straightforward way to facilitate it.

People often don't believe me when I tell them this, but the single biggest obstacle to success for the female business owners in developing countries was style. My doctoral student Mary Johnstone-Louis and I went to the Women Vendors Exhibition held by the International

Trade Centre in Mexico City in 2012. The event was intended to act as a venue for women owners, especially from developing countries, to pitch their wares to big buyers, as well as for WEConnect, then just getting started, to sign them up. As the women and the buyers began to interact, the buyers lamented that the women were not making objects "for the market," meaning the Western consumer market. But we knew that the women in poor countries have little or no exposure to that market, so they don't know how to envision its tastes or its seasons, and they have little understanding of how it operates. For instance, they are often caught by surprise when they learn that their products must be tested for consumer safety or certified against animal cruelty.

International trade shows, usually in places like Shanghai, New York, and Milan, are too expensive for these women to attend, at least on a regular basis. Someone needs to arrange for those shows to go to the women, instead of the women having to go to the shows. It would be expensive, but it would pay off because the women usually "get it" pretty quickly. A single trade show transformed women-owned fashion design businesses in Moldova, for instance.

The designers at Global Goods Partners worked with the Maasai women to come up with jewelry they hoped would be seen as fashionable but that used the traditional beading technique. Despite everyone's best efforts, the bracelets and necklaces sat in Walmart's warehouse for at least a year, being repeatedly discounted but never moving. Walmart absorbed all these costs, but a widespread failure to sell would make scaling EWT into an ongoing global program a no-go.

The Walmart shopper was the final adjudicator of whether EWT was going to work. Most Americans have shopped at Walmart a few times, but the regular Walmart shopper is someone on a tight budget. These shoppers must buy very wisely and therefore shouldn't be asked to pay a high sticker price for the sake of an experimental global development program.

While I was doing this project, people frequently asked me whether Walmart's low price point caused poor women in developing countries to be "cheated." Folks who asked me this question had usually never thought about poor women shopping in Walmart's stores who shouldn't be "cheated," either. It's the Walmart shopper who sets the price limits in those stores. If we are to liberate the Double X Economy, we have to balance the interests of all the women who are implicated in our work.

In some cases, the product could not be made for the price acceptable to Walmart shoppers. Sometimes, a brand could have been developed to sell the object online through a more "upscale" outlet like Sundance or Anthropologie. The whole point of branding is to distinguish something well enough to command a higher price. But brand development is not something the women in the developing countries can do—it's a challenge for them to make things that appeal to the Western market, let alone brand them, too. If trade organizations like the Association of National Advertisers in the United States or the European Brands Association would encourage their members to volunteer as marketing advisors to these women-owned businesses, it would "do good," as businesspeople like to say these days, for a lot of women and their families.

Social media assistance would also be useful. A continuing complaint among EWT partners and suppliers was that the Walmart website did not foreground their products sufficiently. The site relied on buyers either searching for products made by women—an unlikely event—or searching for the products by name—again, unlikely without branding. Though Walmart did "feature" the products at the outset and create a special portal for "women-made" products, I saw that there were too many competing priorities across the whole online interface to sustain this visualization to the degree that would be necessary to build a single business, let alone the whole list of EWT suppliers. If the global community could volunteer independent marketing advice and support, particularly for optimizing digital results, it would be a boon for small suppliers like these.

Marketing a product as "made by a woman-owned business" can offer its own appeal. A consumer survey done by Walmart showed that its women shoppers—who represent the vast majority—would prefer to buy from a woman-owned business, all other things (especially price) being equal. At the same time, male shoppers said they didn't really care one way or another. So Walmart helped WBENC develop a logo

FIGURE 32. This "Women Owned" logo was designed to mark products at the retail level so that consumers can help women by buying from them.

Source: By permission from the Women's Business Enterprise Council; see https://www.womenownedlogo.com for further details

that could be used by all retailers to mark an item as the product of a woman-owned business (Figure 32).

EWT suppliers had difficulty getting the cash to buy materials and pay people to make the things Walmart ordered. None of the firms could afford to tie up working capital for labor and supplies for long, but it was a long wait between shipping, invoicing, processing, and payment. In North America, a bank might extend credit based on the purchase order from Walmart. But because the women in developing countries don't own any land and banks won't loan money without a pledge of real property, the female entrepreneurs can't get a loan, even with a purchase order.

The Priddy brothers worked doggedly on this problem. Banks and social impact investors were approached. No luck. In a couple of cases, they ended up fronting the capital themselves. "Here's the problem," said John Priddy to me on the phone one day. "We want women-owned businesses to grow, but they don't have any capital. So when time comes for them to expand, they have to raise capital, and guess who has it? The men! So let's say they get capital from the Priddy brothers. Much as we want to help them, that would mean their business becomes a male-owned business!"

As a nonprofit social enterprise, Global Goods Partners has access to funding that a for-profit organization does not. Therefore, it provides 50 percent of an order's value up front to enable its producing partners to purchase materials at the outset and pay women artisans during the production process. While not a solution to women gaining equal access to capital, without this funding mechanism, most of the women businesses with which GGP works could not continue to operate.

Now I am seeing some good work on solutions. The World Bank's We-Fi initiative has a fund of about US$300 million to distribute to the regional development banks around the world for use in programs to support female entrepreneurs. The funds are being combined with contributions from other sources that more than triple the total amount of money available. I am honored to be involved in the work of We-Fi, especially because it has given me a window into these possibilities.

Over time, We-Fi proposals have become increasingly gender-aware and have focused on other issues besides credit, including the problem of equity capital. Efforts are now underway that use a variety of incentives, forms, and advocacy measures to help raise equity capital for women. That kind of change takes an organization with the reach and authority of the World Bank to pull off, however, as well as funds to act as stimulant and cushion.

In fact, most of what I have described here would be accomplished more easily if the major international economic bodies like the G7, G20, and APEC, as well as world leaders, would pay more attention. In the end, Walmart concluded that the "ecosystem" for women-owned businesses in developing countries just did not support making contracts with such small enterprises. It decided to focus instead on helping the women-owned businesses among its existing suppliers to grow, and to concentrate on other programs, such as the retail, agriculture, and factory efforts that were already showing good results. I was disappointed with Walmart's decision, but I understood.

In fact, as these and other collaborations between corporations, NGOs, international agencies, various women's organizations, and sometimes national governments have evolved, it has become increasingly clear that the world's ecosystem needs a major overhaul, not just a bunch of single fixes by well-meaning individuals and companies. If women are ever to be equal in the global economy, the people at the top of world economic management have to get gender-friendly. It seems like a tall order, and it is, but Canada's leadership is making me think it can happen.

Canada is surely the first government in world history to boast that it has a feminist prime minister and a feminist foreign policy, but its actions are earning the titles. Canada's new "progressive" approach to trade is nothing less than a vision of a new world order; the government asserts that it will no longer conduct trade under the world's overarching economic philosophy because it is destructive and unsustainable. A focus on gender is, in its view, a primary strategy for moving the world economy toward a humane and sustainable future. Canada's trade commission also estimates that lifting barriers to female participation in world trade would boost its own economy by US$114 billion.

In July 2017, Canada and Chile reached the first international trade agreement ever to have a gender-equality provision. The "Trade and Gender" chapter of the updated Canada-Chile Free Trade Agreement explicitly asserts that trade is *not* gender-neutral and goes further to emphasize "the importance of incorporating a gender perspective into the promotion of inclusive economic growth, and the key role that gender-responsive policies can play in achieving sustainable socioeconomic development."[5]

In the provisions of the agreement, both nations reaffirm their commitments to all international accords on gender equality and commit to promoting public knowledge of their own "gender equality laws, regulations, policies, and practices" domestically. Then, there is a list of activities that Chile and Canada will include in their women's empowerment plans, from financial inclusion for women to increased representation in leadership and decision-making. Sex-disaggregated data will be collected and analyzed by both countries, separately and jointly.

Importantly, for the circumstances I have described in this chapter, the Canada-Chile trade agreement creates a joint committee that is explicitly empowered to work cooperatively with NGOs, the private sector, international agencies, and "other relevant institutions as appropriate" in pursuing gender equality through trade. This provision sets the stage for building the gender-friendly ecosystem that is needed, as recognized by the many organizations already working on the issue.

Canada is actively trying to persuade the rest of the world to follow suit. That's why it was involved in drafting the Declaration on Trade and Women's Economic Empowerment presented at the 2017 World Trade Organization (WTO) meeting in Buenos Aires. The individual behind the declaration was Arancha González, the executive director of the International Trade Centre (ITC).

Arancha had been the opening speaker at Power Shift in 2015. That morning, she impressed all of us with her fiery passion about the disgrace of gender inequality in the global markets. Explaining that only 11 percent of women who own businesses participate in import-export deals, she announced that ITC was officially committing to a goal of getting a million women into the international trade system by 2020. By doing this, ITC expected to increase global GDP by US$148 trillion.

In the written explanations and justifications for the Declaration on Trade and Women's Economic Empowerment, supporters explained that addressing gender could be the first step in turning the WTO toward a more progressive agenda and, therefore, put it back on the path it was originally meant to follow.[6]

Under the United Nations' charter, signed in 1945, international trade was dedicated to a new purpose: supporting peace. Article 55, "International Economic and Social Cooperation," specifically states that the primary objective for the global economy is to create the "conditions of stability and well-being which are necessary for peaceful and friendly relations among nations."[7] The United Nations created several agencies devoted to the new economic agenda, including the World Bank, the International Monetary Fund, the ITC, and the predecessor of the WTO. However, when trade was split off from the rest under the General Agreement on Trade and Tariffs (1948), it divorced economics from the humanitarian mission. At that point, trade policy took up the might-is-right ideology typical of 1950s economics—and stuck with it for the next seventy-five years.

So, in 2017, the activists behind the declaration on behalf of women—who knew well the positive humanitarian effects that come from economic gender inclusion—felt they were proposing a return to the real mission of the United Nations charter by bringing gender to the table. And, with a declaration like this one, women's rights would once again be covered in the global economic, as well as the humanitarian, agendas.

The declaration was a nonbinding but important agreement to enable gender-based analysis to be applied to domestic and international domestic policy, encourage female entrepreneurship and financial inclusion, remove barriers to women's participation in trade, and develop useful gender statistics and research. It was brought to the table by the governments of Iceland and Sierra Leone, and signed by 119 countries (eventually 122), including all the rich nations except the United States. Among the Muslim-majority countries, only Turkey and Pakistan signed. India, with the second-largest population and one of the world's most dismal gender records, did not sign, claiming that gender should not be part of any trade agreement.[8] The 46 naysayers were particularly offended by women asking for procurement contracts and also felt it was just too much work to be taking on women's interests at all.

It was no real surprise that the United States did not sign. The Americans still have not ratified the 1979 international women's bill of rights, called the Convention on the Elimination of All Forms of Discrimination Against Women (CEDAW); it is one of only six countries that have not ratified this important treaty, the others being Iran, Palau, Somalia, Sudan, and Tonga. As I explained earlier, the United States was the original breeding ground for extreme-market philosophy; its representatives still often take the stance that markets should not accommodate social issues, including gender inequality. In recent years, the United States has also been the bully on the playground at the WTO and is not seen as likely to engage positively with a progressive agenda.

The insistence, by India, that the very word *trade* is already defined in a way that excludes gender issues is rooted, once again, in the philosophy that insists markets operate objectively, a premise that is conveniently formulated to ensure that those who benefit from "things as they are" stay on the gravy train. Acceding to this philosophy means supporting the current structure, values, and beneficiaries of the world's exchange system. This view cannot be combined with a gender lens without crumbling, because doing so would acknowledge that there are two different economies operating within the "objective" global system, one half being severely and structurally disadvantaged when compared with the other. India was intent on hewing to a philosophy founded on the falsehood that economics is gender-neutral.

The response from civil society was also disappointing. Some slammed the declaration in what has become a predictable strategy for slowing down progress on gender inclusion. Ostensibly progressive observers oppose any measure to help women until a whole raft of world problems are solved first—or until the world order is burned down and replaced with something else. This stance is a cynical attempt to take women hostage and use them as leverage for other ideological agendas the detractors want to prioritize instead. By frontloading all the world's problems on any tentative start for women, they are shouting, "Women last—everything else first!" It's an unconscionable variation on patriarchal politics, but you increasingly see these supposed progressives anywhere that system-level gender reforms are under consideration, always trying to block the women's cause and proving once again that the left can be the enemy of gender equality just as easily as the right can.

Unfortunately, women's organizations also jumped on this bandwagon, issuing statements that were, ironically, bereft of a gender perspective. More than 160 women's organizations and "allied groups" signed a petition asking their government representatives *not* to sign the declaration. Here are some of the things they said to protest the first-ever gender-equality agreement by the World Trade Organization:

> Women's rights organisations from all continents have rejected this declaration as simply a "pink herring" designed to distract attention from the harm the WTO does. If there was genuine interest in women's human rights, governments would change the rules of international trade that currently drive down women's wages, displace women from their land, privatise public goods to enrich multinational corporations. We are sick of gender equality being used as a cynical ploy to justify neoliberalism.
>
> —KATE LAPPIN, *regional coordinator,*
> *Asia Pacific Forum on Women, Law and Development*

Women peasants have been devastated by free trade policies that open up agricultural markets to foreign investment. Trade liberalization worsens corporate land-grabs that deprive women of their land and livelihood resulting [in] widespread hunger that destroys communities and deepens women's misery.

—ZENAIDA SORIANO,
Amihan, National Federation of Peasant Women, Philippines

Women were the first to show how WTO was institutionalised capitalist patriarchy on a world scale. We will not allow "women" to be used as a trojan horse to expand and extend a system that is destroying the lives and livelihoods of women and children, peasants and workers, and the planet.

—VANDANA SHIVA, *Indian scholar,*
environmental activist, food sovereignty advocate[9]

"Women" in all these statements refers to an indistinguishable subspecies of the downtrodden—there is no recognition that all the downtrodden are not equally disadvantaged, nor that the male "peasants" systematically exclude the female "peasants." Remarkably, women's economic interests are treated as a triviality that can be useful only as superficial cover, a Trojan horse to hide more substantive issues. Nothing done for women can be serious or substantive or beneficial, they imply; therefore, all efforts on their behalf are just a "cynical ploy." Even the mentions of land ownership reveal shocking ignorance: it wasn't the WTO that took land from these women—they never had land in the first place.

No engagement with the WTO is acceptable to these dissidents or to the "progressives" at the NGOs, even for the worthy purpose of helping women and, through them, the poor and the hungry. Not even if the purpose is to put the WTO on a more progressive track—that's only distracting from the harm it has already done. No, there are only two stances possible here—you stand against the WTO or you stand guilty with it—and no path leads anywhere productive from either position.

Neoliberalism is a term used so promiscuously it's hard to know what is meant when you see it. It can refer to an excessive faith in laissez-faire capitalism (what I have been calling extreme-market economics). Or it can be used as a criticism of programs that don't deal with systemic problems but expect individuals to solve their own. Neither of these objections applies to the people trying to persuade the WTO to start working on women's exclusion from the global markets.

In common usage, in fact, *neoliberal* is merely an epithet for anyone who will work within current economic structures, even to empower women and help the poor. To escape these barbs, one must not be working with *any* international economic organization or business, or presumably with any government that sends representatives to the WTO, including all 164 member nations. So, really, according to them, you can't work with any organization currently engaged with "the system" and not be called a "neoliberal." An exception would be made, I surmise, for all the unions that still negotiate with businesses around the world.

Contemporary critics often treat capitalism as if it were the only form of patriarchy there has ever been. The long and horrific experience of women under patriarchy—a singular force with many forms and infinite lives—is denied. From this perspective, there is no Paleolithic patriarchy, forager patriarchy, horticultural patriarchy, nomadic patriarchy, warrior patriarchy, or agricultural patriarchy. Certainly no socialist, communist, or Soviet patriarchy.

This stance doesn't recognize that women suffer from a unique set of constraints that keep them from engaging equally in *any* type of economy. In fact, the implicit suggestion is that women should be set aside, their exclusion allowed to continue, their suffering to go on, while this lot waits for a perfect world.

There is no way out of this box. And there is no room for women in it.

We can wait for a world order without problems before addressing gender inequality. Or we can prioritize women *now*.

Half the population is big enough. Five millennia of brutality is suffering enough. Least equal among all unequal groups is unfairness enough. Securing a hopeful future is reason enough. It's time to let the Double X Economy go first.

14 | THE PATH TO REDEMPTION

umanity's treatment of females is one of the darkest parts of our history. For too long, we have resisted shining a light there, perhaps fearful of confronting a painful reality. An enormous trove of evidence, from histories to statistics, has now brought this tragedy into plain sight. But the data also illuminates a path to redemption. For the sake of justice and compassion, as well as for the material welfare of the whole species, I beseech you to join the women's economic empowerment movement on this important new journey.

All over the world, women suffer from economic practices with roots a thousand years deep. Buying and selling daughters against their will. Burning brides whose dowries have been used up. Forcing a widow to accept sexual humiliation so she and her children will have means to survive. Starving dependent wives as punishment for some minor household offense. Trapping mothers in violent homes because they have no other shelter for themselves and their children.

We can now see that economic mechanisms systematically keep women dependent and unequal in every nation. Male monopoly on capital. Marriage bars against employment. Sexual assault in the workplace. Earnings and family assets appropriated by males. Bigotry about brain power. An unjustified burden of servitude. The motherhood penalty.

But the Double X Economy's exclusions also incur huge costs for entire societies. High adolescent fertility and infant mortality result from selling young daughters into marriage. Widows who have been left with nothing constitute the largest segment of the extreme poor. Food insecurity and world hunger are both worsened because women can't own land. After decades of unequal earnings, elderly women are more likely to depend on government assistance. Where women have no autonomy, the costs in death, property destruction, disease, and trauma are incalculable. Children go hungry, sick, and uneducated because their mothers have no economic power.

There is also a hefty opportunity cost. Women who work are the most reliable source of economic growth. When they are kept home because there is no affordable childcare—or because their husbands won't let them out of the house—they lose and so do their countries. Many societies invest heavily in female education, especially in the West, and then push women out of the workforce—wasting a valuable resource, losing a chance at sustained growth, and widening a skills gap that already threatens their future.

With a deliberate global effort to lift the constraints on the Double X Economy, some of the world's most tragic problems can be solved. Women's economic empowerment has been shown, many times, to be the best available weapon against poverty. Economically autonomous women can walk away from abuse. Providing young women with the means to earn shields them from human trafficking. Gender equality reduces violence of all kinds.

The beneficial effects of full inclusion for women would be visible at the institutional and national levels. Including women in the financial system contributes to institutional profit and also reduces risk, increases transparency and also adds stability for the entire economy. Allowing women to participate in international trade increases a nation's resilience and innovation. When women have money to spend, human capital is cultivated. Community investment and charitable contributions also rise. When women share in economic leadership we see better returns, lower risks, reduced environmental damage, and friendlier workplaces.

Because of its power to generate growth and reduce costs, the Double X Economy, when included, pays for itself. Investments made in affordable childcare, for instance, would be offset by an influx of women into the labor force who otherwise would have to stay home, leading to a rise in GDP, and therefore an increase in tax revenues. Yet data shows that men will not lose jobs if women come into the workforce, because the resulting growth drives the creation of more jobs. Men benefit in other ways when they share economic responsibilities with women: overwork, male-dominant workplaces, and the lone responsibility to provide take a profound toll on men worldwide.

Economic results are best when men and women work in a gender-balanced way, whether at work or at home. Studies show consistently that teams of males and females make better investments, produce better products, generate higher returns, and have fewer failures. At home, couples who share housework and paid work have closer relationships with children, more egalitarian values, less interpersonal tension, and more productivity.

If we want to find a better way to live as a civilization, there is no surer strategy than to remove the constraints on the Double X Economy. Nevertheless, there will be resistance. Some men will be angered by a global movement to include women in the economy because they cannot let go of their attachment to traditional masculinity without serious distress. Their rage will signal danger to all of us—as it always has—but we must resolve to stand together against it.

Economists are also likely to resist. That discipline is heavily invested in an ideology that cannot stretch to explain the systematic exclusion of half the human species. Women's disadvantages, they insist, must be the result of "self-selection"—that is, they ask us to believe that women in *every* country, in *every* time, in *every* industry, in *every* occupation, and in *every* domain of the world economy have either made the same self-defeating choices or have been lacking *whatever* quality was required for success in *all* instances. But the Double X Economy is traceable to a tragic history rather than millions of individual women making the same poor choices or sharing the same inadequacies.

When we look at the persistent disadvantages experienced by the world's women, we see a pattern of structural inequity caused by purposeful exclusion, not a thousand random acts of feminine irrationality. These are the distinguishing marks of humanity's oldest and largest underclass. Let's work together to redeem that ugly history and put a prosperous peace in its place.

A concerted global movement is needed to put an end to the systemic constraints on women. There is much to be done. It won't be easy and it won't be done quickly, but the change will be worth the effort. We can be inspired to take on this task by the promise of a world economy that is not only more inclusive, but free of the patriarchal exploitation that has subjugated women *and* men, while destroying the earth, for thousands of years.

Turning to an ethic of sharing instead of dominance will require nothing less than an evolutionary leap for our species. But agility is our strongest suit. We can do this.

The path is bright and clear, the need is pressing, and the potential is epic. Let's join together, a sisterhood and a brotherhood, to set the Double X Economy free.

EPILOGUE | NEXT STEPS

I n this momentous undertaking, there will be something for every-one to do. I have offered a few suggestions while describing what the Double X Economy is, what its limits are, and how it operates. In this epilogue I will give you a few more ideas. But from there, you should try to do what the rest of us have been doing: think through the limitations women are facing, try to come up with an action that would at least nudge the barriers, and then figure out how you can implement it.

There are also straightforward things that can be done, like using social media to increase people's awareness or giving to women's empowerment charities. These things can be done quickly. And there isn't a moment to lose while the suffering continues.

I am going to divide my remarks into three sets—one for the United States, one for the global community, and one for individuals. I focus first on the United States, because it is at a crossroads that will determine women's fate for many years and will inevitably affect women around the world, too.

UNITED STATES OF AMERICA

I want to remind Americans that Margaret Atwood's novel *The Handmaid's Tale* begins with the retraction of women's economic rights. That loss instantly reduces them to powerlessness, making it much easier for the rulers of Gilead to take over their reproductive rights. These two freedoms are not unrelated and should be protected with equal urgency.

Therefore, it is crucial to divert some of the intense attention being given to the abortion fight—which is justifiably causing outrage and even panic—to protecting economic rights as well. I fear the rollback of Second Wave employment protections has gone unnoticed because radical conservatives have been intentionally pulling public attention toward a single-issue campaign against reproductive freedom. It is essential to pay attention to what has happened—and is happening—to those Second Wave economic achievements.

American women produce almost as much GDP as men, pay substantial taxes, and vote more often. They are the biggest interest group in America. Every other interest group exacts their price for political support, and women should do the same. It's time to pound the table.

Here, then, is my suggested priority list. I have ordered these economic issues according to a combination of impact and ease of achievement.

Priority 1: A federal ban on forced arbitration contracts. The press has been referring to this issue as an "arcane" one, but it is in truth a bread-and-butter matter going unnoticed. These contracts force employees to surrender their job rights as a condition of employment by agreeing to pursue any grievance through arbitration arranged by the employer. The employee usually also signs away the right to join a class action suit. Therefore, these contracts constitute a blanket removal of all employment rights from American workers.

Forced arbitration contracts affect all employees, regardless of gender, race, ethnicity, or religion. However, I think women have more points of vulnerability to discrimination. That's why I identify this issue as a women's matter.

Forced arbitration contracts have been upheld as constitutional by the conservative Supreme Court. This decision will encourage more employers to adopt them. Already, nearly half of American workers are subject to these contracts. I predict that, as a result of the Supreme Court ruling, the number of U.S. workers subject to forced arbitration will grow, possibly until all working Americans are affected.

This fundamental attack on employment rights must be stopped. Fortunately, there is bipartisan support in Congress for doing so. Congress has already demonstrated that it is possible to override the practice by enacting a ban on forced arbitration for cases of sexual harassment. So there is already a template. And because the contracts will affect everyone, this is one issue where a coalition could be put together across a polarized populace. That effort should commence immediately.

However, commercial pressure should also be brought to bear. A list of companies using these contracts should be published. As consumers, citizens should stop buying those employers' products. On the business-to-business side, companies that care about maintaining their public reputation should not only refrain from adopting these contracts but also refuse to buy from or otherwise do business with firms that do have them. The object is to remove any upside advantage for firms to lobby against a ban.

Priority 2: Forgiveness of all student debt. This matter is a women's issue because females hold two-thirds of the debt, have borrowed more money, and—barring progress on equal pay—will have lower salaries to use to pay off the loans. Remember, women are more invested in these loans because they go to college at a higher rate and they have to pursue more credentials in order to win the same jobs as men. For that reason, a limit on the amount of debt the government will forgive per person discriminates against women. Bear in mind that this is not an elite issue: 65 percent of millennials have some kind of postsecondary training. Forgiving student debt will not disproportionately benefit the rich: people with means don't allow their children to take out these predatory loans in the first place. *Everyone* who has one of these loans needs relief.

The government should be looking to lift this burden for economic reasons anyway, so forgiveness should not be treated as a handout or entitlement. The future economy will suffer for having an entire generation burdened like this. The specter of debt will ultimately reduce the number of people going for postsecondary education, which will directly reduce national competitiveness. The debt will affect consumer spending, savings, and investment because it will suck up all those dollars. It will also affect household formation, which will dampen everything from purchase of durable goods to housing starts. The debt will depress the fertility rate and make it harder for this "sandwich generation" to support the elderly, therefore increasing the cost of social and health services to the government. If the federal government can afford to give handouts to banks and billionaires, it can afford to prevent this demographic disaster.

Because of the long-term impact on the economy, the decision to forgive student debt should not be approached as a onetime "expense" to the federal government, taken right off the budget as a line item with no benefits. Instead, the costs and benefits should be calculated according to a capital investment model that assesses the initial outlay as netted out against the present value of all the positive inflows that can be forecast as a result of the investment. The forecast should be compared with a fully fleshed forecast of the damage that will come from keeping the debt on the books. (If you don't get what I just said, keep on reading and don't worry about it. In finance, it's actually a pretty basic calculation, and I am sure *someone* reading this will know how to do it.)

When the impact of student debt forgiveness is calculated correctly, I think it will become clear that leaving this debt outstanding is not only heartless, it is economically *insane*.

Finally, I want to call out to other baby boomers to get behind this idea, because the debt will hurt our own children and grandchildren for decades to come. Those of us who are parents should be ready to take to the streets to get it removed.

Priority 3: Universal childcare. I have given the case for universal childcare in chapter 7. Here I just want to say that it should be a high priority and that I have only listed the other two things first because I think they can be done more quickly. I believe childcare should be available to everyone, including mothers who have chosen to stay home. We should be planning this public service as "early childhood development" and not "day care": we will want all children to have access—and for their parents to *want* access.

Priority 4: Moving the enforcement of equal pay to the executive branch. We now know from our own experience, as well as that in other countries, that putting the burden of equal pay enforcement on individual women was a bad idea. We should look for a radical shift of responsibility. Especially now that the judiciary has been stuffed with conservative judges, we cannot otherwise expect this situation to improve. We must take these decisions away from the courts to the greatest extent possible.

Priority 5: Equal participation in all infrastructure projects. Whether it's the Green New Deal or state highway projects, women should be getting a fair share of the jobs created.

A major source of unequal pay and advancement is the near monopoly males have in construction and other "hard," "heavy" jobs. Working-class women are particularly affected by this form of discrimination. Yet the imagery around infrastructure is all about bringing back "man jobs." Not acceptable. Every time one of these programs comes under consideration, women and their male allies should be demanding equal inclusion.

Priority 6: New protections for stay-at-home wives and mothers. I list this idea last only because it will probably take research to figure out how best to do it before legislation can be drafted. I am unconvinced that higher alimony payments are either the best or the only way to get this done.

Our collective emphasis on working women has overshadowed the personal risk taken by women who are dependent on their husbands for income. Women's advocates inevitably cite the higher number of women who leave work to care for children as a cause of unequal pay and advancement. It is hypocritical not to have a platform for protecting these women.

In *all* these efforts, it is essential to ensure that the rights of minority and poor women are fairly treated, including special adjustments to compensate for their unique disadvantages.

The United States plays a special role in the international community, and could have a particularly positive impact on women's economics if ordinary Americans took a stand.

THE WORLD

Global governance. Women do not have a voice in the global governance of the economy. Even though the G7, the G20, and APEC have instigated outward-facing show-and-tell activities in the past five years, these activities are, to a great extent, merely efforts to pacify women's advocates by providing the appearance of inclusion.

For instance, these economic cooperation summits will have a separate "women's week" where women's economic issues are presented, but the delegates to the main body do not attend. The main meeting will then be held at least six months later—without women's representatives present—and the only connection between the two events will be a short summary of women's key points sent from "women's week" to the delegates. Usually that document is hastily put together by consensus at the women's week, instead of being rooted in evidence and informed by existing practice and policy. I doubt that the points get much attention from the delegates, and *I know* that some nations, behind the scenes, refuse to cooperate on any goals regarding women. We should all be calling out the disingenuous behavior of our national economic representatives.

The shortage of expertise on women in economics is painfully evident in many of these venues, however. For instance, when I spoke at APEC's women's week in 2018, the program lasted four full days and yet there were only three speakers on the entire agenda who gave talks oriented toward economics. The rest were all about reproductive freedom and violence against women (without an economic angle), or they were informal panels by "practitioners" (either businesspeople, mostly sponsors, or local entrepreneurs). At the end, we took a hurried vote about what matters should be taken forward to APEC. That's pretty much how it goes for all these women's weeks. If an actual delegate to APEC had shown up for this women's gathering, he (always a "he") could be excused for concluding that either women know nothing about economics or that their issues are already covered by entities such as the World Health Organization. The perception that women are just breeders is unwittingly underscored by the focus on reproduction in these meetings, at the expense of economics.

Unfortunately, most of the men involved in international economic governance shamelessly refuse to pay any attention to the Double X Economy. About two years ago, I was on a panel at a World Bank internal training meeting that drew professional employees from all over the world. There were four hundred participants. The women's economics panel was one of four offered in one time slot, but only twenty-five people came to it, all but two of them women (and there were very few women at this meeting). That same year, the W20 was invited to give a presentation at the virtually all-male global meeting of the Think Tank 20. The men sat through other presentations, including a long one on environmental issues. But as soon as the W20 went to the stage, the Think Tank 20 got up and walked out.

At other confabs, the absence of a holistic appreciation for the Double X Economy causes the effort to be fragmented and undermined. The recent United Nations High-Level Panel on Women's Economic Empowerment was a once-in-a-lifetime opportunity to get a global understanding and initiative started on behalf of women in the economy. However, the panel mostly fell into a turf war over other interests and ideologies.

Participants in international efforts to address the Double X Economy should be chosen according to their expertise, their commitment to women, and their independence, so that they can focus on women as a whole, and not displace women's interests in favor of other agendas.

There is a pressing need to found and fund an independent global organization to advocate for women's economic interests from an informed perspective. This organization should have a building and staff of its own and be authorized to participate in all the global summits *as* delegates. It should become a repository of research on women's economics and should monitor and report on progress. Despite years of floundering, the W20 now looks like the most likely base from which to start. Queen Máxima of the Netherlands has stepped up to lead the fund-raising and formalization of the W20. It would be a service to all women for that effort to be a success.

More pressure should be put on organizations like the WTO to adopt a gender lens. Canada is posing a good example to follow. The best way to support such efforts is for citizens in each country to put pressure on national governments. It's the national leadership that sets the agenda for each country, which in turn sets the priorities for the world. We cannot keep treating these entities as if what they are doing is gender-neutral. These guys work for us—we should make them accountable.

Leadership and expertise. Leaders like Christine Lagarde at the International Monetary Fund and Justin Trudeau in Canada have made all the difference. Supporting women-friendly leadership in these international economic bodies is essential.

However, supporting leadership in the private sector is important as well. I am dismayed by people who dismiss initiatives like those supporting women on corporate boards as if they were only going to advantage rich women. The leaders of corporations affect everyone who works for them, buys from them, and supplies them, as well as affecting the communities they operate in and the environment. The issues of impact range from equal pay and advancement to worker and product safety to transparency and corruption. We would not dismiss the importance of having women (and sympathetic men) in leadership positions in government, and we should not do so for leadership in the economy, either. It's too important.

There is a lamentable lack of expertise about women in the economy. This is occurring in part because economics departments are so gender-unfriendly. There are feminist economists and others who can offer useful advice scattered through the world's universities, governments, and agencies. These people need to be identified, supported, consulted, and brought together to document and formulate policies, as well as to assist with outreach to convince the rest of the policy community to help. Young women should be encouraged to undertake relevant programs of study so that they will be ready to staff the next generation of posts.

Public and private funding. Appeals should be made to convince international aid and global charities to support women's economic empowerment. In particular, citizens in the donor countries should insist that a growing portion of their international aid budgets go directly to women. Especially given that the rest of the budgets often get absorbed by military spending and corruption, there should be some willingness to support women because we know it's more effective and the money will be used productively.

INDIVIDUAL ACTIONS

Many places in the movement can benefit from individual involvement. Here are a few:

Investment. Individual, impact, and institutional investors should make a point of investing in gender-supportive companies, female entrepreneurs, and large-scale projects that aim to benefit women.

Syndicates of women investors should be formed that will facilitate angel investing by women into women-owned enterprises. Some of these should be made accessible to smaller investors.

Crowdfunding women-owned enterprises, as well as projects that benefit women, is something just about anyone can do. The more women, as well as other investors, motivated to balance the scale who enter this domain, the better.

I know this is a hard one, but when a company comes into the news with an egregious violation of gender equality, moving out of that company's stock puts pressure on it to change. As a general practice, putting money into companies with a good gender rating will support a systems shift toward gender equality.

Consumption. Purposeful consumption along the lines we have already seen in fair trade would be a good idea. Boycotts don't tend to work and often hurt workers. Instead, positive choices of products made by gender-friendly companies helps convince their competitors to reform.

There are many ways to assess whether a producer is "gender-supportive." For instance, you can use the Bloomberg Gender Equality Index for this purpose. Another index is the Edge Certification for employers. This certification is very rigorous and expensive for companies to obtain. If you see a company displaying that seal, it's good to show support with your money. Similarly, there is the Gender Equal brand sign, which is given for good performance on a system of gender indicators for branded products. You can also use an app to look up brands, not just companies, to get a comparative rating within a given category.

Occasionally, retailers and marketing co-ops try out labels indicating that a product is made by a woman-owned business or that a commodity is produced by women farmers. It is good to support these efforts when you see them, because these things are mostly in test form now—which is why they seem to come and go—and even a short bump in sales helps persuade businesses that they should continue to develop these forms of supporting women in the economy.

Employment. Within a workplace, individuals can take actions either as coworkers or managers. Perhaps the most radical is that, where it is legal, employees should share their compensation information. If a way to do this anonymously can be provided, that is best, but informal conversation is effective. The biggest barrier for women in salary negotiation (besides bigotry) is the opacity of pay arrangements.

You don't need a full-blown mentoring program to encourage upcoming women. I do caution against offering too much criticism, as this kind of advice can be more destructive than helpful. A little boost of confidence, however, can go a long way.

To the extent you have the power, getting career-developing opportunities allocated to women and, of course, promoting them would be helpful.

Many experts and management consultancies have recommended that managers be evaluated and incentivized on their diversity achievements. I agree with this recommendation. For years, businesspeople have thought it was enough to have CEO buy-in for diversity objectives. We know now that the problem is at the workbench level and that the managers there care less about company goals than about their own.

Everyone can refuse to go along with denigrating speech about women. Everyone can agree to speak up about sexual harassment. Everyone can stop humoring bigots.

Awareness. We must build our ranks and increase pressure on institutions by raising awareness of the dimensions of women's exclusion, the magnitude of its impact, and the difference change will make. I think this can be done in various ways to different degrees. Nearly everyone who reads this book will, I suspect, have some kind of social media presence. I think it would be good to share your own commitment of support, as well as items of interest published online by or about the movement.

Journalism and other forms of media can cover the cause, especially in mainstream media that reaches large segments of the public. Many interesting people and programs can provide content, both stories and images. Informed representatives of the international movement can be interviewed at the World Bank, the International Finance Corporation, Chatham House, WEConnect, USAID, the Department for International Development, UN Women, and other institutions. The gender teams at big institutions are usually very small; it helps them when they get a shout-out, so please take the time. Whenever you can share or tweet or write, please do so.

Public awareness and support is what pushes governments to act on gender issues, as well as funders, public and private, to put money into helping women. The more the public supports this cause, the easier the work will be.

Speech. There should be a campaign to insist that the terms *implicit bias* and *unconscious bias* be used in settings where there is a reasonable chance the bias is actually unconscious and not just unadmitted. Using those terms to describe outright bigotry should never happen. People who speak and act like gender bigots should be treated as disapprovingly as racial bigots.

A group like Mothers Against Drunk Driving could be formed and funded to call for an end to the motherhood penalty. Public service announcements should dramatize the moral offensiveness inherent in withholding fair pay from someone who must support children, even when that someone is female. This is a despicable attitude that has gone unremarked. Shame should be attached to it until the attitude ceases and the discriminatory behaviors stop.

Charitable giving. Quite a few charities specialize in empowering women economically, and they get a very small share of the gifts given. Try to find room in your donation budget to give to one of them. On the global level, I feel best able to vouch for CARE, but there are women's empowerment efforts at several large charities that you can find online. I do think highly of Women for Women International, which focuses on conflict areas. There aren't many programs available in those countries, likely because people are just afraid of them. Local charities that support women are often effective and thus worthy of our support.

Beyond what I have suggested, I ask everyone to think creatively about your own strengths and try to find ways to apply them. If everyone adds their own voice and skills, the job will be much easier.

I welcome you to one of the most important causes of our time, perhaps in history.

NOTES

SELECTED BIBLIOGRAPHY

ACKNOWLEDGMENTS

INDEX

NOTES

1. THE DOUBLE X ECONOMY

1. Diane Coyle, "Economics Has a Problem with Women," *Financial Times*, August 28, 2017, https://www.ft.com/content/6b3cc8be-881e-11e7-afd2-74b8 ecd34d3b; Mary Daly, "Economics Trails the Sciences in Attracting a Diverse Student Mix," *Financial Times*, May 13, 2018, https://www.ft.com/content /d47e885a-539b-11e8-84f4-43d65af59d43; "Inefficient Equilibrium: Women and Economics," *Economist*, December 19, 2017, https://www.economist.com /christmas-specials/2017/12/19/women-and-economics; Elizabeth Winkler, "'Hotter,' 'Lesbian,' 'Feminazi': How Some Economists Discuss Their Female Colleagues," *Washington Post*, August 22, 2017, https://www.washingtonpost .com/news/wonk/wp/2017/08/22/hotter-lesbian-feminazi-how-some -economists-discuss-their-female-colleagues/; Justin Wolfers, "Evidence of a Toxic Environment for Women in Economics," *New York Times*, August 18, 2017, https://www.nytimes.com/2017/08/18/upshot/evidence-of-a-toxic -environment-for-women-in-economics.html; Justin Wolfers, "Why Women's Voices Are Scarce in Economics," *New York Times*, February 2, 2018, https:// www.nytimes.com/2018/02/02/business/why-womens-voices-are-scarce -in-economics.html; Ann Mari May, "Women Are Missing from Economics. Here's Why That Matters for All of Us," *Huffington Post*, June 11, 2018. But see also Mark J. Perry, "Women's Voices Might Be Scarce in Economics, but They Are Abundant and Over-Represented in Most Academic Fields and Graduate School Overall," *AEIdeas*, February 4, 2018, http://www.aei.org/publication /womens-voices-might-be-scarce-in-economics-but-they-are-abundant -and-over-represented-in-most-academic-fields-and-graduate-school-overall. Perry, a professor at the University of Michigan, makes the usual argument that women are just naturally drawn to other subjects, but he also objects that there are *too many* women in other subjects (admitting also that their

performance is better) and nobody is complaining about that. His argument would be more persuasive if there weren't so much evidence of bullying and harassment of women in economics departments. Alice Wu, *Gender Stereotyping in Academia: Evidence from Economics Job Market Rumors Forum* (thesis, University of California, Berkeley, December 2017), https://growthecon .com/assets/Wu_EJMR_paper.pdf.

2. Wolfers, "Why Women's Voices Are Scarce in Economics"; American Physical Society, "Doctoral Degrees Earned by Women," https://www.aps.org/programs /education/statistics/fraction-phd.cfm. The data goes up to 2017 and is taken from the Integrated Postsecondary Education Data System and the American Physical Society.

3. John T. Harvey, "Do Women Avoid Economics . . . or Does Economics Avoid Women?," *Forbes*, January 11, 2019, https://www.forbes.com/sites/johntharvey /2019/01/11/do-women-avoid-economics-or-does-economics-avoid-women /#642585aa2f32; Winkler, "'Hotter,' 'Lesbian,' 'Feminazi.'"

4. "Market Power: Women in Economics," *Economist*, March 23, 2019, 11–12; Daly, "Economics Trails the Sciences in Attracting a Diverse Student Mix"; Wolfers, "Why Women's Voices Are Scarce in Economics"; "Inefficient Equilibrium"; Winkler, "'Hotter,' 'Lesbian,' 'Feminazi.'"

5. "Inefficient Equilibrium."

6. Coyle, "Economics Has a Problem with Women."

7. The first of these attempts was actually made in 1995 by the United Nations Development Programme's *Human Development Report*. However, there was a long period of silence after that. It was in 2006, when the World Economic Forum published its first *Global Gender Gap Report*, that other institutions began reporting on the links between gender equality and economic health. Between 2006 and 2012, several important reports were released in a row. After that, activity increased every year. *Gender, Equality and Development* (Washington, DC: World Bank Group, 2012); Organisation for Economic Co-operation and Development, *Closing the Gender Gap: Act Now!* (Paris: Organisation for Economic Co-operation and Development, 2011); UNICEF, *State of the World's Children: Women and Children—The Double Dividend of Gender Equality* (New York: UNICEF, 2007). At this point, early 2019, reports from major institutions are released every year.

8. See, for instance, Ronald Inglehart and Pippa Norris, *Rising Tide: Gender Equality and Cultural Change Around the World* (Cambridge, UK: Cambridge University Press, 2003).

9. Katrin Elborgh-Woytek, Monique Newiak, Kalpana Kochlar, Stefania Fabrizio, Kangni Kpodar, Philippe Wingender, Benedict Clements, and Gerd Schwartz, *Women, Work and the Economy: Macroeconomic Gains from Gender Equity* (Washington, DC: International Monetary Fund, 2013); DeAnne Aguirre, Leila Hoteit, Christine Rupp, and Karim Sabbagh, *Empowering the Third Billion: Women and the World of Work* (New York: Booz and Company, 2012); Sandra Lawson and Douglas B. Gilman, *The Power of the Purse: Gender Equality and Middle-Class Spending* (New York: Goldman Sachs Global Market Institute, 2009); Jonathan Woetzel, Anu Madgavkar, Kweilin Ellingrud, Eric Labaye, Sandrine Devillard, Eric Kutcher, James Manyika, Richard Dobbs, and Mekala

Krishnan, *The Power of Parity* (New York: McKinsey Global Markets Institute, 2015); "Pursuing Women's Economic Empowerment, Meeting of the G7 Ministers and Central Bank Governors, June 1–2, 2018, Whistler, Canada," prepared by the staff of the International Monetary Fund, May 31, 2018, https://www.imf.org/en/Publications/Policy-Papers/Issues/2018/05/31 /pp053118pursuing-womens-economic-empowerment; UNICEF, *State of the World's Children.*

10. Woetzel et al., *The Power of Parity*, 26. According to McKinsey, the global average in 2015 was 37 percent. However, the GDP contribution of women is higher in the bigger economies, and it is growing. On this basis, I have conservatively estimated roughly 40 percent at this time. See also Food and Agriculture Organization, "Women in Agriculture: Closing the Gender Gap for Development," in *The State of Food and Agriculture* (Rome: Food and Agriculture Organization of the United Nations, 2011).

11. Ewa Lechman and Harleen Kaur, "Economic Growth and Female Labor Force Participation—Verifying the U-Feminization Hypothesis: New Evidence for 162 Countries over the Period 1990–2012," *Economics and Sociology* 8, no. 1 (2015): 246–57. The discourse about working women and growth builds substantially on the work of the Harvard professor Claudia Goldin. For instance, Claudia Goldin, "The U-Shaped Female Labor Force in Economic Development and Economic History," NBER Working Paper Series, no. 4707 (Cambridge, MA: National Bureau of Economic Research, 1994).

12. UNICEF, *State of the World's Children.*

13. Quentin Wodon and Benedicte De La Briere, *Unrealized Potential: The High Cost of Gender Inequality in Earnings* (Washington, DC: World Bank Group, Children's Investment Fund Foundation, Global Partnership for Education, Canada, 2018).

14. Lawson and Gilman, *The Power of the Purse.*

15. World Economic Forum, *The Global Gender Gap Report*, 2006–2018.

16. Organisation for Economic Co-operation and Development, *Closing the Gender Gap.*

17. For landholders, Food and Agriculture Organization, "Gender and Land Rights Database," http://www.fao.org/gender-landrights-database/en/. For wealth, "Daily Chart: Women's Wealth Is Rising," *Economist*, March 8, 2018, https:// www.economist.com/graphic-detail/2018/03/08/womens-wealth-is-rising.

18. *Measuring Women's Financial Inclusion: The Value of Sex-Disaggregated Data* (Washington, DC: Global Banking Alliance for Women, Data 2X, InterAmerican Development Bank, 2015).

19. Susan Harris Rimmer, *Gender-Smart Procurement Policies for Driving Change* (London: Chatham House, 2017); Romina Kazandjian, Lisa Kolovich, Kalpana Kochhar, and Monique Newiak, "Gender Equality and Economic Diversification," International Monetary Fund Working Paper, WP/16/140, https://www .imf.org/external/pubs/ft/wp/2016/wp16140.pdf.

20. Gerda Lerner, *The Creation of Patriarchy* (Oxford: Oxford University Press, 1986); Janet S. Hyde, Sara M. Lindberg, Marcia C. Linn, Amy B. Ellis, and Caroline C. Williams, "Gender Similarities Characterize Math Performance," *Science* 321 (2008): 494–95; E. Zell, Z. Krizen, and S. R. Teeter, "Evaluating

Gender Similarities and Differences Using Metasynthesis," *American Psychologist* 70 (2015): 10–20.

21. *WHO Multi-country Study on Women's Health and Domestic Violence Against Women: Summary Report—Initial Results on Prevalence, Health Outcomes and Women's Responses* (Geneva: World Health Organization, 2005); Anke Hoeffler and James Fearon, "Conflict and Violence Assessment Paper," Copenhagen Consensus Center, August 22, 2014; Bjørn Lomborg and Michelle A. Williams, "The Cost of Domestic Violence Is Astonishing," *Washington Post*, February 22, 2017; Valerie Hudson, Bonnie Ballif-Spanvill, Mary Caprioli, and Chad Emmett, *Sex and World Peace* (New York: Columbia University Press, 2014).

22. Max Roser, "War and Peace," Our World in Data, https://ourworldindata.org/war-and-peace. See also Steven Pinker, *The Better Angels of Our Nature: Why Violence Has Declined* (New York: Viking, 2011).

23. For a review and discussion of statistics, see Conor Seyle, "Is the World Getting More Peaceful?," OEF Research, a program of One Earth Future, https://oefresearch.org/think-peace/world-getting-more-peaceful.

24. Dwight D. Eisenhower, address to the American Society of Newspaper Editors, April 16, 1953, available online.

25. Kevin Bales, *Disposable People: New Slavery in the Global Economy* (Berkeley: University of California Press, 2017).

26. Marianne Egger de Campo, "Contemporary Greedy Institutions: An Essay on Lewis Coser's Concept in the Era of the 'Hive Mind,'" *Czech Sociological Review* 49, no. 6 (2013): 969–86. The original concept of "greedy institutions" was the brainchild of Lewis Coser. See Lewis Coser, *Greedy Institutions: Patterns of Undivided Commitment* (New York: Free Press, 1974). See, for instance, M. G. Marmot, G. Rose, M. Shipley, and P. J. Hamilton, "Employment Grade and Coronary Heart Disease in British Civil Servants," *Journal of Epidemiology and Community Health* 32, no. 4 (1978): 244–49.

27. Kellie A. McElhaney and Sanaz Mobasseri, *Women Create a Sustainable Future* (San Francisco: University of California, Center for Responsible Business, Haas Business School, 2012), https://www.eticanews.it/wp-content/uploads/2012/11/Report-Women_Create_Sustainable_Value.pdf.

2. BEHIND THE BIG DATA

1. At the time we were starting this study, the only other scholar looking at the question was Dr. Marni Sommer, of the Mailman School of Public Health at Columbia University, New York. We knew and worked with Dr. Sommer, who experienced the same kind of skepticism we did. She has since gone on to found a global community of academics and professionals focused on the impact of sanitary-care issues on poor schoolgirls.

2. Neil Andersson, Sergio Paredes-Solís, Deborah Milne, Khalid Omer, Nobantu Marokoane, Ditiro Laetsang, and Anne Cockcroft, "Prevalence and Risk Factors for Forced or Coerced Sex Among School-Going Youth: National Cross-Sectional Studies in 10 Southern African Countries in 2003 and 2007," *BMJ Open* 2 (2012): e000754.

3. Quentin Wodon, Claudio Montenegro, Hoa Nguyen, and Adenike Onagoruwa, *Missed Opportunities: The High Cost of Not Educating Girls* (Washington, DC: World Bank Group, 2018), https://openknowledge.worldbank.org/handle /10986/29956; Quentin Wodon, C. Male, A. Nayihouba, A. Onagoruwa, A. Savadogo, A. Yedan, J. Edmeades, et al., *Economic Impacts of Child Marriage: Global Synthesis Report* (Washington, DC: World Bank and International Center for Research on Women, 2018), https://www.icrw.org/wp-content/uploads /2017/06/EICM-Global-Conference-Edition-June-27-FINAL.pdf.

4. Linda Scott, Paul Montgomery, Laurel Steinfield, Catherine Dolan, and Sue Dopson, "Sanitary Pad Acceptability and Sustainability Study," October 2013, https:// www.doublexeconomy.com/wp-content/uploads/2010/09/7PageReport.pdf.

5. Julie Hennegan, Paul Montgomery, Catherine Dolan, MaryAlice Wu, Laurel Steinfield, and Linda Scott, "Menstruation and the Cycle of Poverty: A Cluster Quasi-randomised Control Trial of Sanitary Pad and Puberty Education Provision in Uganda," *PLOS ONE* 11, no. 12 (2016): e0166122.

6. "Women Faculty Face Bias at UCLA," *Los Angeles Times*, October 8, 2015; Melissa Korn, "Gender Bias Alleged at UCLA's Anderson Business School," *Wall Street Journal*, June 4, 2014; Jodi Kantor, "Harvard Business School Case Study: Gender Equity," *New York Times*, September 7, 2013; Katy Waldman, "Harvard Business School Apologizes for Sexism on Campus," *Slate*, January 29, 2014.

7. Linda Scott, "Let's Be Honest About Gender Discrimination at Business Schools," *Bloomberg*, July 28, 2014. See also David Moltz, "The B-School Glass Ceiling," *Inside Higher Education*, February 23, 2010.

8. Bhagwan Chowdhry, "Would a Push to Hire More Women Reduce Gender Pay-Gap? Not Until We Fix the Pipeline," *Huffington Post*, November 30, 2014; Larry Gordon, "Women Faculty Face Bias at UCLA," *Los Angeles Times*, October 4, 2015.

9. UCLA faculty expressed this belief to me in 2014; however, an analysis by management consultancy Korn Ferry, based on empirical data from the school, also pointed to the dean's lack of commitment to gender diversity and identified it as a block to progress. Korn Ferry, *Gender Equity Final Report*, July 2015, https://www.anderson.ucla.edu/documents/areas/adm/dean/Korn -Ferry-Gender-Study-FINAL.pdf. The *Los Angeles Times* also reported that the school leadership had "not demonstrated the focused intention and proactive behavior required to increase diversity." Gordon, "Women Faculty Face Bias at UCLA."

10. I figured this out by visiting each school's website, going to its finance department page, clicking on every member's CV, and looking at the dates they finished their education. I then counted the percentage of older men versus younger ones, and compared the total number of finance faculty members to the total number of professors across the school.

11. Korn Ferry's *Gender Equity Final Report* also alludes to UCLA finance faculty wives being at home. I also asked respondents in my interviews about wives of finance faculty, and most answered that their wives stayed at home. Sreedhari D. Desai, Dolly Chugh, and Arthur P. Brief, "The Implications of

Marriage Structure for Men's Workplace Attitudes, Beliefs, and Behaviors Toward Women," *Administrative Science Quarterly* 59, no. 2 (2014): 330–65. Korn Ferry, *Gender Equity Final Report.*

12. Waldman, "Harvard Business School Apologizes for Sexism on Campus."

13. Korn Ferry, *Gender Equity Final Report.*

14. Valerie Hudson, Bonnie Ballif-Spanvill, Mary Caprioli, and Chad Emmett, *Sex and World Peace* (New York: Columbia University Press, 2014), 85–86.

15. Joseph A. Vandello, Jennifer K. Bosson, Rochelle M. Burnaford, Jonathan R. Weaver, and S. Arzu Wasti, "Precarious Manhood and Displays of Physical Aggression," *Personality and Social Psychology Bulletin* 35, no. 5 (May 2009): 623–34; Joseph A. Vandello and Jennifer K. Bosson, "Precarious Manhood and Its Links to Action and Agression," *Association for Psychological Science* 20, no. 2 (2011); Joseph A. Vandello and Jennifer K. Bosson, "Hard Won and Easily Lost: A Review and Synthesis of Theory and Research on Precarious Manhood," *Psychology of Men and Masculinity* 14, no. 2 (2013): 101–13; Michael M. Copenhaver, Steve J. Lash, and Richard M. Eisler, "Masculine Gender-Role Stress, Anger, and Male Intimate Abusiveness: Implications for Men's Relationships," *Sex Roles* 42, nos. 5–6 (2000): 405–15; Natasha Kosakowska, "If My Masculinity Is Threatened I Won't Support Gender Equality? The Role of Agentic Self-Stereotyping in Restoration of Manhood and Perception of Gender Relations," *Psychology of Men and Masculinity* 17, no. 3 (July 2016): 274–84.

3. CONTROLLED BY NECESSITIES

1. I used a large number of sources for this section, some of them specifically addressing land rights and others that were about marital rights or financial activities, including ownership and inheritance of land. Works specifically about women's property rights include L. Muthoni Wanyeki, *Women and Land in Africa* (Cape Town, South Africa: David Philip, 2003); Janet Walsh, *Double Standards: Women's Property Rights Violations in Kenya* (New York: Human Rights Watch, 2003); Amy Porter, *Their Lives, Their Wills* (Lubbock: Texas Tech University Press, 2015); Rebecca Sharpless and Melissa Walker, *Work, Family, and Faith* (Columbia, MO: University of Missouri Press, 2006); Carmen Diana Deere and Magdalena León, *Empowering Women: Land and Property Rights in Latin America* (Pittsburgh: University of Pittsburgh Press, 2001); Bipasha Baruah, *Women and Property in Urban India* (Vancouver: University of British Columbia, 2010); Bina Agarwal, *A Field of One's Own* (Cambridge, UK: Cambridge University Press, 1995); Cema Bolabola, *Land Rights of Pacific Women* (Fiji: Institute of Pacific Studies, University of the South Pacific, 1986); Gale Summerfield and Irene Tinker, *Women's Rights to House and Land: China, Laos and Vietnam* (Boulder, CO: Lynne Rienner Publishers, 1999).

2. "Married to the Mortgage," *Economist*, July 13, 2013, https://www.economist.com/china/2013/07/13/married-to-the-mortgage; "Watering the Gardens of Others: China's Women Are Being Shut Out of the Land and Housing Markets," *Economist*, June 12, 2015, https://www.economist.com/asia/2015/06/12/watering-the-gardens-of-others.

3. Food and Agriculture Organization, "Gender and Land Rights Database," http://www.fao.org/gender-landrights-database/data-map/statistics/en/, accessed June 13, 2019.

4. FAO data is the percentage of landholders who are either male or female. However, it emphasizes that, because men tend to own larger plots, their share of the farmland is higher than their representation as landholders.

5. I am drawing on my own experiences and observations in Uganda throughout this section, but also on the following sources: Constitute Project, "Uganda's Constitution of 1995 with Amendments Through 2005" (Constitute Project, 2017), https://www.constituteproject.org/constitution/Uganda_2005.pdf?lang=en; Rachel Loftspring, "Inheritance Rights in Uganda: How Equal Inheritance Rights in Uganda Would Reduce Poverty and Decrease the Spread of HIV/AIDS in Uganda," *University of Pennsylvania Journal of International Law* 29, no. 1 (2014); Valerie Bennett, Ginger Faulk, Anna Kovina, and Tatjana Eres, "Report: The Inheritance Law in Uganda; The Plight of Widows and Children," *Georgetown Journal of Gender and Law* 7 (December 2006): 451.

6. Human Rights Watch, *Just Die Quietly: Domestic Violence and Women's Vulnerability to HIV in Uganda* (New York: Human Rights Watch, 2003), 35.

7. Walsh, *Double Standards*, 13.

8. Walsh, *Double Standards*, 1.

9. Food and Agriculture Organization, "The State of Food and Agriculture: Women in Agriculture, Closing the Gender Gap for Development" (Rome: Food and Agriculture Organization, Economic and Social Development Department, 2010), 3; World Food Programme, "Women and Hunger: 10 Facts," https://www.wfp.org/our-work/preventing-hunger/focus-women/women-hunger-facts.

10. Food and Agriculture Organization, "State of Food and Agriculture."

11. Mary Johnstone-Louis, *Case Study: International Women's Coffee Alliance*, Power Shift: The Oxford Forum for Women in the World Economy, 2013, https://www.doublexeconomy.com/wp-content/uploads/2019/09/Power-Shift-IWCA-Case.pdf.

12. Linda Scott, *Private Sector Engagement with Women's Economic Empowerment: Lessons Learned from Years of Practice* (Oxford: Saïd Business School Series, University of Oxford, November 2017), https://www.doublexeconomy.com/wp-content/uploads/2018/10/RES-0054-GBCWEE-Report-171117-BOOKLET.pdf.

13. Scott, *Private Sector Engagement with Women's Economic Empowerment.*

14. Food and Agriculture Organization, "State of Food and Agriculture," vi.

15. Women for Women International, *Ending Violence Against Women in Eastern Congo*, Winter 2007, 20–22, quoted in Valerie Hudson, Bonnie Ballif-Spanvill, Mary Caprioli, and Chad Emmett, *Sex and World Peace* (New York: Columbia University Press, 2014).

16. *WHO Multi-country Study on Women's Health and Domestic Violence Against Women: Summary Report—Initial Results on Prevalence, Health Outcomes and Women's Responses* (Geneva: World Health Organization, 2005).

17. Victim blaming is common in incidents of domestic violence. Consequently, surveys assessing the prevalence of and attitudes toward intimate partner

violence often use a standard set of questions asking the reasons for which it is acceptable to beat a woman. "Burning the dinner" is a standard checklist item. In 2016, for instance, 68 percent of respondents in Nepal said a woman could be beaten if she neglects the children, argues with her husband, refuses sex, or burns the dinner. The same victim-blaming behavior is common in the developed nations as well. Enrique Gracia, "Intimate Partner Violence Against Women and Victim-Blaming Attitudes Among Europeans," *World Health Organization Bulletin* 92, no. 5 (May 1, 2014): 380–81; Saraswati Sundas, "Bhutan Tackles Violence Against Women for 'Refusing Sex, Burning the Dinner,'" Reuters World News, March 22, 2016, https://uk.reuters.com/article/us-bhutan -women-abuse/bhutan-tackles-violence-against-women-for-refusing-sex -burning-the-dinner-idUSKCN0WP04E.

18. Amber Peterman, Audrey Pereira, Jennifer Bleck, Tia M. Palermo, and Kathryn M. Yount, "Women's Individual Asset Ownership and Experience of Intimate Partner Violence: Evidence from 28 International Surveys," *American Journal of Public Health* 107, no. 5 (May 2017): 747–55.

19. Erin Lentz, "In the Fight Against Hunger, Why Don't We Prioritize Women?," *The Hill*, November 21, 2016, https://lbj.utexas.edu/fight-against-hunger-why -dont-we-prioritize-women.

20. Malala Yousafzai, *I Am Malala: The Girl Who Stood Up for Education and Was Shot by the Taliban* (New York: Back Bay, 2015), 22.

21. The gender nutrition index is described on Erin Lentz's faculty profile page at the University of Texas at Austin, Lyndon B. Johnson School of Public Affairs, https://lbj.utexas.edu/lentz-erin.

22. World Food Programme, "Women and Hunger: 10 Facts," https://www.wfp.org /our-work/preventing-hunger/focus-women/women-hunger-facts.

23. José Villar, Leila Cheikh Ismail, Cesar G. Victora, Eric O. Ohuma, Doug G. Altman, Aris T. Papageorghiou, Maria Carvalho, et al., for the International Fetal and Newborn Growth Consortium for the 21st Century, "International Standards for Newborn Weight, Length, and Head Circumference by Gestational Age and Sex: The Newborn Cross-Sectional Study of the INTERGROWTH-21st Project," *Lancet* 384 (2014): 857–68; Francesca Giuliani, Eric Ohuma, Elena Spada, Enrico Bertina, Ayesha S. Al Dhaheri, Douglas G. Altman, Agustin Conde-Agudelo, Stephen H. Kennedy, José Villar, and Leila Cheikh Ismail, "Systematic Review of the Methodological Quality of Studies Designed to Create Neonatal Anthropometric Charts," *Acta Pediatrics* 104, no. 10 (2015): 987–96; José Villar, Aris T. Papageorghiou, Ruyon Pang, Ann Lambert, Eric O. Ohuma, Manorama Purwar, Leila Cheikh Ismail, et al., "The Likeness of Fetal Growth and Newborn Size Across Non-Isolated Populations in the INTERGROWTH-21st Project: The Fetal Growth Longitudinal Study and Newborn Cross-Sectional Study," *Lancet: Diabetes and Endocrinology* 2, no. 10 (2014): 781–92; Fernando C. Barros, Aris T. Papageorghiou, Cesar G. Vicora, Julia A. Noble, Ruyang Pang, J. Iams, Anna Lambert, et al., for the International Fetal and Newborn Growth Consortium for the 21st Century, "The Distribution of Clinical Phenotypes of Preterm Birth Syndrome: Implications for Prevention," *JAMA Pediatrics* 169, no. 3 (2015): 229; Cesar G. Vic-

tora, José Villar, Fernando C. Barros, Julia A. Noble, Manorama Purwar, Leila Cheikh Ismail, Cameron Chumlea, Aris T. Papageorghiou, et al., for the International Fetal and Newborn Growth Consortium for the 21st Century, "Anthropometric Characterization of Impaired Fetal Growth: Risk Factors for and Prognosis of Newborns with Stunting or Wasting," *JAMA Pediatrics* 169, no. 7 (2015): e151431; José Villar, Fabien A. Puglis, Tanis R. Fenton, Leila Cheikh Ismail, Eleonora Staines-Urias, Francesca Giuliani, Eric O. Ohuma, et al., "Body Composition at Birth and Its Relationship with Neonatal Anthropometric Ratios: The Newborn Body Composition Study of the INTERGROWTH-21st Project," *Pediatric Research* (May 31, 2017).

24. Food and Agriculture Organization, "State of Food and Agriculture," vii, 13.
25. Ester Boserup, *Woman's Role in Economic Development* (London: Earthscan, 1970).
26. Bernice Yeung and Grace Rubenstein, "Female Workers Face Harassment in U.S. Agriculture Industry," NPR, June 25, 2013; Food and Agriculture Organization, "State of Food and Agriculture," 8, 10.
27. Sara Kominers, "Working in Fear: Sexual Violence Against Women Farmworkers in the United States," OXFAM, 2015, https://www.northeastern.edu/law/pdfs/academics/phrge/kominers-report.pdf.
28. Food and Agriculture Organization, "State of Food and Agriculture," 18.
29. Organisation for Economic Co-operation and Development, *SIGI 2019 Global Report: Transforming Challenges into Opportunities*, Social Institutions and Gender Index (Paris: OECD Publishing, 2019), https://doi.org/10.1787/bc56d212-en. To support the statement here about the connection between farmwork and SIGI scores, I took data about women's participation in farmwork by country and matched it to the SIGI scores for the same nation.
30. S. El Feki, B. Heilman, and G. Barker, *Understanding Masculinities: Results from the International Men and Gender Equality Survey (IMAGES)—Middle East and North Africa* (Cairo and Washington, DC: UN Women and Promundo-US, 2017), https://promundoglobal.org/wp-content/uploads/2017/05/IMAGES-MENA-Multi-Country-Report-EN-16.

4. INADEQUATE EXCUSES, INEXCUSABLE TREATMENT

1. Pew Research Center, "Breadwinner Moms," May 29, 2013, http://www.pewsocialtrends.org/2013/05/29/breadwinner-moms/; Alexandra Petri, "Science Says Males Must Dominate, According to Erick Erickson," *Washington Post*, May 30, 2013, https://www.washingtonpost.com/blogs/compost/wp/2013/05/30/science-says-males-must-dominate-according-to-erick-erickson.
2. Kay Prüfer, Kasper Munch, Ines Hellmann, Keiko Akagi, Jason R. Miller, Brian Walenz, Sergey Koren, et al., "The Bonobo Genome Compared with the Chimpanzee and Human Genomes," *Nature, International Journal of Science* 486, no. 7404 (June 28, 2012): 527–31.
3. In addition to Prüfer et al., "The Bonobo Genome Compared with the Chimpanzee and Human Genomes," and the sources on warrior chimps cited later, sources for material on bonobos and chimpanzees include Jane Goodall, *Though a Window: My Thirty Years with the Chimps of Gombe* (New York:

Mariner Books, 2010); Richard Wrangham, *The Goodness Paradox: The Strange Relationship Between Virtue and Violence in Human Evolution* (New York: Pantheon Books, 2017); Richard Wrangham and Dale Peterson, *Demonic Males: Apes and the Origins of Human Violence* (New York: Mariner Books, 1997); Jared Diamond, *The Third Chimpanzee: The Evolution and Future of the Human Animal* (New York: HarperCollins, 1992); Barbara Smuts, "Apes of Wrath," *Discover Magazine*, August 1995, http://discovermagazine.com /1995/aug/apesofwrath548; Malini Suchak, Jen Crick, Timothy M. Eppley, Matthew W. Campbell, and Frans B. M. de Waal, "The Roles of Food Quality and Sex in Chimpanzee Sharing Behaviour (*Pan troglodytes*)," *Behavior* 150, no. 11 (2013): 1220–24; Martin N. Muller, Sonya M. Kahlenberg, Melissa Emery Thompson, and Richard Wrangham, "Male Coercion and the Costs of Promiscuous Mating for Female Chimpanzees," *Proceedings of the Royal Society, Biological Sciences* 274, no. 1612 (2007): 1009–14; Kristina Cawthon Lang, "Chimpanzee *Pan troglodytes*," Primate Factsheets, April 13, 2006, University of Wisconsin, http://pin.primate.wisc.edu/factsheets/entry/chimpanzee; J. D. Pruetz, P. Bertolani, K. Boyer Ontl, S. Lindshield, M. Shelley, and E. G. Wessling, "New Evidence on the Tool-Assisted Hunting Exhibited by Chimpanzees (*Pan troglodytes verus*) in a Savannah Habitat at Fongoli, Sénégal," *Royal Society Open*, April 2015, https://doi.org/10.1098/rsos.140507; Henry Nicholls, "Do Bonobos Really Spend All Their Time Having Sex?," BBC, March 17, 2016, http://www.bbc.com/earth/story/20160317-do-bonobos-really -spend-all-their-time-having-sex; Brian Hare and Suzy Kwetuenda, "Bonobos Voluntarily Share Their Own Food with Others," *Current Biology* 20, no. 5 (2010); Emily E. Wroblewski, Carson M. Murray, Brandon F. Keele, Joann C. Schumacher-Stanley, Beatrice H. Hahn, and Anne E. Pusey, "Male Dominance Rank and Reproductive Success in Chimpanzees, *Pan troglodytes schweinfurthii*," *Animal Behavior* 77, no. 4 (2009): 873–85; James K. Rilling, Jan Scholz, Todd M. Preuss, Matthew F. Glasser, Bhargav K. Errangi, and Timothy E. Behrens, "Differences Between Chimpanzees and Bonobos in Neural Systems Supporting Social Cognition," *Social Cognitive and Affective Neuroscience* 7, no. 4 (2012): 369–79; Richard W. Wrangham, Michael L. Wilson, and Martin N. Muller, "Comparative Rates of Violence in Chimpanzees and Humans," *Primates* 47, no. 1 (2006): 14–26; Ewen Callaway, "Loving Bonobos Have a Carnivorous Dark Side," *New Scientist*, October 13, 2008, https://www .newscientist.com/article/dn14926-loving-bonobos-have-a-carnivorous-dark -side/; John Horgan, "Chimp Violence Fails to Support Deep-Roots Theory of War," *Scientific American*, September 17, 2014; Joseph T. Feldblum, Emily E. Wroblewski, Rebecca C. Rudicall, Beatrice H. Hahn, Thais Paiva, Mine Cetinkaya-Rundel, Anne E. Pusey, and Ian C. Gilby, "Sexually Coercive Male Chimpanzees Sire More Offspring," *Current Biology* 24 (December 1, 2014): 2855–60; Stefano Kaburu and Nicholas E. Newton-Fisher, "Egalitarian Despots: Hierarchy Steepness, Reciprocity and the Grooming-Trade Model in Wild Chimpanzees, *Pan troglodytes*," *Animal Behavior* 99 (2015): 61–71.
4. Smuts, "Apes of Wrath"; Melissa Emory Thompson, "Sexual Conflict: Nice Guys Finish Last," *Current Biology* 24, no. 23 (December 1, 2014): R1125–27.

5. John C. Mitani, Thomas T. Struhsaker, and Jeremiah S. Lwanga, "Primate Community Dynamics in Old Growth Forest Over 23.5 Years at Ngogo, Kibale National Park, Uganda: Implications for Conservation and Census Methods," *International Journal of Primatology* 21, no. 2 (April 2000): 269–86; David P. Watts and John C. Mitani, "Infanticide and Cannibalism by Male Chimpanzees at Ngogo, Kibale National Park," *Primates* 41, no. 4 (2000): 357–65; J. S. Lwanga, T. T. Struhsaker, P. J. Struhsaker, T. M. Butynski, and J. C. Mitani, "Primate Population Dynamics over 32.9 Years at Ngogo, Kibale National Park, Uganda," *American Journal of Primatology* 73 (2011): 997–1011; David P. Watts and John C. Mitani, "Hunting Behavior of Chimpanzees at Ngogo, Kibale National Park, Uganda," *International Journal of Primatology* 23, no. 1 (February 2002): 1–28; John C. Mitani, David P. Watts, and Sylvia J. Amsler, "Lethal Intergroup Aggression Leads to Territorial Expansion in Wild Chimpanzees," *Current Biology* 20, no. 12 (June 22, 2010): R507–508; Mike Cummings, "Yale-Led Study: Wild Chimpanzees Have Surprisingly Long Life Spans," *Yale News*, March 20, 2017; Alok Jha, "Chimpanzees Expand Their Territory by Attacking and Killing Neighbors," *Guardian*, June 21, 2010; Cheyenne McDonald, "Being a Gangster Pays Off: Members of Uganda's Notoriously Violent Ngogo Chimp Gang Live Twice as Long as Their Neighbors," *Daily Mail*, March 21, 2017; Nicholas Wade, "Chimps, Too, Wage War and Annex Rival Territory," *New York Times*, June 21, 2010; "The Ngogo Chimpanzee Project," http://ngogochimpanzeeproject.org; John C. Mitani, "Diet of Chimpanzees (*Pan troglodytes schweinfurthii*) at Ngogo, Kibale National Park, Uganda, 1. Diet Composition and Diversity," *American Journal of Primatology* 74 (2012): 114–29; Jessica Hamzelou, "Male Chimpanzee Seen Snatching Seconds-Old Chimp and Eating It," *New Scientist*, October 13, 2017; "Female Chimpanzees Know Which Males Are Most Likely to Kill Their Babies," *Science Daily*, October 18, 2018, https://www.sciencedaily.com/releases/2018/10/181018095026.htm.

6. Ann Gibbons, *The First Human: The Race to Discover Our Earliest Ancestors* (New York: Anchor Books, 2007); Kate Wong, "40 Years Afer Lucy: The Fossil That Revolutionized the Search for Human Origins," *Scientific American*, November 24, 2014; Yuval Noah Harari, *Sapiens: A Brief History of Humankind* (New York: Harper Perennial, 2018); Wrangham, *The Goodness Paradox*. Also on brain evolution: Rilling et al., "Differences Between Chimpanzees and Bonobos in Neural Systems Supporting Social Cognition"; Michael Balter, "Brain Evolution Studies Go Micro," *Science* 315, no. 5816 (2007): 1208–11; Simon Neubauer, Jean-Jacques Hublin, and Philipp Gunz, "The Evolution of Modern Human Brain Shape," *Science Advances* 24, no. 1 (January 2018): eaao5961; Javier DeFelipe, "The Evolution of the Brain, the Human Nature of Cortical Circuits, and Intellectual Creativity," *Frontiers in Neuroanatomy* 5 (May 16, 2011): 29.

7. The literature on social dominance is quite large. This source gives the basic definitions and also documents the discovery of a genetic component: Thomas Haarklau Kleppesto, Nikolai Olavi Czajkowski, Olav Vassend, Espen Roysamb, Nikolai Haahjem Eftedal, Jennifer Sheehy-Skeffington, Jonas R. Kunst, and Lotte Thomsen, "Correlations Between Social Dominance Orientation and

Political Attitudes Reflect Common Genetic Underpinnings," *PNAS* 116, no. 38 (September 3, 2019): 17741–46.

8. Wrangham, in *The Goodness Paradox*, claims that humans are peaceable, compared with other primates, on the basis of their having less lethal conflict between the male members of the same group; however, they are more lethal in war than any other primate. It does appear that neither number includes violence against females.

9. Harari, *Sapiens*.

10. Michael Gurven and Kim Hill, "Why Do Men Hunt? A Reevaluation of 'Man the Hunter' and the Sexual Division of Labor," *Current Anthropology* 50, no. 1 (2009): 51–74.

11. John D. Speth, "Seasonality, Resource Stress, and Food Sharing in So-Called 'Egalitarian' Societies," *Journal of Anthropological Archaeology* 9, no. 2 (1990): 148–88.

12. Speth, "Seasonality, Resource Stress, and Food Sharing in So-Called 'Egalitarian' Societies," p. 161, quoting Basil S. Hetzel, "The Chance Nutrition of Aborigines in the Ecosystem of Central Australia," in *The Nutrition of Aborigines in Relation to the Ecosystem of Central Australia: Papers Presented at a Symposium, CSIRO, 23–26 October 1976, Canberra*, ed. B. S. Hetzel and H. J. Frith (Melbourne: Commonwealth Scientific and Industrial Research Organization, 1978), 148–88.

13. Speth, "Seasonality, Resource Stress, and Food Sharing in So-Called 'Egalitarian' Societies."

14. L. R. Lukacs and L. M. Thompson, "Dental Caries Prevalence by Sex in Pre-History: Magnitude and Meaning," in *Technique and Application in Dental Anthropology*, ed. Joel D. Irish and Greg C. Nelson (Cambridge, UK: Cambridge University Press, 2008), 136–77.

15. Alison A. Macintosh, Ron Pinhasi, and Jay T. Stock, "Prehistoric Women's Manual Labor Exceeded That of Athletes Through the First 5500 Years of Farming in Central Europe," *Science Advances* 3, no. 11 (November 29, 2017): eaao3893. Other sources on females in prehistory include Rosemary A. Joyce, *Ancient Bodies, Ancient Lives: Sex, Gender, and Archaeology* (New York: Thames and Hudson, 2008); J. M. Adovasio, Olga Soffer, and Jake Page, *The Invisible Sex: Uncovering the True Roles of Women in Prehistory* (Walnut Creek, CA: Left Coast Press, 2007); Kelley Hays-Gilpin and David S. Whitley, *Reader in Gender Archaeology* (New York: Routledge, 1998); and Margaret Ehrenberg, *Women in Prehistory* (London: British Museum Publications, 1989).

16. Wrangham, *The Goodness Paradox*.

17. Wrangham, *The Goodness Paradox*.

18. Lisbeth Skogstrand, "The Role of Violence in the Construction of Prehistoric Masculinities," in *Archaeologies of Gender and Violence*, ed. Uroš Matié and Bo Jensen (Oxford: Oxford University Press, 2017), 77–102.

19. Julie Farrum, "Gender and Structural Violence in Prehistoric Peru," in *Archaeologies of Gender and Violence*, ed. Uroš Matié and Bo Jensen (Oxford: Oxford University Press, 2017), 247–62.

20. Cynthia Eller, *The Myth of Matriarchal Prehistory* (Boston: Beacon Press, 2000)

21. Stephanie Coontz, *Marriage, a History: How Love Conquered Marriage* (London: Penguin Books, 2006).

22. Tim Worstall, "The Gender Pay Gap Is the Result of Being a Parent, Not Discrimination," *Forbes*, October 1, 2015, https://www.forbes.com/sites /timworstall/2015/10/01/the-gender-pay-gap-is-the-result-of-being-a-parent -not-discrimination/#2732829aac7f.

23. Sarah Hrdy, *Mother Nature: Maternal Instincts and How They Shape the Human Species* (New York: Ballantine, 2000).

24. Hrdy, *Mother Nature*.

25. Steve Tobak, "The Gender Gap Is a Complete Myth," CBS News, April 11, 2011, https://www.cbsnews.com/news/the-gender-pay-gap-is-a-complete-myth/.

26. Jonathan Gibbons, *Global Study on Homicide* (Vienna: United National Office of Drugs and Crime, 2013). See Federal Bureau of Prisons, May 2019, https:// www.bop.gov/about/statistics/statistics_inmate_gender.jsp, and World Prison Brief, February 2016, http://www.prisonstudies.org/news/more-1035-million -people-are-prison-around-world-new-report-shows; Kathryn E. McCollis- ter, Michael T. French, and Hai Feng, "The Cost of Crime to Society: New Crime-Specific Estimates for Policy and Program Evaluation," *Drug and Alco- hol Dependency* 100, nos. 1–2 (April 1, 2010): 98–109; Dorian Furtuna, "Male Aggression: Why Are Men More Violent?," *Psychology Today*, September 22, 2014, https://www.psychologytoday.com/us/blog/homo-aggressivus/201409 /male-aggression.

27. James Owen, "Men and Women Really Do See Things Differently," *National Geographic*, September 6, 2012, https://www.nationalgeographic.com/news /2012/9/120907-men-women-see-differently-science-health-vision-sex/.

28. Man the Hunter was more than a cultural myth; it was also the name given to a school of primatology and evolutionary theory that was heavily popularized during the 1950s and 1960s. Man the Hunter is a name still used to refer to this school of thought in many fields today, including anthropology, archaeol- ogy, and primatology, although it is used to designate an influential way of thinking, once seen as legitimate, that has now been falsified and is thus out of date. A key publication was a collection of essays following a 1966 academic conference that brought together the influential people working under the theory for the first time: R. B. Lee and I. Devore, eds., *Man the Hunter* (Chi- cago: Aldine, 1968), 293–303. Robert Ardrey also wrote a four-book series on the topic, beginning with *African Genesis* in 1961; some of those books were made into documentaries for television. Perhaps the most popular transla- tion of the theory to the public was Desmond Morris's *The Naked Ape* (1967), which was first serialized in the *Daily Mail* and eventually published in book form in 1967. In 2011, *Time* listed *The Naked Ape* as one of the "100 All-Time Non-Fiction Books," http://entertainment.time.com/2011/08/30/all-time-100 -best-nonfiction-books/slide/the-naked-ape-by-desmond-morris/.

29. Rebecca Solnit, "Shooting Down Man the Hunter," *Harper's Magazine*, Septem- ber 1, 2015.

30. Robert W. Sussman, *Man the Hunted: Primates, Predators, and Human Evolu- tion* (New York: Basic Books, 2005); Robert W. Sussman, "The Myth of Man

the Hunter, Man the Killer, and the Evoluation of Human Morality," *Zygon* 34, no. 3 (1999): 453–71.

31. Ester Boserup, *Woman's Role in Economic Development* (London: Earthscan, 1970).

32. Alberto Alesina, Paola Giuliano, and Nathan Nunn, "On the Origins of Gender Roles: Women and the Plough," *Quarterly Journal of Economics* 128, no. 2 (2013): 469–530; "The Plough and the Now," *Economist*, July 21, 2011, https://www.economist.com/node/18986073. See also Fernand Braudel, *On History* (Chicago: University of Chicago Press, 1982).

33. Judy Barrett Litoff and David C. Smith, "To the Rescue of the Crops," *National Archives' Prologue Magazine* 25, no. 4 (1993), https://www.archives.gov/publications/prologue/1993/winter/landarmy.html; Melissa Walker and Rebecca Sharpless, *Work, Family and Faith: Rural Southern Women in the Twentieth Century* (Columbia: University of Missouri Press, 2006); Sue Kazeman Balcolm, *Women Behind the Plow: Work Makes Life Sweet* (North Dakota: Tri County Alliance, 2017); Elaine Weiss, *Fruits of Victory: The Woman's Land Army of America in the Great War* (Lincoln, NE: Potomac Books, 2008); Susan Hagood Lee, *Rice Plus: Widows and Economic Survival in Rural Cambodia* (London: Routledge, 2012); H. Elaine Lindgren, *Land in Her Own Name: Women as Homesteaders in North Dakota* (Fargo: North Dakota Institute for Regional Studies, 1991).

34. Theophilus Liefeld, *Faces and Phases of German Life* (New York: Fowler & Wells, 1910).

35. See, for instance, Peter Frankopan, *The Silk Roads: A New History of the World* (London: Bloomsbury, 2015).

36. Laurel Bossen and Hill Gates, *Bound Feet, Young Hands: Tracking the Demise of Footbinding in Village China* (Stanford, CA: Stanford University Press, 2017).

37. Beginning in the 1970s, there was, among feminists, a strong belief in and desire to document an ancient matriarchy, mostly to prove that patriarchy was not necessary, natural, or unchangeable. However, extensive efforts on the part of scholars looking for this (or any) matriarchal society have now put that hope to rest. See Eller, *The Myth of Matriarchal Prehistory*. That still doesn't mean, however, that patriarchy is natural, necessary, or unchangeable.

38. Robert M. Sapolsky and Lisa J. Share, "A Pacific Culture Among Wild Baboons: Its Emergence and Transmission," *PLOS Biology* 2, no. 4 (April 13, 2004): e106. Also see Robert M. Sapolsky, *A Primate's Memoir* (New York: Scribner, 2001); Mark Schwartz, "Robert Sapolsky Discusses Physiological Effects of Stress," *Stanford Report*, March 7, 2007, https://news.stanford.edu/news/2007/march7/sapolskysr-030707.html; and "Of Monkeys and Men: Robert Sapolsky Talks About His Years Spent with a Troop of Baboons," *Atlantic*, April 2001, https://www.theatlantic.com/magazine/archive/2001/04/of-monkeys-and-men/303047/.

39. Robert M. Sapolsky, "The Endocrine Stress-Response and Social Status in the Wild Baboon," *Hormones and Behavior* 16, no. 3 (1982): 279–92. The same finding came from the famous Whitehall studies in Britain, only the subjects

were human employees of the civil service. M. G. Marmot, G. Rose, M. Shipley, and P. J. Hamilton, "Employment Grade and Coronary Heart Disease in British Civil Servants," *Journal of Epidemiology and Community Health* 32, no. 4 (1978): 244–49; M. G. Marmot, G. Davey Smith, S. Stansfield, et al., "Health Inequalities Among British Civil Servants: The Whitehall II Study," *Lancet* 337, no. 8754 (1991): 1387–93.

40. Robert M. Sapolsky and Lisa J. Share, "A Pacific Culture Among Wild Baboons: Its Emergence and Transmission," *PLOS Biology*, April 13, 2004, https://journals.plos.org/plosbiology/article?id=10.1371/journal.pbio.0020106.

5. FOR LOVE, NOT MONEY

1. Gayle Rubin, "The Traffic in Women," in *Toward an Anthropology of Women*, ed. Rayna R. Reiter (New York: Monthly Review Press, 1975), 157–210.

2. Robert W. Sussman, *Man the Hunted: Primates, Predators, and Human Evolution* (New York: Basic Books, 2005); George Murdock, *The Ethnographic Atlas*, http://eclectic.ss.uci.edu/~drwhite/worldcul/atlas.htm; Leta Hong Fincher, *Leftover Women: The Resurgence of Gender Inequality in China* (London: Zed Books, 2014).

3. Marcel Mauss, *The Gift: The Form and Reason for Exchange in Archaic Societies*, trans. W. D. Halls (New York: W. W. Norton, 1954), 14.

4. Richard Wrangham, *The Goodness Paradox: The Strange Relationship Between Virtue and Violence in Human Evolution* (New York: Pantheon, 2019), 207, referring to A. P. Elkin, *The Australian Aborigines* (Sydney: Angus and Robertson, 1938).

5. Gordon F. McEwan, *The Incas: New Perspectives* (New York: W. W. Norton, 2006); María Emma Mannarelli, *Private Passions and Public Sins: Men and Women in Seventeenth-Century Lima*, trans. Sidney Evans and Meredith D. Dodge (Albuquerque: University of New Mexico Press, 2007).

6. Jenny Jochens, *Women in Old Norse Society* (Ithaca, NY: Cornell University Press, 1995); A. S. Altekar, *The Position of Women in Hindu Civilization* (Delhi: Motilal Banarsidass, 1956).

7. I am, of course, indebted to Gerda Lerner for pioneering the importance of the cultures of Mesopotamia and the first written laws to the history of patriarchy. Gerda Lerner, *The Creation of Patriarchy* (Oxford: Oxford University Press, 1986).

8. Deuteronomy 22:28–29.

9. Lerner, *The Creation of Patriarchy*.

10. Susan Pomeroy, *Goddesses, Whores, Wives, and Slaves: Women in Classical Antiquity* (New York: Schocken Books, 1975); Lloyd Llewellyn Jones, *Aphrodite's Tortoise: The Veiled Women of Ancient Greece* (Wales, UK: Classical Press of Wales, 2003); Stephanie Coontz, *Marriage, a History: How Love Conquered Marriage* (London: Penguin Books, 2006); Marilyn Yalom, *A History of the Wife* (New York: Perennial, 2001); Kecia Ali, *Marriage and Slavery in Early Islam* (Cambridge, MA: Harvard University Press, 2010); Altekar, *The Position of Women in Hindu Civilization*; Mannarelli, *Private Passions and Public Sins*.

11. Judith K. Brown, "A Note on the Division of Labor by Sex," *American Anthropologist* 72 (1970): 1073–78. Some readers will be surprised I have listed "convent" here, thinking these institutions have only been retreats for nuns. However, throughout the medieval period and up to at least the early nineteenth century, women who were unmarried, whether by death, divorce, desertion, or simply being the daughter of a family with insufficient funds to make a match, have been sent off to live in convents.

12. Shereen El Feki, Gary Barker, and Brian Heilman, *Understanding Masculinities: Results from the International Men and Gender Equality Survey (IMAGES)— Middle East and North Africa* (Cairo and Washington, DC: UN Women and Promundo-US, 2017), https://promundoglobal.org/wp-content/uploads/2017/05/IMAGES-MENA-Multi-Country-Report-EN-16May2017-web.pdf.

13. Malcolm Potts and Thomas Hayden, *Sex and War: How Biology Explains Warfare and Terrorism and Offers a Path to a Safer World* (Dallas: Benbella Books, 2008).

14. Stephanie Pappas, "APA Issues First-Ever Guidelines for Practice with Men and Boys," *American Psychological Association* 50, no. 1 (2019), https://www.apa.org/monitor/2019/01/ce-corner. See also "Harmful Masculinity and Violence," *In the Public Interest*, American Psychological Association, September 2018, https://www.apa.org/pi/about/newsletter/2018/09/harmful-masculinity.

15. International Labour Organization and Walk Free Foundation, *Global Estimates of Modern Slavery* (Geneva: International Labour Office, 2017).

16. To be fair, in a significant number of such marriages, the kidnapping is staged by the couple so that the groom can avoid the cost and the bride can choose her husband. So, it's important where there are numbers available to break out the consensual from nonconsensual bride kidnapping. In the Kyrgyzstan example, a third of all "marriage by rape" is really elopement, which represents about 20 percent of total marriages. The number I have cited in the text reflects only the coercive instances.

17. Roderick Phillips, *Untying the Knot: A Short History of Divorce* (Cambridge, UK: Cambridge University Press, 1991); Coontz, *Marriage, a History.*

18. Phillips, *Untying the Knot*; Sandra Cavallo and Lyndan Warner, eds., *Widowhood in Medieval and Early Modern Europe* (Harlow, UK: Pearson, 1999).

19. Phillips, *Untying the Knot*, 98.

20. Phillips, *Untying the Knot*, 98.

21. David Herlihy, "Land, Family, and Women in Continental Europe, 701–1200," in *Women in Medieval Society*, ed. Susan Mosher Stuard (Philadelphia: University of Pennsylvania Press, 1976), 13–43.

22. Martha C. Howell, *Women, Production, and Patriarchy in Late Medieval Cities* (Chicago: University of Chicago Press, 1986); Heather Swanson, *Medieval Artisans: An Urban Class in Late Medieval England* (Oxford: Basil Blackwell, 1989); Lindsey Charles and Lorna Duffin, eds., *Women and Work in Preindustrial England* (London: Croom Helm, 1985).

23. Susan Mosher Stuard, "Women in Charter and Statute Law: Medieval Ragusa/Dubrovnik," in *Women in Medieval Society*, ed. Susan Mosher Stuard (Philadelphia: University of Pennsylvania Press, 1976), 199–208; Shulamith Shahar,

The Fourth Estate: A History of Women in the Middle Ages (New York: Routledge, 1983); Coontz, *Marriage, a History*; Jack Goody, *The Development of the Family and Marriage in Europe* (Cambridge, UK: Cambridge University Press, 1983).

24. Stuard, "Women in Charter and Statute Law," 204.

25. Phillips, *Untying the Knot*; Coontz, *Marriage, a History*.

26. Nina Nichols Pugh, "The Evolving Role of Women in the Louisiana Law: Recent Legislative and Judicial Changes," *Louisiana Law Review* 42, no. 5 (special issue, 1982), https://digitalcommons.law.lsu.edu/lalrev/vol42/iss5/8.

27. Valerie Hudson, Bonnie Ballif-Spanvill, Mary Caprioli, and Chad Emmett, *Sex and World Peace* (New York: Columbia University Press, 2014).

28. Coontz, *Marriage, a History*, 241.

6. ESCAPE FROM THE KITCHEN

1. Amartya Sen, *Development as Freedom* (Oxford: Oxford University Press, 1999).

2. Claudia Goldin, "The U-Shaped Female Labor Force in Economic Development and Economic History," NBER Working Paper Series, no. 4707 (Cambridge, MA: National Bureau of Economic Research, 1994), https://www.nber.org/papers/w4707; Ewa Lechman and Harleen Kaur, "Economic Growth and Female Labor Force Participation—Verifying the U-Feminization Hypothesis; New Evidence for Two Countries over the Period 1990–2012," *Economics and Sociology* 8, no. 1 (2015): 246–57; Paolo Verme, "Economic Development and Female Labor Participation in the Middle East and North Africa: A Test of the U-Shape Hypothesis," *IZA Journal of Labor and Development* 4, no. 1 (2015), http://documents.worldbank.org/curated/en/184611468278682448/Economic-development-and-female-labor-participation-in-the-Middle-East-and-North-Africa-a-test-of-the-u-shape-hypothesis; Constance Sorrentino, "International Comparisons of Labor Force Participation, 1960–81," *Monthly Labor Review* 106, no. 2 (1983): 23–36.

3. Kate Bahn and Annie McGrew, "A Day in the U.S. Economy Without Women," Center for American Progress, March 7, 2017, https://www.americanprogress.org/issues/economy/news/2017/03/07/427556/a-day-in-the-u-s-economy-without-women/; Jason Gold, "Women Are the Key to Economic Growth: Leaving Our Greatest Economic Asset on the Sideline Should Not Be an Option," *U.S. News and World Report*, December 18, 2017, https://www.usnews.com/opinion/economic-intelligence/articles/2017-12-18/women-are-the-key-to-unlocking-americas-economic-growth.

4. Though most historians have focused on the aristocratic Puritan women of the abolition movement, a number of professionals were equally, if not more, prominent in their time. Some of them, including Jane Croly and Ellen Demorest, founded Sorosis, the predecessor to the General Federation of Women's Clubs. Jennifer Scanlon, *Inarticulate Longings* (New York: Routledge, 1995); Linda Scott, *Fresh Lipstick: Redressing Fashion and Feminism* (New York: Palgrave Macmillan, 2004).

5. Eleanor Flexner, *Century of Struggle: The Woman's Rights Movement in the*

United States (Cambridge, MA: Belknap Press of Harvard University Press, 1959); Karen J. Blair, *The Clubwoman as Feminist: True Womanhood Redefined, 1868–1914* (New York: Homes and Meier, 1980); Glenna Matthews, *The Rise of Public Woman: Woman's Power and Woman's Place in the United States, 1630–1970* (Oxford: Oxford University Press, 1992).

6. Marilyn Power, Ellen Mutari, and Deborah M. Figart, "Beyond Markets: Wage Setting and the Methodology of Feminist Political Economy," in *Toward a Feminist Philosophy of Economics*, ed. Drucilla K. Barker and Edith Kuiper (New York: Routledge, 2003), 70–86.

7. Janet Saltzman Chafetz and Anthony Gary Dworkin, *Female Revolt: Women's Movements in Global Perspective* (Totowa, NJ: Rowman and Allanheld, 1986), 42.

8. Research conducted by U.K. Aid funded the Work and Opportunities for Women (WOW) program, 2018. I learned about these findings in a special presentation made to the Global Business Coalition for Women's Economic Empowerment in November 2018. The project was not yet finished when this book went to press, but I am reporting these results with permission from the leadership on the work.

9. Rebecca Traister, *All the Single Ladies: Unmarried Women and the Rise of an Independent Nation* (New York: Simon and Schuster, 2016); Marian Botsford Fraser, *Solitaire: The Intimate Loves of Single Women* (Canada: Macfarlane Walter and Ross, 2001); Betsy Israel, *Bachelor Girl: The Secret History of Single Women in the Twentieth Century* (New York: William Morrow, 2002); Scott, *Fresh Lipstick*; Kathy Peiss, *Cheap Amusements: Working Women and Leisure in Turn-of-the-Century New York* (Philadelphia: Temple University Press, 1986).

10. Jacob Mincer, "Labor Force Participation of Married Women: A Study of Labor Supply," in *Aspects of Labor Economics*, ed. National Bureau Committee for Economic Research (Princeton, NJ: Princeton University Press, 1962), 63–105; Nancy Folbre, *Greed, Lust, and Gender: A History of Economic Ideas* (Oxford: Oxford University Press, 2009).

11. Betty Friedan, *The Feminine Mystique* (New York: W. W. Norton, 1963).

12. Ryan Nunn and Megan Mumford, "The Incomplete Progress of Women in the Labor Market," *The Hamilton Project* (Washington, DC: Brookings Institution, 2017); Jonathan Woetzel, Anu Madgavkar, Kweilin Ellingrud, Eric Labaye, Sandrine Devillard, Eric Kutcher, James Manyika, Richard Dobbs, and Mekala Krishnan, *The Power of Parity* (New York: McKinsey Global Markets Institute, September 2015).

13. "President Ronald Reagan's message to Phyllis Schlafly and Eagle Forum members," https://www.youtube.com/watch?v=rON6dgi1W3A.

14. Chafetz and Dworkin, *Female Revolt*.

15. One-third of the decline is from having no family support.

16. Francine Blau and Lawrence M. Kahn, "Female Labor Supply: Why Is the U.S. Falling Behind?," in *Discussion Paper Series* (Bonn, Germany: Institute for Study of Labor [IZA], 2013).

7. PUNISHING MOTHERHOOD

1. Damian Carrington, "Want to Fight Climate Change? Have Fewer Children," *Guardian*, July 12, 2017.

2. Phillip Longman explains the implications of the "point of no return" and gives a good, accessible explanation for why the fertility bust is so ominous in economic terms. Phillip Longman, *The Empty Cradle: How Falling Birthrates Threaten World Prosperity and What to Do About It* (New York: Basic Books, 2004).

3. For the numbers on fertility, I used the 2017 figures in the CIA's *World Factbook*, https://www.cia.gov/library/publications/the-world-factbook/rankorder/2127rank.html. Also United Nations, World Population Ageing, 2015, https://www.un.org/en/development/desa/population/publications/pdf/ageing/WPA2015_Report.pdf.

4. Though I have been presenting this argument myself in public lectures for a number of years, I was pleased to have the additional support of Population Action International's excellent analysis to help with this chapter: Elizabeth Leahy with Robert Engelman, Carolyn Gibb Vogel, Sarah Haddock, and Todd Preston, *The Shape of Things to Come: Why Age Structure Matters to a Safer, More Equitable World* (Washington, DC: Population Action International, 2007).

5. Peter McDonald, "Societal Foundations for Explaining Low Fertility: Gender Equity," *Demographic Research* 28, no. 34 (2013): 991–94; Peter McDonald, "Gender Equity in Theories of Fertility Transition," *Population and Development Review* 26, no. 3 (2000): 427–39; Melinda Mills, Katia Begall, Letizia Mencarini, and Maria Letizia Tanturri, "Gender Equity and Fertility Intentions in Italy and the Netherlands," *Demographic Research* 18 (2008), https://www.demographic-research.org/volumes/vol18/1/default.htm.

6. Paul Collier, *The Bottom Billion* (Oxford: Oxford University Press, 2007).

7. World Economic Forum, *The Global Gender Gap Report* (Geneva: World Economic Forum, 2018).

8. Leahy, *The Shape of Things to Come*.

9. For the fragile states measure, I used the Fund for Peace Fragile State Index, https://fundforpeace.org/2019/04/10/fragile-states-index-2019/.

10. Valerie Hudson, Bonnie Ballif-Spanvill, Mary Caprioli, and Chad Emmett, *Sex and World Peace* (New York: Columbia University Press, 2014).

11. Elizabeth Mendes, Lydia Saad, and Kyley McGeeney, "Stay-at-Home Moms Report More Depression, Sadness, Anger," Gallup News, May 18, 2012, https://news.gallup.com/poll/154685/stay-home-moms-report-depression-sadness-anger.aspx.

12. For these figures, I have used Euromonitor's measures of private household composition: https://ec.europa.eu/eurostat/statistics-explained/index.php?title=File:Private_households_by_household_composition,_2007-2017_(number_of_households_in_1_000_and_%25_of_household_types)_new.png.

13. World Economic Forum, *The Corporate Gender Gap Report* (Geneva: World Economic Forum, 2010).

14. Wendell Steavenson, "Ceausescu's Children," *Guardian*, December 10, 2014, https://www.theguardian.com/news/2014/dec/10/-sp-ceausescus-children.

See also Amy MacKinnon, "What Actually Happens When a Country Bans Abortion," *Foreign Policy*, May 16, 2019, https://foreignpolicy.com/2019/05/16 /what-actually-happens-when-a-country-bans-abortion-romania-alabama/; Dirk J. van de Kaa, "Temporarily New: On Low Fertility and the Prospect of Pro-natal Policies," *Vienna Yearbook of Population Research* 4 (2006): 193–211.

15. Some employers do provide or allow maternity leave, but they are under no obligation to do so, as in other countries. Maternity is not a right, in other words.

16. "Employment Characteristics of Families," U.S. Bureau of Labor Statistics, April 18, 2019, https://www.bls.gov/news.release/famee.nr0.htm.

17. "Employment in Families with Children in 2016," *TED: The Economics Daily*, U.S. Bureau of Labor Statistics, April 27, 2017, https://www.bls.gov/opub/ted /2017/employment-in-families-with-children-in-2016.htm.

18. Sarah Jane Glynn, "Breadwinning Mothers Are Increasingly the U.S. Norm," *American Progress*, December 19, 2016, https://www.americanprogress.org /issues/women/reports/2016/12/19/295203/breadwinning-mothers-are -increasingly-the-u-s-norm/.

19. "How Big Is the Wage Penalty for Mothers?," *Economist*, January 28, 2019, https://www.economist.com/graphic-detail/2019/01/28/how-big-is-the-wage -penalty-for-mothers; Henrik Kleven, Camille Landais, Johanna Posch, Andreas Steinhauer, and Josef Zweimüller, "Child Penalties Across Countries: Evidence and Explanations," NBER Working Paper no. 25524, February 2019, https://www.nber.org/papers/w25524.

20. "Analysis: Women Hold Two-Thirds of Country's $1.4-Trillion Student Debt," American Association of University Women, May 21, 2018, https://www.aauw .org/article/women-hold-two-thirds-of-college-student-debt/; "Graduating to a Pay Gap," a report from the American Association of University Women, https://www.aauw.org/research/graduating-to-a-pay-gap/.

21. Rachel G. Lucas-Thompson, Wendy A. Goldberg, and JoAnn Prause, "Maternal Work Early in the Lives of Children," *Psychological Bulletin* 126, no. 6 (2010): 915–42, https://www.apa.org/pubs/journals/releases/bul-136-6-915.pdf.

22. Frances Goldscheider, Eva Bernhardt, and Trude Lappegård, "The Gender Revolution: A Framework for Understanding Changing Family and Demographic Behavior," *Population and Development Review* 41, no. 2 (June 2015): 207–39; Christin Munsch, Matthew Rogers, and Jessica Yorks, "Relative Income, Psychological Well-Being, and Health: Is Breadwinning Hazardous or Protective?," presented at the 111th Annual Meeting of the American Sociological Association, 2016, https://www.asanet.org/press-center/press-releases /being-primary-breadwinner-bad-mens-psychological-well-being-and -health; Michael M. Copenhaver and Richard M. Eisler, "Masculine Gender Role Stress: A Perspective on Men's Health," *Handbook of Diversity Issues in Health Psychology*, ed. Pamela M. Kato and Traci Mann (New York: Plenum Press, 1996), 219–35; Joanna Syrda, "Spousal Relative Income and Male Psychological Distress," *Personality and Social Psychology Bulletin* (October 2019), https://doi.org/10.1177/0146167219883611.

23. Kathleen L. McGinn, Mayra Ruiz Castro, and Elizabeth Long Lingo, "Learning from Mum: Cross-National Evidence Linking Maternal Employment

and Adult Children's Outcomes," *Work, Employment, and Society* 33, no. 3 (April 30, 2018): 374–400.

24. World Economic Forum, *The Corporate Gender Gap Report* (Geneva: World Economic Forum, 2010).

25. John Davis, "Spain's New Sex Czar," A Voice for Men, August 13, 2018, https://www.avoiceformen.com/feminism/spains-new-sex-czar/.

26. Matthew MacWilliams, "The One Weird Trait That Predicts Whether You're a Trump Supporter," *Politico*, January 20, 2016, https://www.politico.com/magazine/story/2016/01/donald-trump-2016-authoritarian-213533.

27. Steve Hendrix, "He Always Hated Women. Then He Decided to Kill Them," *Washington Post*, June 7, 2019, https://www.washingtonpost.com/graphics/2019/local/yoga-shooting-incel-attack-fueled-by-male-supremacy/; Emmet Rensin, "The Internet Is Full of Men Who Hate Feminism. Here's What They Are Like in Person," *Vox*, August 18, 2015, https://www.vox.com/2015/2/5/7942623/mens-rights-movement; "Male Supremacy," Southern Poverty Law Center, https://www.splcenter.org/fighting-hate/extremist-files/ideology/male-supremacy.

28. Aaron Karp, *Estimating Global Civilian-Held Firearms Numbers*, Small Arms Survey (Geneva: Graduate Institute on International and Development Studies, June 2018), http://www.smallarmssurvey.org/fileadmin/docs/T-Briefing-Papers/SAS-BP-Civilian-Firearms-Numbers.pdf; National Institute of Mental Health, "Suicide," https://www.nimh.nih.gov/health/statistics/suicide.shtml; Christopher Ingraham, "There Are Now More Guns Than People in the United States," *Washington Post*, October 5, 2015, https://www.washingtonpost.com/news/wonk/wp/2015/10/05/guns-in-the-united-states-one-for-every-man-woman-and-child-and-then-some/; Kim Parker, Juliana Menasce Horowitz, Ruth Igielnik, J. Baxter Oliphant, and Anna Brown, "The Demographics of Gun Ownership," Pew Research Center, June 22, 2017, https://www.pewsocialtrends.org/2017/06/22/the-demographics-of-gun-ownership/; American Foundation for the Prevention of Suicide, "Suicide Statistics," https://afsp.org/about-suicide/suicide-statistics/; Bindu Kalesan, Marcos D. Villarreal, Katherine M. Keyes, and Sandro Galea, "Gun Ownership and Social Gun Culture," *Injury Prevention* 0 (2015): 1–5, https://injuryprevention.bmj.com/content/injuryprev/early/2015/06/09/injuryprev-2015-041586.full.pdf?keytype=ref&ijkey=doj6vx0laFZMsQ2; Lindsay Lee, Max Roser, and Esteban Ortiz-Ospina, "Suicide," Our World in Data, July 2016, https://ourworldindata.org/suicide; Sally C. Curtin, Margaret Warner, and Holly Hedegaard, "Increase in Suicide Rates in the United States, 1999–2014," NCHS Data Brief No. 241, National Center for Health Statistics, April 2016, https://www.cdc.gov/nchs/products/databriefs/db241.htm; Helene Schumacher, "Why More Men Than Women Die by Suicide," BBC Future, March 18, 2019, http://www.bbc.com/future/story/20190313-why-more-men-kill-themselves-than-women.

29. "Asia's Lonely Hearts," *Economist*, August 20, 2011, https://www.economist.com/leaders/2011/08/20/asias-lonely-hearts.

30. Josh Levs, *All In: How Our Work-First Culture Fails Dads, Families, and Businesses—and How We Can Fix It Together* (New York: Harper One, 2015).

31. Grover J. "Russ" Whitehurst, "Why the Federal Government Should Subsidize Childcare and How to Pay for It," March 9, 2017, https://www.brookings.edu

/research/why-the-federal-government-should-subsidize-childcare-and-how
-to-pay-for-it/.

32. Jon Greenberg, "If Women Worked as Much as Men, Would US GDP Jump
5 Percent?," Politifact, December 12, 2018, https://www.politifact.com/truth-o
-meter/statements/2018/dec/12/christine-lagarde/if-women-worked-much
-men-would-gdp-jump-5/.

8. BRAIN BIGOTS

1. Steve Connor, "The Hardwired Difference Between Male and Female Brains
Could Explain Why Men Are 'Better at Map Reading,'" *Independent*, December 2013.

2. Cliodhna O'Connor, "'Brain Study Confirms Gender Stereotypes': How Science Communication Can Fuel Modern Sexism," *Impact Blog*, London School
of Economics, February 4, 2015, http://blogs.lse.ac.uk/impactofsocialsciences
/2015/02/04/science-communication-gender-stereotypes-sexism/; Cliodhna
O'Connor and Helene Joffe, "Gender on the Brain: A Case Study of Science
Communication in the New Media Environment," *PLOS ONE* 9, no. 10 (2014).

3. Hannah Devlin, "Science Museum Under Fire over Exhibit Asking If Brains
Are Pink or Blue," *Guardian*, September 14, 2016, https://www.theguardian
.com/world/2016/sep/14/science-museum-under-fire-exhibit-brains-pink
-blue-gender-stereotypes; Mahatir Pasha, "Museum Under Fire for Quiz on
Male, Female Brains," CNN, September 14, 2016, https://www.cnn.com/2016
/09/14/health/science-museum-brain-quiz-controversy-trnd/index.html.

4. Sarah Ashley O'Brien and Seth Fiegerman, "Fired Engineer: Google Tried to
Shame Me," CNN Business, August 17, 2017; Connie Loizo, "James Damore
Just Filed a Class Action Lawsuit Against Google, Saying It Discriminates
Against White Male Conservatives," *TechCrunch*, https://techcrunch.com/2018
/01/08/james-damore-just-filed-a-class-action-lawsuit-against-google-saying
-it-discriminates-against-white-male-conservatives/.

5. Michael J. Coren, "James Damore Has Proven the Alt-Right Playbook Can
Work in Silicon Valley," *Quartz*, August 19, 2017; Sara Ashley O'Brien and
Laurie Segall, "Former Google Engineer: 'I Do Not Support the Alt-Right,'"
CNN Business, https://money.cnn.com/2017/08/15/technology/culture/james
-damore-interview/index.html.

6. Lutz Jänke, "Sex/Gender Differences in Cognition, Neurophysiology, and Neuroanatomy," PMC, published online June 20, 2018, https://www.ncbi.nlm.nih
.gov/pmc/articles/PMC6013760/; Cordelia Fine, *Delusions of Gender: How Our
Minds, Society, and Neurosexism Create Difference* (New York: W. W. Norton,
2010); Rebecca Jordan-Young and Raffaella I. Rumiati, "Hardwired for Sexism? Approaches to Sex/Gender in Neuroscience," *Neuroethics* 5 (2012): 305–
15; Daphna Joel, Zohar Berman, Ido Tavor, Nadav Wexler, Olga Gaber, Yaniv
Stein, Nisan Shefi, et al., "Sex Beyond the Genitalia: The Human Brain Mo-
saic," *PNAS* 112, no. 50 (2015): 15468–73. See also Angela Saini, *Inferior: How
Science Got Women Wrong and the New Research That's Rewriting the Story*
(Boston: Beacon Press, 2017).

7. Lise Eliot, "Single-Sex Education and the Brain," *Sex Roles* 69 (2013): 363–81;

Jonathan M. Kane and Janet E. Mertz, "Debunking Myths About Gender and Mathematics Performance," *Notices of the American Medical Society* 59, no. 1 (2012): 10–21.

8. Julie Bort, "Over Half of Google Employees Polled Say the Web Giant Shouldn't Have Fired the Engineer Behind the Controversial Memo," *Business Insider*, August 9, 2017, https://www.businessinsider.com/many-google -employees-dont-think-james-damore-should-have-been-fired-2017-8.

9. Jenessa R. Shapiro, Amy M. Williams, and Mariam Hambarchyan, "Are All Interventions Created Equal? A Multi-Threat Approach to Tailoring Stereotype Threat Interventions," *Journal of Personality and Social Psychology* 104, no. 2 (2014).

10. Cordelia Fine, "Explaining, or Sustaining, the Status Quo? The Potentially Self-Fulfilling Effects of 'Hard-Wired' Accounts of Sex Differences," *Neuroethics* 5 (2012): 285–94; Claude M. Steele, "A Threat in the Air: How Stereotypes Shape Intellectual Identity and Performance," *American Psychologist* 52, no. 6 (1997): 613–29; Thomas A. Morton, Alex Haslam, and Matthew J. Hornsey, "Theorizing Gender in the Face of Social Change: Is There Anything Essential About Essentialism?" *Journal of Personality and Social Psychology* 96, no. 3: 653–64; Vincent Yzerbyt, Steve Rocher, and Georges Schadron, "Stereotypes as Explanations: A Subjective Essentialist View of Group Perception," in *The Social Psychology of Stereotyping and Group Life*, ed. Russell Spears, Penelope J. Oakes, Naomi Ellemers, and S. Alexander Haslam (Cambridge, UK: Blackwell, 1997), 20–50; Johannes Keller, "In Genes We Trust: The Biological Component of Psychological Essentialism and Its Relationship to Mechanisms of Motivated Social Cognition," *Journal of Personality and Social Psychology* 88 (2005): 686–702; Jessica Cundiff and Theresa Vescio, "Gender Stereotypes Influence How People Explain Gender Disparities in the Workplace," *Sex Roles* 75, no. 3–4 (2016): 126–38.

11. O'Connor, "Gender on the Brain."

12. O'Connor, "Gender on the Brain."

13. O'Connor, "Gender on the Brain."

14. O'Connor, "Gender on the Brain."

15. Fine, *Delusions of Gender*; Margaret M. McCarthy and Arthur P. Arnold, "Reframing Sexual Differentiation of the Brain," *Nature Neuroscience* 14, no. 6 (2011): 677–87. Also Jordan-Young and Rumiati, "Hardwired for Sexism?"

16. Robin McKie, "Why It's Time for Brain Science to Ditch the 'Venus and Mars' Cliche," *Guardian*, December 7, 2013.

17. Camilla Persson Benbow and Julian C. Stanley, "Sex Differences in Mathematical Ability: Fact or Artifact?," *Science* 210 (December 1980): 1262–64; Camilla Persson Benbow and Julian C. Stanley, "Sex Differences in Mathematical Reasoning Ability: More Facts," *Science* 222 (1983): 1029–31.

18. Janet S. Hyde, Elizabeth Fennema, and Susan J. Lamon, "Gender Differences in Mathematics Performance: A Meta-Analysis," *Psychological Bulletin* 107, no. 2 (1990): 139–55; Jacqueline S. Eccles, "Understanding Women's Educational and Occupational Choices: Applying the Eccles et al Model of Achievement-Related Choices," *Psychology of Women Quarterly* 8, no. 4 (1994): 585–610;

Judith L. Meece, Jacquelynne E. Parsons, Caroline M. Kaczala, and Susan B. Goff, "Sex Differences in Math Achievement: Toward a Model of Academic Choice," *Psychological Bulletin* 91, no. 2 (1982): 324–48; National Science Foundation, "Science and Engineering Indicators" (2006), https://wayback.archive -it.org/5902/20160210153725/http://www.nsf.gov/statistics/seind06/. For an overview of the narrative, see Janet S. Hyde and Janet E. Mertz, "Gender, Culture, and Mathematics Performance," *PNAS* 106, no. 22 (2009): 8801–807. For a critical review, see Elizabeth S. Spelke, "Sex Differences in Intrinsic Aptitude for Mathematics and Science? A Critical Review," *American Psychologist* 60, no. 9 (2005): 950–58.

19. Janet S. Hyde, "The Gender Similarities Hypothesis," *American Psychologist* 60 (2005): 581–92; Janet S. Hyde, Sara M. Lindberg, Marcia C. Linn, Amy B. Ellis, and Caroline C. Williams, "Gender Similarities Characterize Math Performance," *Science* 321 (2008): 494–95; and Janet S. Hyde, "Sex and Cognition: Gender and Cognitive Functions," *Current Opinion in Neurobiology* 38 (June 2016): 53–56.

20. Luigi Guiso, Ferdinando Monte, Paola Sapienza, and Luigi Zingales, "Culture, Gender, and Math," *Science* 320 (2008): 1164–65.

21. Jing Feng, "Playing an Action Video Game Reduces Gender Differences in Spatial Cognition," *Psychological Science* 18 (2007): 850–55; Jennifer A. Lachance and Michele M. M. Mazzocco, "A Longitudinal Analysis of Sex Differences in Math and Spatial Skills in Primary School-Age Children," *NIH Public Access Manuscript* 116, no. 3 (2006): 195–216. See also D. H. Uttal, N. G. Meadow, E. Tipton, L. L. Hand, A. R. Alden, C. Warren, and N. S. Newcombe, "The Malleability of Spatial Skills: A Meta-Analysis of Training Studies," *Psychological Bulletin* 139 (2013): 352–402.

22. Merim Bilalić, Kerim Smallbone, Peter McLeod, and Fernand Gobet, "Why Are (the Best) Women So Good at Chess?," *Proceedings of the Royal Society* 23, doi:10.1098/rspb.2008.1576; Neil Charness and Yigal Gerchak, "Participation Rates and Maximal Performance: A Log-Linear Explanation for Group Differences, Such as Russian and Male Dominance in Chess," *Psychological Science* 7, no. 1 (1996): 46–51.

23. Hyde, "Gender Similarities Hypothesis."

24. Sebastian Seung, *Connectome: How the Bran's Wiring Makes Us Who We Are* (New York: Mariner Books, 2013); Catherine Vidal, "The Sexed Brain: Between Science and Ideology," *Neuroethics* 5, 295–303.

25. Amber Dance, "A Massive Global Effort Maps How the Brain Is Wired," *Nature*, October 2, 2015, https://www.scientificamerican.com/article/a-massive -global-effort-maps-how-the-brain-is-wired/.

26. Sue V. Rosser and Mark Zachary Taylor, "Why Are We Still Worried About Women in Science?," AAUP, May–June 2009, https://www.aaup.org/article/why -are-we-still-worried-about-women-science.

27. I just want to say for the benefit of readers with liberal arts backgrounds that I don't agree with the assessment that those areas of study are either easy or impractical. I majored in English myself.

28. For instance, Jonathan Zimmerman, "Why Are Schools Discriminating Against Women?," *Christian Science Monitor*, April 8, 2014.

29. Christina Hoff Sommers, *The War Against Boys: How Misguided Feminism Is Harming Our Young Men* (New York: Simon and Schuster, 2001).

30. Vivienne Ming, "The Hidden Tax on Being Different," *HR*, November 23, 2016.

31. The *Global Gender Gap Report* of the World Economic Forum has shown, in all the years it has been published, that men are more often employed, make more money, and dominate leadership posts in both the private and public sectors of every country in the world.

32. Claudia Goldin, "The Quiet Revolution That Transformed Women's Employment, Education, and Family," *AEA Papers and Proceedings* 96, no. 2 (2006).

33. American Physical Society, "Doctoral Degrees Earned by Women," https://www.aps.org/programs/education/statistics/fraction-p.cfm. The data goes up to 2017 and is taken from the Integrated Postsecondary Education Data System and the American Physical Society.

34. Fine, *Delusions of Gender*, 76.

35. "The Elephant in the Valley," https://www.elephantinthevalley.com.

36. Cary Funk, "Women and Men in STEM Often at Odds Over Workplace Equity," Pew Research Center, January 9, 2018, https://www.pewsocialtrends.org/2018/01/09/women-and-men-in-stem-often-at-odds-over-workplace-equity/.

37. Derek Thompson, "Health Care Just Became the US's Largest Employer," *Atlantic*, January 9, 2018.

9. THE FAILURE OF EQUAL PAY

1. Amelia Gentleman, "'I'm Beyond Anger': Why the Great Pay Gap Reveal Is an Explosive Moment for Gender Equality," *Guardian*, February 28, 2018, https://www.theguardian.com/news/2018/feb/28/gender-pay-gap-reveal-explosive-moment-equality.

2. Gentleman, "'I'm Beyond Anger.'"

3. Hannah Murphy, "UK Pay Data Force Companies to Mind Their Gender Gap," *Financial Times*, September 26, 2017, https://www.ft.com/content/dd21e03e-634a-11e7-8814-0ac7eb84e5f1.

4. BBC Reality Check Team, "Equal Pay: What Is the Extent of the Problem?," BBC News, January 8, 2018, https://www.bbc.com/news/uk-42611725.

5. The original provision from which the positive discrimination doctrine comes appears to be in section 1, the second paragraph, in which the act says that the provisions "are framed with reference to women and their treatment relative to men, but are to be read as applying equally in a converse case to men and their treatment relative to women." Equal Pay Act 1970, chapter 41, http://www.legislation.gov.uk/ukpga/1970/41/enacted/data.xht?view=snippet&wrap=true.

6. Noreen Burrows and Muriel Robison, "Positive Action for Women in Employment: Time to Align with Europe?," *Journal of Law and Society* 33, no. 1 (March 2006): 24–41; Julie C. Suk, "Gender Quotas After the End of Men,"

Boston Law Review 93 (2013): 1123–40; Ivana Krstić, "Affirmative Action in the United States and the European Union: Comparison and Analysis," Facta Universitatis, Law and Politics Series 1, no. 7 (2003): 825–43.

7. Claire Suddath, "New Numbers Show the Gender Pay Gap Is Real," *Bloomberg Businessweek*, March 29, 2018.

8. Linda Babcock and Sara Laschever, *Women Don't Ask* (New York: Bantam, 2007).

9. I have summarized this literature, with references, at Linda Scott, "Why Women Can't Negotiate for Equal Pay," Double X Economy, https://www.doublexeconomy.com/2015/04/14/why-women-cant-negotiate-for-equal-pay/.

10. May Bulman, "Women in the UK Losing Out on £140 Billion Due to Gender Pay Gap, Figures Show," *Independent*, January 27, 2018; Gentleman, "'I'm Beyond Anger.'"

11. Alexander J. S. Colvin, "The Growing Use of Mandatory Arbitration," *Economic Policy Institute*, April 6, 2018.

12. Justice White, "Separate Opinion," Legal Information Institute, 438 U.S. 265, Regents of the University of California v. Bakke (No. 7811), argued October 12, 1977, decided June 28, 1978, https://www.law.cornell.edu/supremecourt/text/438/265#writing-USSC_CR_0438_0265_ZX1.

13. European Commission, "International Perspectives on Positive Action Measures," 2009, EU Publications, http://bim.lbg.ac.at/files/sites/bim/International%20Perspectives%20on%20Positive%20Action%20Measures.pdf.

14. Petra Foubert, *The Gender Pay Gap in Europe from a Legal Perspective* (Brussels: European Union, 2010). See also Sanchari Roy, *Discriminatory Laws Against Women: A Survey of the Literature*, Policy Research Working Paper 8719 (Washington, DC: World Bank Group, 2019), https://www.ssrn.com/abstract=3324761.

15. European Commission, "International Perspectives on Positive Action Measures."

10. THE 80 PERCENT CHRISTMAS

1. "How Is Our Economy Impacted by the Holiday Season?," Export-Import Bank of the United States, January 25, 2018, https://grow.exim.gov/blog/how-is-our-economy-impacted-by-the-holiday-season; Larry Light, "Why Holiday Shopping Is So Important for the U.S. Economy," CBS News, November 28, 2016, https://www.cbsnews.com/news/why-holiday-shopping-is-so-important-for-the-economy/; "Consumers Will Spend 4.1 Percent More Than Last Year During Winter Holidays," National Retail Federation, October 24, 2018, https://nrf.com/media-center/press-releases/consumers-will-spend-41-percent-more-last-year-during-winter-holidays; Rod Sides, Bryan Furman, Rama Krishna V. Sangadi, and Susan K. Hogan, "2018 Deloitte Holiday Retail Survey: Shopping Cheer Resounds This Year," Deloitte Insights, October 23, 2018, https://www2.deloitte.com/insights/us/en/authors/h/susan-k-hogan.html.

2. Tom Hancock, "China's Lunar New Year Spending Growth Slowest Since 2005," *Financial Times*, February 11, 2019.

3. The dates for Ramadan fluctuate from year to year, moving gradually across the calendar. In 2019, it's in May/June; in 2020, it will be in April/May. "The Ramadan Effect: How Islam's Holy Month Impacts Business," Harding Loevner, April 2018, https://www.hardingloevner.com/fundamental-thinking/ramadan -effect-how-islams-holy-month-impacts-businesses/; "Big Indian Festivals and Their Effects on the Indian Economy," Economics Club: IMI New Delhi, October 1, 2017; Eileen Fischer and Stephen J. Arnold, "More Than a Labor of Love: Gender Roles and Christmas Gift Shopping," *Journal of Consumer Research* 17, no. 3 (December 1990): 333–45; Michael Solomon, Gary Bamossy, Søren Askegaard, and Margaret Hogg, *Consumer Behavior: A European Perspective* (London: Financial Times/Prentice Hall, 2005).

4. Michael J. Silverstein and Kate Sayre, "The Female Economy," *Harvard Business Review*, September 2009.

5. Mary Douglas and Baron Isherwood, *The World of Goods* (New York: W. W. Norton, 1982).

6. Douglas and Isherwood, *The World of Goods*, 4.

7. Silverstein and Sayre, "The Female Economy."

8. Linda Scott, Mary Johnstone-Louis, and Catherine Dolan, "Pampers and UNICEF, Part 1: The Marketing Campaign," Saïd Business School Teaching Notes, University of Oxford, October 2011, https://www.doublexeconomy .com/wp-content/uploads/2011/05/Pampers-Unicef-Case-Teaching-Note-Part -1.pdf; Linda Scott, Mary Johnston-Louis, and Catherine Dolan, "Pampers and UNICEF, Part 2: Delivering the Vaccine," Saïd Business School Teaching Notes, University of Oxford, October 2011, https://www.doublexeconomy .com/wp-content/uploads/2011/05/Pampers-Unicef-Case-Part-2.pdf.

9. Dayna Evans, "The Only Way to Know If Striking Works Is to Do It," *New York*, March 7, 2017; Mary Emily O'Hara, "Women's Strike: 'A Day Without a Woman' Events Take Place Worldwide," NBC News, March 8, 2017; Glosswitch, "What Would Happen If the World's Women Went on Strike?," *New Statesman America*, February 9, 2017.

11. MONEY BULLIES

1. Kessler Psychological Distress Scale, https://www.tac.vic.gov.au/files-to-move /media/upload/k10_english.pdf.

2. L. I. Pearlin and C. Schooler, "The Structure of Coping," *Journal of Health and Social Behavior* (1978): 2–21, https://www.hsph.harvard.edu/health-happiness /pearlin-mastery-scale/.

3. E. Yoon, K. Adams, I. Hogge, J. P. Bruner, S. Surya, and F. B. Bryant, "Development and Validation of the Patriarchal Beliefs Scale," *Journal of Counseling Psychology* 62, no. 2 (2015): 264–79.

4. The project was called the Moldova Second Competitiveness Enhancement Project (CEP-II).

5. Pierella Paci, *Gender in Transition* (Washington, DC: World Bank Group, 2002), http://documents.worldbank.org/curated/en/892681468751807453/pdf /multi0page.pdf; Andrei Kutuzov and Brenda R. Haskins, *Moldova Country Brief: Property and Land Markets* (Madison, WI: Land Tenure Center,

University of Wisconsin, 2003), https://www.nelson.wisc.edu/ltc/docs/moldova brief.pdf.

6. Majority Report of the U.S. Senate Committee on Small Business and Entrepreneurship, "21st Century Barriers to Women's Entrepreneurship," July 23, 2014, https://www.sbc.senate.gov/public/_cache/files/3/f/3f954386-f16b-48d2 -86ad-698a75e33cc4/F74C2CA266014842F8A3D86C3AB619BA.21st-century -barriers-to-women-s-entrepreneurship-revised-ed.-v.1.pdf.

7. I saw several sources on the internet that said women employed 9 million people in the United States. This figure cannot be correct, because there are 12 million women-owned businesses—and 9 million employees among them would mean a substantial percentage had negative numbers of people working for them. So I decided to go with sources that instead calculated a standard number of employees from the sales revenue. The number I finally settled on, 23 million, is from the National Women's Business Council, which is the U.S. government's official agency representative for women's entrepreneurship. The figure is found on this site: https://www.nwbc.gov/2009/10/27/the-economic -impact-of-women-owned-businesses-in-the-united-states/.

8. Linda Scott and Elizabeth Paris, "Women Entrepreneurs and Effective Banking in Emerging Markets: BLC Bank Lebanon Proves a Strategy for Financial Inclusion" (Oxford: Saïd Business School Series, University of Oxford, 2019).

9. *MSME Finance Gap: Assessment of the Shortfalls and Opportunities in Financing Micro, Small and Medium Enterprises in Emerging Markets* (Washington, DC: International Finance Corporation, 2017), http://documents.worldbank .org/curated/en/653831510568517947/MSME-finance-gap-assessment-of -the-shortfalls-and-opportunities-in-financing-micro-small-and-medium -enterprises-in-emerging-markets.

10. International Finance Corporation, *MSME Finance Gap 2019* (Washington, DC: International Finance Corporation, 2019); World Bank, *Women, Business and the Law 2014* (Washington, DC: World Bank Group, 2014).

11. Linda Scott and Jiafei Jin, "Finance After Hours" (Oxford: Saïd Business School Series, University of Oxford, 2014).

12. The bank in this case was a real bank but was given a fictitious name for publication.

13. Claire Suddath, "New Numbers Show the Gender Pay Gap Is Real," *Bloomberg Businessweek*, March 29, 2018.

14. Maureen Sherry, "The Brutal Truth About Being a Woman on Wall Street," *Fortune*, August 6, 2016.

15. Sam Polk, "How Wall Street Bro Talk Keeps Women Down," *New York Times*, July 7, 2016.

16. Polk, "How Wall Street Bro Talk Keeps Women Down."

17. Here is just a sampling of the literature. Several of these articles also contain extensive reviews. Jean-Claude Dreher, Simon Dunne, Agnieszka Pazderska, Thomas Frodl, John J. Nolan, and John P. O'Doherty, "Testosterone Causes Both Prosocial and Anti-Social Status-Enhancing Behaviors in Human Males," *Proceedings of the National Academy of Science* 113, no. 41 (2016): 11633–38; Gary D. Sherman, Jennifer S. Lerner, Robert A. Josephs, Jonathan Renshon, and James J. Gross, "The Interaction of Testosterone and Cortisol Is

Associated with Attained Status in Male Executives," *Journal of Personality and Social Psychology* 110, no. 6 (2016): 921–29; Ed Leefelt, "This Is a Man's Brain on Testosterone," CBS News, May 4, 2017, https://www.cbsnews.com /news/this-is-a-mans-brain-on-testosterone/; "Testosterone Makes Men Less Likely to Question Their Impulses: Sex Hormone Connected with Greater Reliance on Gut Instincts and Less Self Reflection," *Science Daily*, April 28, 2017, https://www.sciencedaily.com/releases/2017/04/170428154556.htm; Gideon Nave, Amos Nadler, David Zava, and Colin Cramer, "Single Dose Testosterone Administration Impairs Cognitive Reflection in Men," *Psychological Science*, August 3, 2017, https://journals.sagepub.com/doi/abs/10.1177 /0956797617709592.

18. For a review, see Meredith A. Jones, *Women of the Street* (New York: Palgrave Macmillan, 2015), 7–22.

19. Melissa S. Fisher, *Wall Street Women* (Durham, NC: Duke University Press, 2011).

20. Andrea Turner Moffitt, *Harness the Power of the Purse: Winning Women Investors* (Los Angeles: Rare Bird Books, 2015).

21. Sylvia Ann Hewlett and Andrea Turner Moffitt with Melinda Marshall, *Harnessing the Power of the Purse: Female Investors and Global Opportunities for Growth* (New York: Center for Talent Innovation, 2014), http://www .talentinnovation.org/publication.cfm?publication=1440.

12. OWNING IT

1. Dame Stephanie Shirley, *Let It Go* (London: Acorn Books, 2013).

2. Louise Tickle, "We Were Part of a Crusade to Get Women into Business," *Guardian*, March 8, 2017; Melissa Pandika, "How Dame Shirley Jumped over the Gender Gap in Tech in the 1960s," NPR, June 12, 2014.

3. Jenna Burch, "Why One Woman Went by the Name Steve," *Self*, April 9, 2015.

4. Linda Scott, *Fresh Lipstick: Redressing Fashion and Feminism* (New York: Palgrave Macmillan, 2004).

5. Yes, this statistic is true. I have fact-checked it. Those who are also surprised may want to think about the fact that the whole world is not Christian, but Avon is in some very big non-Christian countries (e.g., China and India); and while most Christians have only one Bible (or one for the family), the Avon catalog comes out every eight weeks.

6. Mohamed Seedat, "Violence and Injuries in South Africa," *Lancet* 374, no. 9694 (September 19, 2009): 1011–22.

7. Linda Scott, Catherine Dolan, Mary Johnstone-Louis, Maryalice Wu, and Kim Sugden, "Enterprise and Inequality," *Entrepreneurship, Theory and Practice* 36, no. 3 (May 1, 2012): 543–68.

8. Catherine Dolan and Linda Scott, "Lipstick Evangelism: Avon Trading Circles and Gender Empowerment in South Africa," *Gender and Development* 17, no. 2 (July 15, 2009): 203–18.

9. The project was called the Moldova Second Competitiveness Enhancement Project (CEP-II). Tarik Sahovic, Noa Catalina Gimelli, and Galina Cicanci, *Supporting Women's Enterprise in Moldova* (Washington, DC:

World Bank Group, 2018), http://documents.worldbank.org/curated/en /411391516856355553/Supporting-women-s-entrepreneurship-in-Moldova -review-assessment-and-recommendations.

10. Dana Kanze, Laura Huang, Mark A. Conley, and E. Tory Higgins, "Male and Female Entrepreneurs Get Asked Different Questions by VCs—and It Affects How Much Funding They Get," *Harvard Business Review*, June 27, 2017; Dana Kanze, Laura Huang, Mark A. Conley, and E. Tory Higgins, "We Ask Men to Win and Women Not to Lose: Closing the Gender Gap in Startup Funding," *Academy of Management Journal* 61, no. 2 (2018), https://journals.aom.org/doi /abs/10.5465/amj.2016.1215.

11. Saheel Raina, "The Gender Gap in Startup Success Disappears When Women Fund Women," *Harvard Business Review*, July 19, 2016.

12. Lucy Kellaway, "Justine Roberts of Mumsnet," *Financial Times*, December 9, 2013.

13. Natalie Robehmed, "Next Billion-Dollar Startup: Entrepreneurs Create $750M Bra Business by Exposing Victoria's Weakness," *Forbes*, October 18, 2018, https://www.forbes.com/sites/natalierobehmed/2018/10/18/next-billion -dollar-startup-entrepreneurs-create-750m-bra-business-by-exposing-victorias -weakness/.

14. Robehmed, "Next Billion-Dollar Startup."

15. Sally Herships, "Why Female Entrepreneurs Get Less Funding Than Men," *Marketplace*, October 25, 2017.

16. Herships, "Why Female Entrepreneurs Get Less Funding Than Men."

17. Eleanor Steifel, "I Was Told I Didn't Look the Part: The Funding Gap Prevent- ing Millions of Women from Starting Their Own Businesses," *Telegraph*, March 8, 2018.

18. Jenny Tooth, "The Barriers and Opportunities for Women Angel Investing in Europe," UK Business Angels Association, https://www.beangels.eu/wp -content/uploads/2018/03/WA4E-UKBAA-Women-Angels-Report-February -2018-WEB-003.pdf.

13. JOINING THE GLOBAL MARKET

1. Sue Harris Rimmer, *Gender-Smart Procurement: Policies for Driving Change* (London: Chatham House, 2017), https://www.chathamhouse.org/publication /gender-smart-procurement-policies-driving-change.

2. Linda Scott, *Private Sector Engagement with Women's Economic Empowerment: Lessons Learned from Years of Practice* (Oxford: Saïd Business School Series, University of Oxford, 2017), https://www.doublexeconomy.com/wp-content /uploads/2018/10/RES-0054-GBCWEE-Report-171117-BOOKLET.pdf.

3. See, for instance, Linda Scott, Catherine Dolan, and Laurel Steinfield, *Women's Empowerment Through Access to Markets: Maasai Women Development Orga- nization (MWEDO), Arusha, Tanzania* (Oxford: Saïd Business School Series, University of Oxford, 2015), https://www.doublexeconomy.com/wp-content /uploads/2019/02/mwedo-casestudy-final-may2015.pdf; Linda Scott, Laurel Steinfield, and Catherine Dolan, *Women's Empowerment Through Access to Markets: Katchy Kollections, Nairobi, Kenya* (Oxford: Saïd Business School

Series, University of Oxford, 2015), https://www.doublexeconomy.com/wp-content/uploads/2019/02/katchy-kollections-casestudy-final-may2015.pdf.

4. Angélica Fuentes, "The Link Between Corruption and Gender Inequality: A Heavy Burden for Development and Democracy," Wilson Center blog, July 2, 2018, https://www.wilsoncenter.org/publication/the-link-between-corruption-and-gender-inequality-heavy-burden-for-development-and; Naomi Hossain, Celestine Nyamu Musembi, and Jessica Hughes, *Corruption, Accountability and Gender: Understanding the Connections* (New York: United Nations Development Program and United Nations Development Fund for Women, 2010), https://www.undp.org/content/dam/aplaws/publication/en/publications/womens-empowerment/corruption-accountability-and-gender-understanding-the-connection/Corruption-accountability-and-gender.pdf; Sangeetha Purushothaman, Tara Tobin, Shruthi Vissa, Priya Pillai, Sarah Silliman, and Carolina Pinheiro, *Seeing Beyond the State: Grassroots Women's Perspectives on Corruption and Anti-Corruption* (New York: United Nations Development Programme, 2012), https://www.undp.org/content/dam/undp/library/Democratic%20Governance/Anti-corruption/Grassroots%20women%20and%20anti-corruption.pdf.

5. "Appendix II, Chapter N *bis*–Trade and Gender," Canada-Chile Free Trade Agreement, 2017, https://www.international.gc.ca/trade-commerce/trade-agreements-accords-commerciaux/agr-acc/chile-chili/index.aspx?lang=eng#a5.

6. *Reshaping Trade Through Women's Economic Empowerment: Special Report* (Geneva: International Trade Centre, 2018), https://www.cigionline.org/reshaping-trade-through-womens-economic-empowerment.

7. Charter of the United Nations, Chapter IX, "International Economic and Social Cooperation," Article 55, 1945, http://legal.un.org/repertory/art55.shtml.

8. "119 Nations Back Move to Remove Barriers Limiting Women's Participation in Trade," *Hindu*, December 13, 2017, https://www.thehindu.com/business/Economy/119-nations-back-move-to-remove-barriers-limiting-womens-participation-in-trade/article21581261.ece/.

9. Asia Pacific Forum on Women, Law, and Development, "Women's Rights Groups Call on Governments to Reject the WTO Declaration on 'Women's Economic Empowerment,'" press release, December 12, 2017, https://apwld.org/press-release-164-womens-rights-groups-call-on-governments-to-reject-the-wto-declaration-on-womens-economic-empowerment/.

SELECTED BIBLIOGRAPHY

More than one thousand works went into this book as source material. It was not practical in a book of this length to include all of them. I have cited sources as appropriate in the endnotes. This short list is a bibliography selected to give a sense of the works that had an impact on my thinking.

Agarwal, Bina. *A Field of One's Own: Gender and Land Rights in South Asia.* Cambridge, UK: Cambridge University Press, 1995.

Bales, Kevin. *Disposable People: New Slavery in the Global Economy.* Berkeley: University of California Press, 2000.

Blau, Francine D., and Lawrence M. Khan. "Changes in the Labor Supply Behavior of Married Women 1980–2000." Cambridge, MA: National Bureau of Economic Research, 2005.

———. "Female Labor Supply: Why Is the U.S. Falling Behind?" In *Discussion Paper Series.* Bonn, Germany: Institute for Study of Labor (IZA), 2013.

———. "Gender Differences in Pay." In NBER Working Paper Series, no. 7732. Cambridge, MA: National Bureau of Economic Research, 2000.

Boserup, Ester. *Woman's Role in Economic Development.* London: Earthscan, 1970.

Coontz, Stephanie. *Marriage, a History: How Love Conquered Marriage.* London: Penguin Books, 2006.

Drakeman, Cynthia. *Leave No One Behind: Taking Action for Transformational Change on Women's Economic Empowerment.* UN Secretary General's High Level Panel on Women's Economic Empowerment, 2017.

Eller, Cynthia. *The Myth of Matriarchal Prehistory.* Boston: Beacon Press, 2000.

Ferber, Marianne A., and Julie A. Nelson. *Beyond Economic Man: Feminist Theory and Economics.* Chicago: University of Chicago Press, 1993.

Fernandez, Raquel. "Culture as Learning: The Evolution of Female Labor Force Participation Over a Century." Cambridge, MA: National Bureau of Economic Research, 2007.

Folbre, Nancy. *Greed, Lust, and Gender: A History of Economic Ideas*. Oxford: Oxford University Press, 2009.

Food and Agriculture Organization. *The State of Food and Agriculture: Women in Agriculture, Closing the Gender Gap for Development*. Rome: Food and Agriculture Organization, Economic and Social Development Department, 2010.

Gibbons, Ann. *The First Human: The Race to Discover Our Earliest Ancestors*. New York: Anchor Books, 2007.

Goldin, Claudia. "Life-Cycle Labor-Force Participation of Married Women: Historical Evidence and Implications." In NBER Working Paper Series, no. 1251. Cambridge, MA: National Bureau of Economic Research, 1983.

———. "Marriage Bars: Discrimination Against Married Women Workers, 1920's to 1950's." In NBER Working Paper Series, no. 2747. Cambridge, MA: National Bureau of Economic Research, 1988.

———. "The Quiet Revolution That Transformed Women's Employment, Education, and Family." *AEA Papers and Proceedings* 96, no. 2 (May 2006).

———. "The U-Shaped Female Labor Force in Economic Development and Economic History." In NBER Working Paper Series, no. 4707. Cambridge, MA: National Bureau of Economic Research, 1994.

Hays-Gilpin, Kelley, and David S. Whitley. *Reader in Gender Archaeology*. London: Routledge, 1998.

Hrdy, Sarah. *Mother Nature: Maternal Instincts and How They Shape the Human Species*. New York: Ballantine, 2000.

Hudson, Valerie, Bonnie Ballif-Spanvill, Mary Caprioli, and Chad Emmett. *Sex and World Peace*. New York: Columbia University Press, 2014.

Inglehart, Ronald, and Pippa Norris. *Rising Tide: Gender Equality and Cultural Change Around the World*. Cambridge: Cambridge University Press, 2003.

Jaggar, Alison. *Feminist Politics and Human Nature*. Maryland: Rowman and Littlefield, 1988.

Joyce, Rosemary A. *Ancient Bodies, Ancient Lives: Sex, Gender, and Archaeology*. New York: Thames and Hudson, 2008.

Kristoff, Nicholas D., and Sheryl WuDunn. *Half the Sky: Turning Oppression into Opportunity for Women Worldwide*. New York: Vintage, 2010.

Lechman, Ewa, and Harleen Kaur. "Economic Growth and Female Labor Force Participation—Verifying the U-Feminization Hypothesis; New Evidence for 162 Countries over the Period 1990–2012." *Economics and Sociology* 8, no. 1 (2015): 246–57.

Lerner, Gerda. *The Creation of Patriarchy*. Oxford: Oxford University Press, 1986.

Mauss, Marcel. *The Gift: The Form and Reason for Exchange in Archaic Societies*. Translated by W. D. Halls. New York: W. W. Norton, 1954.

Nussbaum, Martha. *Sex and Social Justice*. Oxford: Oxford University Press, 2000.

Phillips, Roderick. *Untying the Knot: A Short History of Divorce*. Cambridge, UK: Cambridge University Press, 1991.

Potts, Malcolm, and Thomas Hayden. *Sex and War: How Biology Explains Warfare and Terrorism and Offers a Path to a Safer World*. Dallas: Benbella Books, 2008.

Prahalad, C. K. *The Fortune at the Bottom of the Pyramid: Eradicating Poverty Through Profits*. Upper Saddle River, NJ: Wharton School Publishing, 2004.

Sachs, Jeffrey. *The End of Poverty.* New York: Penguin, 2006.

Sapolsky, Robert M. *A Primate's Memoir: A Neuroscientist's Unconventional Life Among the Baboons.* New York: Simon and Schuster, 2001.

———. *Behave: The Biology of Humans at Our Best and Worst.* New York: Penguin, 2017.

———. *The Trouble with Testosterone and Other Essays on the Biology of the Human Predicament.* New York: Scribner, 1997.

Seifried, Charlene Haddock. *Pragmatism and Feminism: Reweaving the Social Fabric.* Chicago: University of Chicago Press, 1996.

Sorrentino, Constance. "International Comparisons of Labor Force Participation, 1960–81." *Monthly Labor Review* 106, no. 2 (February 1983): 23–36.

Tyson, Laura, and Jeni Krugman. *Leave No One Behind: A Call to Action for Gender Equality and Women's Economic Empowerment.* United Nations Secretary-General's High Level Panel on Women's Economic Empowerment, 2016.

United Nations Children's Fund. *State of the World's Children: Women and Children, the Double Dividend of Gender Equality.* Geneva: UNICEF, 2007.

United Nations Foundation. "A Roadmap for Promoting Women's Economic Empowerment." United Nations Foundation, ExxonMobil Foundation, 2013.

World Bank. *Women, Business and the Law Report*, 2012–2018. Washington, DC: World Bank Group, 2014.

World Economic Forum. *The Global Gender Gap Report.* Geneva: World Economic Forum, 2006–2018.

Wrangham, Richard. *The Goodness Paradox: The Strange Relationship Between Virtue and Violence in Human Evolution.* New York: Pantheon, 2019.

Yunus, Muhammad. *Creating a World Without Poverty: Social Business and the Future of Capitalism.* New York: Public Affairs, 2007.

ACKNOWLEDGMENTS

This book, and the research that led to it, rested on the support of many individuals and organizations. I particularly want to thank Catherine Dolan and Paul Montgomery, who were my first collaborating colleagues in this work. They continued to work with me for several years and are still among my dearest friends. Amanda Berlan and Sue Dopson were also involved in the early work, as were Caitlin Ryus and Gillian Stevens. Maryalice Wu has been analyzing and collecting data with me since 2008. I am grateful to all of these wonderful people.

I have also been blessed with passionate and energetic doctoral students who helped with this work, especially Laurel Steinfield and Mary Johnstone-Louis, who were there in the early days. Anna Custers was invaluable in my most recent large-scale project on financial inclusion in Uganda. Kelly Northridge, Astrid Van Den Bossche, and Tania Jain provided important support to various projects, and Lina Rothman, then a Cambridge student, gave me help with the work, as well as much-appreciated moral support. Marko Blazekovich was there from the start.

Julia Flynn saved my life by becoming my assistant when the enormous Empowering Women Together project opened up. Many people at the Saïd Business School in Oxford were essential, including Pegram Harrison, Simon Johnson, Nick Riley, Christopher Brook-Hollidge, Claire

Fisher, Josie Powell, Anita Jassi, Nils Nordal, Andrew Morgan-Giles, Arta Gerguri, and Emily Baro. I want to thank Amanda Poole, Grant Phillips, and Edward David, who helped create Power Shift. Elizabeth Paris not only helped give birth to Power Shift but also invited me in to the Goldman Sachs 10,000 Women work and, along the way, taught me a lot about women, entrepreneurship, and finance.

My college at Oxford, Green Templeton, was generous with both financial and moral support. I am especially grateful to Ian Scott, Stephen Kennedy, Michael Earl, and the late Sir David Watson.

While I was writing the book, Cindy Drakeman and Asia Elsner carried the ball for DoubleXEconomy, LLC, which kept a roof over my head and theirs. They also made the past few years a lot of fun.

There are people in women's economic empowerment who, like me, have been around for a while, and their support has also been important: Elizabeth Vazquez, Stéphane Dubois, Wade Channel, Christine Svarer, Henriette Kolb, Mayra Buvenic, and Noa Gimelli are just a few. I am grateful to Melanne Verveer for her inspiring leadership in this movement. I thank Donnetta Campbell for helping build the women's economic empowerment social media network, especially my part of it, as well as for her unflagging enthusiasm and dedication.

I was fortunate to have important organizations as partners in my work, including CARE International, the World Bank, Plan International, UNICEF, the U.K.'s Department for International Development, Avon, and Procter & Gamble. In this regard, I am particularly grateful to the members of the Global Business Coalition for Women's Economic Empowerment—James Jones, Jenny Grieser, Charlotte Oades, Sarah Thorne, Paul George, Bethan Grillo, Chris McGrath, Lisa Mac-Dougall, Cristina Shapiro, Ashley Keenan, Angie Rozas, Angela Baker, Walt Macnee, Payal Dalal, Nancy Swartout, Jamila Belabidi, and Hazel Culley—who represent Coca-Cola, ExxonMobil, Goldman Sachs, MasterCard, Mondelēz, Marks & Spencer, Procter & Gamble, PwC, Qualcomm, and Walmart.

I will always be grateful to those who funded the work, including the John Fell Fund of the Oxford University Press, the ExxonMobil Foundation, the Bill and Melinda Gates Foundation, CARE UK, the

Economics and Social Research Council of the United Kingdom, the Saïd Foundation, the Saïd Business School, the Pears Foundation, the Skoll Foundation, and the Department for International Development, in addition to Green Templeton College.

In the field, I have had so much help, it is impossible to name everyone. In Ghana, I must thank Boatema Asiedu, Sylvia Hinson-Ekong, and Thomas Okyere, as well as Barbara Korsah, Mavis Appiah, George Appiah, Bright Brobby, and many others who helped with the research. In Uganda, I owe a great deal to Sam Mugisha, Rose Manana, and Claire Wambazu, as well as to Carolyne Kagoya, Kisozi Zacchaeus, Agnes Akwi, Joyce Achan, Reeta Nabuzale, Tinah Nassali, Gloria Titi, Edison Nsubuga, and Ester Nanjovu. In Bangladesh, I am of course indebted to Saif Al Rashid and Asif Ahmed, as well as our local research assistants, Jannatul Farjana Niladria, Leena Fhameda, Radia Mehnaz Anis, and Antora Khan, and to Melea Press for joining the project from the U.K. In the Avon project in South Africa, I am grateful to Andrea Jung for giving her permission to do the research, as well as to Mike Gudgin, Yvonne Khoele, and Eunice Maseko, for helping to bring it about. My colleagues Brian Brady, Tim Dowding, and Melea Press made it possible to cover a lot more ground with interviews on the Walmart project than I could ever have done on my own. MiKaela Wardlaw Lemmon, Dana Towsey, Jenny Grieser, Gina Lopez, Joan Shifrin, Catherine Shimony, and John Priddy made the Walmart research enjoyable as well as enlightening. In my current work in Uganda, I am honored to be working with Christian Pennotti, Grace Majara, and Melch Natukunda, as well as with the professionals at IPSOS and Innovations for Poverty Action.

Making all this experience fit into a book has been quite a challenge. I want to thank my agent, Erin Harris, who helped me through the most daunting moments and provided invaluable advice. I am grateful to Laura Hassan at Faber & Faber for having the inspiration to ask me about doing a book. I was blessed by the sponsorship of Ileene Smith at Farrar, Straus and Giroux, who saw what I saw—a chance to support a new wave of activism on behalf of women at a crucial moment in history. Jackson Howard, Rowan Cope, Rebecca Caine, M. P. Klier, and Nick Humphrey were central to producing the final book. Special thanks also to Emma Cheshire, Lizzie Bishop, Hannah Styles, and Hattie Cooke for ushering the book out into the world for translation. I thank all these people for helping me bring my life's work into a single, focused form.

I want to recognize Jim Hecimovich, for having been with me from start to finish. Lastly, but most importantly, I thank my daughters, Eliza and Caitlin, who were not always sure where in the world I was, but nevertheless always understood exactly why I was there.

—*Linda Scott*

INDEX

Page numbers in *italics* refer to figures and captions.

Sign up for free

Become a Faber Member and discover the best *in the arts and literature*

Sign up to the Faber Members programme and enjoy specially curated events, tailored discounts and exclusive previews of our forthcoming publications from the best novelists, poets, playwrights, thinkers, musicians and artists.

Join Faber Members for free at faber.co.uk

faber
members